D0034823

THE SHOW THAT NEVER ENDS

THE SHOW THAT NEVER ENDS

THE RISE AND FALL OF PROG ROCK

DAVID WEIGEL

W. W. NORTON & COMPANY

Independent Publishers Since 1923

New York • London

Copyright © 2017 by David Weigel

A portion of this book appeared in earlier form in *Slate*.

All rights reserved
Printed in the United States of America
First Edition

For information about permission to reproduce selections from this book,
write to Permissions, W. W. Norton & Company, Inc., 500 Fifth Avenue,
New York, NY 10110

For information about special discounts for bulk purchases,
please contact W. W. Norton Special Sales at specialsales@wwnorton.com
or 800-233-4830

Manufacturing by Berryville Graphics
Book design by Chris Welch
Production manager: Julia Druskin

Library of Congress Cataloging-in-Publication Data
Names: Weigel, David, 1981– author.
Title: The show that never ends : the rise and fall of prog rock / David Weigel.
Description: First edition. | New York : W. W. Norton & Company, [2017] |
Includes bibliographical references and index.
Identifiers: LCCN 2017012885 | ISBN 9780393242256 (hardcover)
Subjects: LCSH: Progressive rock music—History and criticism. |
Rock music—1971–1980—History and criticism. |
Rock music—1961–1970—History and criticism.
Classification: LCC ML3534 .W436 2017 | DDC 781.6609/047—
dc23 LC record available at https://lccn.loc.gov/2017012885

W. W. Norton & Company, Inc., 500 Fifth Avenue, New York, N.Y. 10110
www.wwnorton.com
W. W. Norton & Company Ltd., 15 Carlisle Street, London W1D 3BS

1 2 3 4 5 6 7 8 9 0

For Alex, Eileen, and Phil.

CONTENTS

INTRODUCTION

e are the most uncool people in Miami, and we can hardly control our bliss. On a warm April morning, thousands of us have packed into the city's port; one hand on the suitcase, one hand gripping the passport. One tedious line is the only thing keeping us from the "Cruise to the Edge," four nights and five days in paradise with the living gods of progressive rock.

Once we beat that line, the naysayers—millions of them, tens of millions—will be separated from us by international waters. Miami's port is as anonymous as a government building gets, but as we shuffle forward, we feel a growing safety in our numbers. Hawaiian shirts unfurl, revealing tattered Yes tour tees and gear from forgotten festivals. The cruise company takes over the PA system, and obscure progressive music pipes in. "What's this?" asks one cruisemate, hearing a minor-key piano playing under a flanging guitar. "It sounds like Nektar."

It's a good guess, one that only a small number of music heads would make. I use my last minutes of terrestrial cell service to identify the song—"Parted Forever," by Pineapple Thief, a revivalist band that sounds frozen in 1972. The song is eighteen minutes long. Progressive rock is perfect for lengthy, bureaucratic travel tangles.

The "prog rock cruise," which people have paid thousands of dollars to ride, had been an easy subject for mockery. To enjoy a cruise un-ironically is to give up one's cool card and set it to the torch. To enjoy "prog rock"—well, what were you doing with that card in the first place? You forged it, didn't you?

After boarding, and after taking in a few acts, I meet with the people who designed this tour. Larry Morand, manager at Union Entertainment Group, has converted a cigar lounge into a temporary office. It's been filling up with paper and problems for two weeks, as the Cruise to the Edge is the third of three consecutive music vacations on this 1,092-foot-long ship.

There was "Monsters of Rock," the metal cruise; everyone understood the marriage of hair metal and poolside mojitos. Then there was the nostalgic Moody Blues cruise, which skewed older and a bit less American. To fill out the Moody Blues bill, UEG had booked some of the band's contemporaries, like the virtuosic drummer Carl Palmer.

"We were looking at these bands like: Wow, this is another genre, isn't it?" Morand remembers, after relocating from the cigar lounge to an Italian-style café. "To state the obvious, it was prog, but we learned a lot about the music and the audience on the spot. We called Yes's manager, and he called back right away: 'Yes would like to do it.' And we were off to the races."[1]

THIS IS A NARRATIVE HISTORY of progressive rock, told by the people who made it. Many of them told it in real time to the music publications that flowered in the late 1960s, and to the first generation of rock journalists. Most of the stories flow from those sources, though I've also relied on memoirs, radio interviews, TV interviews, third-party band histories, and my own conversations with musicians, producers, and fans to reconstruct time and place.

This is also an argument *for* progressive rock as a grand cultural detour that invented much of the music that's popular now. As the reader will discover—or already knows—"prog's" reputation has never quite recovered from a series of crises in 1977 and 1978. Punk won over the critics, disco won over the teens, and the major progressive bands deflated like punctured blimps.

As of this writing, the blimp's been patched up and given a second look, but not allowed to fly. *The Rock Snob's Dictionary*, originally serialized in *Vanity Fair*, defined prog as the "single most deplored genre of postwar pop music." *Rolling Stone*'s quasi-annual "best albums ever" lists include some Pink Floyd albums but disregard all other prog. In *Rip It Up and Start Again*, a history of postpunk, there is little mystery about what "it" is or whether its fate was earned.

Rock historians wished it all away. When used in a movie, a Funkadelic or Foghat or Blondie song says "1970s." A rare prog note in a movie, like Vincent Gallo's credit of King Crimson and Yes in *Buffalo '66*, is meant to invite us into something broken and strange. More often, prog is quoted as a goof—think of Dr. Venture playing prog for his son in *The Venture Bros.*, then panicking when the kid gets stuck "in a Floyd hole."

Ask a fan how he (yes, usually *he*) feels about Yes and ELP and Jethro Tull being stonewalled from the Rock & Roll Hall of Fame while the Red Hot Chili Peppers—*the Red Hot Chili Peppers*—make it in.

But prog was fabulously popular for years—and for years, critics liked it. It emerged as a direct response to the throwaway three-minute pop song, the format everyone was trying to emulate after the Beatles perfected it.

Prog was more arty and ambitious than anything else in rock. It was a decadent musical feast in contrast to these pop music popovers. *Rolling Stone* panned Led Zeppelin's output and raved about the first Emerson, Lake & Palmer record: "Such a good album it is best heard as a whole," wrote Lloyd Grossman.[2] Of ELP, the music press declared that they had taken "rock to college." It was a compliment, not a slur.

PROG'S OUTSIDER STATUS was irrelevant on the "Karn Evil Cruise." (I wish I could claim credit for the term, but it belongs to the music journalist Jeremy D. Larson.) The audience of some three thousand fans skewed boomer; the T-shirts were more often faded by time then faded ironically by Target. Everywhere they turned, there was a prog fan, or a musician.

There was Roger Dean, the artist of so many space-scape album covers, putting together a salad from the buffet—delicately, so it did not stain his vest.

There was John Wetton, whose sobriety was not yet well enough known to stop fans from offering him drinks from the Campari bar.

And there was Tony Levin, the famously mustachioed and head-shaved bassist for King Crimson and Peter Gabriel and countless side projects that this crew had actually bought and heard.

"Is there any chance you'll play Estonia?" pleads one fan.

"It's not up to us," Levin says grimly.

Progressive rock did not fade across the world as it faded in Britain or the United States. In some countries—countries, sadly, that did not get music labels to build strategies around them—progressive rock music and its forebears remained popular, if cultish. Forty nations were represented on the cruise, a United Nations for people who loved odd time signatures.

"Anybody can play a 4×4 beat," said Paul Boswell, a fifty-five-year-old cruiser from Jacksonville who was taping every show he could get into. "If you've got a box of oats and a pair of hands, you can play 4×4. This is pure chops, what you're hearing right now."

For many of the musicians, the cruise was an invitation to be trapped with people who idolized them. The phenomenon wasn't entirely new. As this music had fallen out of fashion, its obsessives had paid premiums to access it in more intimate ways. The musicians, who could no longer count on large tours or even notice from the media, indulged.

Sometimes that meant VIP packages, and priceless photos with the band. Sometimes, as Mark Howell discovered, it meant you could pay to spend a vacation at a fantasy band camp with Yes. He had discovered the band in 1973, realized "it was everything I'd been searching for," and then many years and dollars later, found himself jamming with its rhythm section. "Me and Alan White played 'Pinball Wizard' together," said Howell, stopping by a bar between shows. "Good times. I don't know how else you get memories in life like these cruises. Last year I had a lot of one-on-one time with Carl Palmer."

BEFORE THEY WERE middle-aged—before they were the sort of people who could decamp for a weeklong cruise—who were the fans of progressive music? Who were the progressive musicians?

Hippies. Teenagers. Fans who were sure there was something more out there. People who wanted to drop acid and have their pupils bombarded by lasers. Arty types who wanted to find meaning in music, and who—rather than searching for it in short pop songs based on American blues—found it in the quirky Britishness of prog, equal parts twee and subversive.

The musicians, and the audiences, had grown up with rock. They took it seriously. But they didn't feel constrained. They were more interested in personalizing or stretching the forms passed down to them. Everybody loved the Beatles, but they loved them best when they got weird. "The Beatles," said guitarist and producer Robert Fripp, "achieve probably better than anyone the ability to make you tap your foot first time round, dig the words sixth time round, and get into the guitar slowly panning the twentieth time."[3]

This was supposed to be *rebellious* music. The Louis XVI of the time was the standard pop song structure—creative kryptonite. In a 1974 feature on Yes for *Let It Rock* magazine, Dave Laing explained that the "basic impetus was a justified discontent with the limitations of the pre-*Pepper* pop approach—the glorification of image, the three-minute single, the pressure towards repetition of the already successful formula."[4]

Rejecting the three-minute single in favor of the suite meant rejecting the "establishment" in every way. "It was felt after *Sgt. Pepper* anybody could do anything in music," said Yes/King Crimson drummer Bill Bruford in a 1982 interview. "It seemed the wilder the idea musically, the better."[5]

Prog songwriters weren't interested in writing "Love Me Do." They weren't even interested in *love*—at least not with a real person. When a woman appeared in a progressive song, she was a presence, not a sex object. King Crimson's "Lady of the Dancing Water" is captured in a moment of seduction ("pouring my wine in your eyes caged mine glowing"), but instead of being objectified, she's transformed into a muse.

Yes's Jon Anderson, who wrote some of the most mystical lyrics in the genre, told me he was trying to convey "discovery of the self and connection with the divine."[6]

Lots of people were. In the late 1960s, Peter Sinfield was a bored computer programmer and aspiring songwriter. He wrote lyrics for the original iteration of King Crimson, then got hired by prog supergroup Emerson, Lake & Palmer. "We just thought we were trying to combine music that hadn't been combined much before," he says now. "Elements of jazz, and of classical. People think Emerson, Lake & Palmer were a progressive band, but they were just playing classical music."[7]

Like a lot of the progressives, Sinfield uses the P word only when pushed. "It's a word invented by journalists, really," he says. "We didn't think of ourselves as progressives—not any of us. Not Yes, not Pink Floyd."

Maybe, but there was pretty wide acceptance of what "progressive" music was. Promoting *A Quick One*, which features "A Quick One, While He's Away," the Who's nine-minute, six-movement ballad of infidelity, Keith Moon called the album "the kind of progressive material which should enable us to break into America."[8] Rock critics and record sellers used the term to denote complex music—complicated by long instrumentals, or symphonic parts, or intricate conceptual structure. These were traits that migrated from the European orchestral tradition into prog.

"Most rock music," says Greg Lake, "was based upon the blues and soul music, and to some extent country and western, gospel. Whereas a lot of progressive music takes its influence from more European roots."[9]

Lake was King Crimson's first singer and bassist before he became ELP's middle initial. "It appealed to some people a lot, but perhaps for the average person—if there is such a thing— it was too complex, too involved, too much to have to think about, too much to have to wrestle with. It's much easier to have a three-minute song; you can sing the hook because you can remember it, and it's done with. Bing, bang."[10]

Prog songwriters wanted to shake up the assumptions listeners brought to pop music. In his 1997 history *Rocking the Classics*, the music theorist Edward Macan argues that the progressives built their sound by "uniting masculine and feminine musical characteristics."[11] The electric guitar and the mellotron tape can dominate different sections of the music; neither sound is wasted as filler. The flute, if you gave it to Jethro Tull's Ian Anderson or Focus's Thijs van Leer, could be played in a rough way that let the listener hear the exertion and breaths of the flautists. On another song it could be played in the classic style, but high and loud in the mix, as vital as the rhythm section.

The masculine/feminine dynamics led to purposefully unsettling music. *In the Court of the Crimson King* starts with "21st Century Schizoid Man," which is easiest to categorize as proto–heavy metal. It begins with Fripp playing a distorted nine-note riff, then playing it again but jumping up an octave for the last three notes, then repeating that, until the riff becomes a sort of elephant squeal. Kanye West sampled the first note for 2010's "Power." (On his last tour, Lake opened his shows with the Kanye song playing as lasers sprayed the stage.) But "Schizoid Man" doesn't stay in the proto-metal mode. Ian McDonald, a multi-instrumentalist who had played with army bands, introduces fast, spitting saxophone lines, turning the next sections of the song into hyperactive jazz.

Humans have spent tens of thousands of years learning to perk up when they hear surprising sounds. You needed to tell a saber-toothed tiger from a gust of wind. So the conflicting attitudes, discordant instrumentation, and jerky rhythms and tempos of prog keep us constantly on edge. Even a prog act's poppiest song, like Pink Floyd's "Money," attempts to undermine the assumptions of radio rock. Roger Waters wrote it in 7/4 time (LOUD-*quiet*-LOUD)—ONE and TWO and *one two three* | ONE and TWO and *one two three* . . . The groove is born out of that tiny moment of suspense. Many progressive epics change time signatures from bar to bar.

Defining or categorizing this music is basically impossible. *Progression* magazine, a glossy quarterly journal that's been around for more than twenty years, identified at least nineteen sub-genres, including "neo-progressive," "neo-classical progressive," and "rock in opposition"—the last one coined by Chris Cutler, a drummer for Henry Cow, to describe music *you can't describe.*

Better to think of "progressive rock" as a lab for three kinds of musical modes. The first was all *retrospection*, trying to replace the standard American-derived influences of pop rock with English and European influences—à la Renaissance, or early Genesis, or early Barclay James Harvest.

The second was *futurism*, and the use of new sounds and new nonrock influences to replace the standard musical modes. Think the continental European bands: Amon Düül II, or Premiata Forneria Marconi, or Magma, the French act that contrived a new language (Kobaïan) for its lyrics.

The third mode was *experimentation*. "We thought of ourselves as English rock musicians doing our own thing," said Egg/National Health keyboard player Dave Stewart to Paul Stump, a British music journalist. "*Progressive*, we thought, was Genesis and Yes, and all that stuff, which we hated."[12]

Instead, Stewart wrote music with "19/8 rhythms, poly-rhythms, polytonality. It was hard to learn, hard to play, and probably hard to listen to." It was music that copied nothing and could be replicated by nobody.

THE CRUISE TO THE EDGE is not a sarcophagus, though it has its tombs. Yes, it quickly becomes clear, are not interested in mingling. Most of the boat's cabins occupy a tranche of floors in the middle and back of the vessel. The members of Yes, like other headliners, are situated in cabins at the front. If they so choose, they can avoid mixing with the public.

For the most part, that is what they do. Geoff Downes, the ex–Buggles synthesizer player who handles the keyboard in this iteration of the band, mingles with fans. So does Jon Davison, the lead singer who's been elevated from the next-generation act Glass Hammer to replace original lead singer Jon Anderson. He sits with fans for an ear-splitting performance by Patrick Moraz, the flamboyant Swiss keyboard player made famous by one album with Yes. He takes most of the questions for "Storytellers," the occasional interview sessions that are featured parts of the cruise.

Almost every interview is proctored by Jon Kirkman, a Liverpudlian radio personality and author whose qualifications include universal superfandom. He beseeches Italy's PFM to play more shows in the United Kingdom. He asks Edgar Froese, the Tangerine Dream synthesizer guru, if the band would be up for playing on a boat on the Thames. He encourages everyone to be themselves, to talk about the new album.

"It's the first time I can really make my statement, something that can be 100 percent reflective of my voice," says Davison, at the windblown Yes interview.[13]

The interviews do not seem to be the highlights of the week for artists. They clamber off at the port of Cozumel, Mexico, for historical excursions of Mayan ruins. Froese, wrapped in a scarf to protect a recent throat surgery, pokes around the ancient stones and evades the actors playing tribal warriors. Steve Hackett, the former Genesis guitarist whose band reinterprets the songs he worked on, enjoys a "Coco Loco" cocktail in the place where a lost civilization once stored grain.

Every cruiser deals in his own way with the pervasive absurdity. "I've never been on a cruise ship," says Mark Kelly, the keyboard player for Marillion, which along with Yes, is the week's big draw. "It's nice—when you're in the theater, you could be anywhere. Well, apart from the slight side-to-side movement."

There are cynics on board, but they begin to melt too. Two of the less storied acts onboard are Three Friends and Soft Machine Legacy—continuations of the iconic Gentle Giant and Soft Machine, respectively. Three Friends pack every room solid with renditions of intricate, baroque-inspired music. The Legacy spellbinds the small Black and White Lounge with improvisational jazz fusion.

"Roy Babbington is a big figure on bass," says Jim Meneses, a drummer and experimental—or "new music"—artist from Philadelphia. "Obviously, the drummer is a big deal too. Program-wise, this is very hip, in this setting, on this goddamn boat with Yes next door and Queensrÿche upstairs."

But the big draw remains the least surprising. Yes had preceded the cruise with a series of lucrative shows that featured no new music. They had jumped aboard the trend of playing entire albums in single goes—something they'd done decades before that was trendy, when all eighty minutes of *Tales from Topographic Oceans* pummeled the audiences of 1973 and 1974. "It adds some excitement for the audience, in terms of knowing what the next track is, of knowing which track follows the other," bassist Chris Squire says, cheerfully. "It's a good concept."

The unquiet secret of Cruise to the Edge is that the concept doesn't quite come off. By playing three classic albums, note for note, Yes makes the muffed notes more noticeable. A video before each forty-minute block is synced to "The Firebird," the Stravinsky-inspired song that Yes used to play on stage. The composer's strings would build, and shudder, and then the band would stroll in, grabbing the melody to toss it elsewhere.

Nice touch. Maybe a bit sepulchral now. On the walk from the theater to one of the all-night lounges, you can hear mega-fans grumble about what went wrong.

They make the best of it. Every night, a too-small bar near the ship's main theater is co-opted for a "prog jam." This is not tipsy karaoke; it is a meticulously organized cycle of cover songs, planned months in advance, with the amateur players hauling their instruments onboard. Greg Bennett, a Florida musician with the nom de plume "Jack the Riffer," even brings his business cards.

The anorak bands are tight, and word spreads. On the second-to-last night of the cruise, they play "The Gates of Delirium," Yes's longest and most melodically complex song, inspired by *War and Peace* and grounded by Squire's floor-rumbling bass lines. Squire and his family walk in on the performance, unannounced. The crowd grows. A casino just one floor down is nearly empty; the bar at the back of the boat is the only place to be. Squire sits on a wraparound leather couch, listening to people who grew up on his music play through every note as if it were an orchestral score. He dabs away tears. When the performance ends—twenty-two minutes later—he leads the standing ovation.

THE SHOW
THAT NEVER
ENDS

1

CHILDREN OF THE BLITZ

The British music press simply did not get it. In the second week of May 1840, the Hungarian-born piano virtuoso Franz Liszt alighted in London to begin his first tour of England. He was twenty-eight years old and had little left to prove on the mainland. His prodigy had blossomed into genius. Later that year he played in Hamburg, where the audience included the poet and fairy tale adapter Hans Christian Andersen.

No grasper for words, Andersen struggled to describe what he'd seen. "The instrument appears to be changed into a whole orchestra; this is produced by ten fingers which possess an expertness that may be called fanatical," he wrote. "When Liszt had ceased playing, flowers showered around him: beautiful young girls, and old ladies who had once been young and beautiful, cast each her bouquet. He had cast a thousand bouquets of tones into their hearts and heads."[1]

Liszt had had the same plan for London. After a solo debut at the Hanover Square Rooms—walking where Bach had walked, playing where Bach had played—he joined the full philharmonic. Liszt adapted Carl Maria von Weber's *Konzertstück in F*

Minor; "passages were doubled, tripled, inverted, and transmogrified." This was not the right way to play it, yet somehow it was celebrated like a conquest. "Liszt has been presented by the Philharmonic Society with an elegant silver breakfast service, for doing that which would cause every young student to receive a severe reprimand—viz., thumping and partially destroying two very fine pianofortes," marveled the short-lived *Musical Journal*.[2]

Europe had seen prodigies before. In his work, Liszt poured all the history of the composers who had come before him. When explaining his craft, he could come off like a madman. "For a whole fortnight my mind and my fingers have been working like two lost souls," Liszt wrote to a pupil. "Homer, the Bible, Plato, Locke, Byron, Hugo, Lamartine, Chateaubriand, Beethoven, Bach, Hummel, Mozart, Weber are all around me. I study them, meditate on them, devour them with fury; besides this, I practice four to five hours of exercises (thirds, sixths, octaves, tremolos, repetition of notes, cadenzas, etc.) Ah! Provided I don't go mad, you will find in me an artist."[3]

So he was, and the momentum built wherever he played. "His portrait was worn on brooches and cameos," wrote Liszt biographer Alan Walker. "Swooning lady admirers attempted to take cuttings of his hair, and they surged forward whenever he broke a piano string in order to make it into a bracelet. Some of these insane female 'fans' even carried glass phials about their persons into which they poured his coffee dregs. Others collected his cigar butts, which they hid in their cleavages."[4]

The next year, as Liszt toured the continent, the skeptical critic O. G. Sonneck struggled to understand what was new about this: "Strange, thought I, these Parisians, who have seen Napoleon, who had to win one battle after another in order to hold their attention! Now they are acclaiming our Franz Liszt."[5]

Sonneck consulted a doctor, a specialist in "female diseases," and asked him to explain the power of music played this way. "[He] smiled in the strangest manner," wrote Sonneck, "and at the same time said all sorts of things about magnetism, galvanism, electricity, of the contagion of a close hall filled with countless wax lights and several hundred perfumed and perspiring human beings, of historical epilepsy, of the phenomenon of tickling, of musical cantherides, and other scabrous things."[6]

The doctor could not define the condition. The writer could. This was "Lisztomania," a frenzy induced by music—surely some kind of a fluke.

POPULAR MUSIC, in the century before rock and roll, was bolder than it had ever been. Folk music, with its simple chords and grab-and-go instrumentation, had always existed outside the strictures of "professional" music. All of these features appeared in early rock; the roots of progressive rock went into the nineteenth century, and earlier. "The progressive rock piano style is marked by virtuoso scalar runs and rolling arpeggios in the right hand, arpeggiated or melodically active accompaniments in the left hand, grandiose block chords, and sustained, impressionist chordal backdrops that make ample use of the damper pedal," wrote the music theorist Edward Macan, in a successful attempt to explain the linkage.[7]

Some classical music echoed especially loudly in the progressive era. The decades in which Liszt played and composed were marked by increasingly complex musical forms. The end of the nineteenth century saw a kind of reaction begin. Liszt, inspired by the composer Hector Berlioz, came up with the "tone poem," a classical-music type that abandoned form to follow an idea within one movement. "In the so-called classical music the return and development of themes is determined by formal rules which are regarded as inviolable," Liszt wrote in 1855. "In program music, in contrast, the return, change, variation and modulation of the motives is conditioned by their relation to a poetic idea."[8]

Composers began looking to folk music or other sources of more digestible melody; Modest Mussorgsky was one of the first. In 1874 he composed a suite of songs called *Pictures at an Exhibition*. The melody of its theme, "Promenade," was unbarred; other sections relied on block chords, with the sound of church music. "Musorgsky's music I send to the devil," Tchaikovsky told one of his brothers, coincidentally also named Modest. "It is the most vulgar and vile parody on music."[9]

At the start of the twentieth century, that opinion was shared by every well-meaning defender of the old music. In his *Summary of the History and Development of Mediaeval and Modern European Music*, a primer meant to be definitive, C. Hubert H. Parry warned English readers that the sort of music Mussorgsky wrote—any ecstatic classical music with colors of folk music— was cultural poison.[10]

"The qualities of races but little advanced from primitive temperamental conditions are even more conspicuous in the Russian music which has almost submerged the world, especially England, in the closing years of the century," Parry wrote, despondently. "The music has naturally appealed to the awakening intelligence of the musical masses by vehement emotional spontaneity, orgiastic frenzy, dazzling effects of colour, barbaric rhythm, and unrestrained abandonment to physical excitement which is natural to the less developed races."[11]

That was the point, however diligently the critics decided to miss it. The flamboyance of Liszt outlived the composer; the deconstruction of classical music, without any departure from craft, continued in the twentieth century. A turning point came in 1913, when the composer Igor Stravinsky, just thirty-one, wrote *The Rite of Spring* and trained an orchestra to get over its disbelief and play it.

Stravinsky's experiments with tone and melody challenged classical music, without entirely changing it. Progressive rock, which would not come into existence for more than fifty years, grew up in Stravinsky's shadow. Introduced to the music as children, or as adults who sought something outside of the rock tropes, the prog rockers came to see *The Rite of Spring* as proof of experimentation's fruits. "I didn't, and don't, have the technical qualifications or capacity to 'know' what was involved," Fripp recollected in 2001. "We might recall that the young Stravinsky of The ROS didn't 'know' what he was doing either: for him it was more an instinctive and intuitive process."[12]

Some of the early-twentieth-century's music stayed closer to the lines but found new power in repetitive sounds. Maurice Ravel began writing *Boléro*, which he called "a piece for orchestra without music," by hitting one key on a piano, repeatedly, until the hook was infectious.[13]

Karlheinz Stockhausen, a German composer who started publishing in the 1950s, went even further in collecting influences. In 1958, Stockhausen joined friends at a club to see Count Basie. He marveled at the spontaneous invention, watching Basie extend a song until his singer ran out of words and started making sounds in time with the music. "For two hours I listened intently to music being played with incomparable skill," Stockhausen recalled, excitedly describing the act. "It taught me a lot, both about instrumentation and about playing technique."[14]

In "How Time Passes By," an essay from the same period, Stockhausen imagined a technological advance that could allow new music to be written over the limitations of analog. He envisioned a key on which, "if one presses only very lightly, the oscillation keeps a constant phase—the pitch remains the same. The heavier the pressure, the more irregular become the phase-relationships and the more indeterminate the pitch."

"It is impossible to say how long we shall have to wait," wrote Stockhausen, "but one may expect that some day such an instrument will exist."[15]

CHRISTOPHER DAVID ALLEN was born in Melbourne in January 1938, a couple of years and thousands of miles away from the pop mainstream. "I was a teen Beat Gen jazz & poetry performer in late 1950s Melbourne and there were very few venues other than those we created ourselves," Allen remembered. Local drinking laws closed down bars at 6 p.m., but Allen gravitated toward the artist scene at the Swanston Family Hotel. "A youthful and indomitable Germaine Greer was the chief obstacle to masculine superiority. I lost every debate I ever started with her."[16]

The displaced bohemian sought an escape route, and then found it. In 1957, he obtained an "immaculately maintained 1928 long chassis Lancia convertible" and sold it to a priest, for enough money to get him to Europe. "It broke down quite thoroughly under its new owner several hundred yards down the road," said Allen. "This event strengthened my innate atheism considerably."

Allen kept trying, and by 1960 he had a ticket on the *Patris* ocean liner, which could get him from Australia to Greece. "My sole ambition was to roam the central nervous system of world creativity until I found the cities where inspiration was peaking at that moment," he recalled. "I wanted to ride the unpredictable waves of art's contemporary cutting edge and feed off its juices."

The quest took him to England, where, under the new name Daevid (he would never change it back) Allen took up lodging with two other Swanston Family Hotel exiles who had stowed away on the ship. All of them slid easily into the Beat scene; Allen even met William Burroughs. Pale and tall, Allen was a natural musician—untrained, but aware of what his audience wanted.

"He wanted me to play music at his poetry readings—I was a jazzer back then—so he suggested we first go up to his room where he got behind this desk like some Brooklyn insurance salesman," recalled Allen. " 'Well, Daevid,' he said, 'there are two ways of doing this. One way will take ten minutes, the other will take the rest of your life.' I assumed the first way might have involved sodomy so I opted for the latter.' "[17]

Allen quickly switched directions. "I wanted to find a cheap rental in the countryside to develop my new fascination for free jazz," he said. Inside an issue of the center-left *New Statesman*, he saw an ad for a rental in the town of Lydden, near Canterbury, a country town southeast of London. The Wellington House, another community of artists, had a room. A fifteen-year-old Robert Wyatt lived there with his parents. "I went down to see the family and I immediately saw Robert," Allen told a journalist. "The first thing we did is look at each other's record collections, and they were almost identical."[18]

Allen had met just the right teenager. He remembered "an intellectual equality"[19] with Wyatt, who had been experimenting with music for years, to the bemusement of his psychologist father and journalist mother. "I took up violin early on," Wyatt would recall, "but when I swapped it for trumpet he [Wyatt's father] was horrified. He said, 'There aren't any great concertos for a trumpet.' "[20]

At the Simon Langton Grammar School for Boys, between bouts of boredom, Wyatt had befriended Hugh Hopper after a fight that started pointlessly and ended harmlessly. "His parents were Conservative, mine were Labour, so we had a fight," according to Wyatt.[21] He'd met Mike Ratledge, a keyboard player two years his senior, after the prefect asked to borrow a Cecil Taylor record that Wyatt happened to own.

There was no band yet; there was only a circle of artists collaborating and whiling the night away with parties at Wellington House. In 1961, the house got its first visit from a seventeen-year-old guitarist named Kevin Ayers, who had come east to Canterbury after a drug arrest. "The magistrate said I should leave London because it was obviously a bad influence," he explained.[22]

Wyatt was fifteen years old when Daevid Allen dropped his bags at the door. We were "the same intellectual age," Allen said, by way of mocking himself and sincerely praising the young musician.[23]

"I couldn't understand reading music, and I wasn't getting better," Wyatt said. "I thought, 'I suppose I could learn to do that, but I really don't want to. I want to stop right now.' So I just decided to try and do that. It was just a practical decision."[24]

What he "decided" was to attempt suicide, by downing the sleeping pills his father took for the pain of his multiple sclerosis. He survived; he transferred to art college. Nothing altered Wyatt's momentum until he visited the poet and author Robert Graves, an old friend, at his home in Mallorca. "There were always lots of people around, and everybody had to do something at these meals," recalled Wyatt. "I used to do vocal percussion duets."[25]

When Wyatt returned, he relocated to London. There was a place to stay with Kevin Ayers and Hugh Hopper. "It was quite a big room, with a permanent smell of hot curry coming up the staircase and a pregnant prostitute in a little room next door."[26]

Daevid Allen had moved to London too. He quickly convinced Wyatt and Hopper to complete his Daevid Allen Trio, an avant-garde jazz group, which was promptly ejected by managers wondering why a man was reciting Beat poetry over the music. An audience settling in for "Song of the Jazzman" heard a shuffling beat obscured by clear-ringing Allen doggerel.

"I am a bird, with aching claws," he would talk-sing. "I am a moon and the evening stars and I can't find the sky." Allen was predating psychedelia by half a decade. There is a problem with being too early for a scene. "We probably did sound pretty damned awful," said Hugh Hopper.[27]

When the band splintered, Wyatt returned to his wanderings. He joined Allen in Paris, where the poet-jazzer had reunited with Burroughs. The minimalist composer Terry Riley, a newer arrival, had joined the group for a life that varied "from the houseboat to the beat hotel."[28] Riley took over a newspaper delivery job when Allen grew sick of it; Riley taught Allen about tape loops, as Allen taught Riley about everything else.

"Daevid was a much hipper guy than me," Riley told the journalist Anil Prasad years later. "He was more into the Beat and pre-hippie scenes. I was a straight UC Berkeley graduate who experimented a lot with weird music, so we had that connection. I educated him about musical ideas and he showed me things about the free bohemian life you could lead in Paris. I really liked Daevid's fantasy drawings, poems, and the funny Australian language elements he'd use. It was captivating for me. He was very influential on me. He showed me a new kind of life, even though his was chaos."[29]

Paris proved more welcoming to the musical improvisers. Wyatt, as Riley remembered, fit right in. "He had a trumpet with him with a turned-up bell, like the one Dizzy Gillespie played," remembered Riley. "I had a little spinet piano there and as I remember, the three of us spent the afternoon jamming."[30]

By 1965, when Allen and Wyatt returned to Britain, the culture had started to open up. The music was still derivative. But that could change.

THEY WERE BORN in the first years after the Blitz. They grew up in the growing shadow of London, or in a countryside that was being repopulated and reorganized under the newness of the welfare state. Their parents, in many cases, had fought in the war and rescued prosperity and opportunity for their children. They were English, at the exact moment when invocation of the word no longer instilled confidence.

"The only reason I've been able to come up with as to why we became musicians was because there wasn't anything to rebel or fight against," remembered future King Crimson drummer Michael Giles, raised near Portsmouth, well south of London. "We weren't doing it with another agenda as a means to escape. If we were seeking to escape, then it would have been from a kingdom of nothingness."[31]

Many of the musicians who became "progressive" said the same. Keith Emerson was raised only a short distance away, in Worthing, a seaside town equipped with cold beaches, algae, pensioners, and not much else. "The elderly came there in droves to die," Emerson would recall. "Once there they conveniently forgot to."[32]

The circle expanded. Not very far from Worthing was the town of Wimborne Minster, where Robert Fripp had entered the world, and where he first learned to be an isolated, bored youth. "I suppose when you're young you think it's a fault not having friends," Fripp said, with a shrug, to one interviewer. He corrected that instinct.[33]

Gordon Haskell, a Fripp classmate with his own musical

ambitions, diagnosed his friend's life as "strange" and distant. "His mother and father didn't seem to share their life with him and so he was left to his own devices."[34]

Other children, growing up around the same time, were more naturally outgoing and naturally inaugurated into music. The Shulman brothers, Derek and Ray, grew up in Portsmouth— their father had been stationed there during the war, and decided to relocate—in what Ray called a house "full of musicians and middle-aged dropouts."[35] Tony Banks grew up in Sussex, with a mother who introduced him to music through her piano.[36] In Canterbury, George Ellidge introduced his son Robert to music, only to watch the trainee drift into jazz.[37]

Jazz was easier to come across than the first stirrings of rock and roll. In Hounslow, an anonymous borough of London, the young Phil Collins heard commercial pop on Radio Luxembourg and drummed along to the music he saw on TV: "I play whenever possible."[38] Peter Brockbanks asked for an instrument from his musician father, and got a ukulele. "Whenever a guitar player was on," said Brockbanks (who later shortened his name to Banks), "like Lonnie Donegan, I'd be glued to the screen, and just watching what his fingers would do."[39]

Television, with its carefully selected windows into the attainable culture, introduced countless young Brits to new sounds. "Around the age of twelve or thirteen I had come under the way of jazz," Bill Bruford would say. It "was being broadcast on BBC TV every Saturday night."[40]

The Church of England was another common tutor for the boys growing up in postwar England. Its inheritance included the popular hymns that wedded the previous century's music to lyrics with the ambition to be timeless. Greg Lake, growing up on the seacoast, remembered the power that "Jerusalem" carried even when the message did not move him. " 'Bring me my bow of burning gold / Bring me my arrows of desire'—what a fantastic line," Lake would say. "All Brits love that song."[41]

"Those songs were terrific," said Bruford of the Church of England's music. "I still think they're great. Wonderful bits of writing for the popular common man to sing."[42]

Tony Banks would attend chapel every day. "Twice on Sundays," Banks said. "There were half a dozen real favorites amongst the classic hymns, with some wonderful melodies such as 'Dear Lord and Father of Mankind.' . . . That sort of thing was an influence on the way Genesis wrote, there's no doubt about it. There's something about hymns, they're simple and they're direct but they have a kind of connection."[43]

Greg Lake remembered seamen in the British navy bringing guitars ashore. "The local kids would buy the guitars and they would also buy records since a lot of those came over off the boats too," he said. "And there you have the leaping off point really for British rock music."[44]

The first records that the young Robert Fripp purchased were typical of the prevailing trends: *Hound Dog* and *Singing the Blues*. He got a guitar at Christmas, learning it right-handed: "Rock at 11, trad at 13, modern jazz at 15."[45]

But he found the rock style limiting, even then. "When I was eleven," said Fripp to an interviewer years later, "I understood that the conventional methods for teaching guitar were poor. Good rock 'n' roll guitarists have always refused to take lessons. This symptom proved that guitar manuals were inefficient. At 13, I was teaching guitar. At 14, I drew my own exercises."[46]

Fripp sought out new teachers wherever he could. "I took lessons from Don Strike who was a very good player in the Thirties' style," he said. "At one time, I bought a good standard flamenco guitar and decided to take up finger style. A little while later I had ten lessons from a jazz guitarist. I don't, however, feel myself to be a jazz guitarist, a classical guitarist, or a rock guitarist. I don't feel capable of playing in any one of those idioms, which is why I felt it necessary to create, if you like, my own idiom."[47]

By the early 1960s, anyone comfortable with the rock idiom was doing just fine. Ian Anderson, born in Scotland but growing up in Blackpool, remembered his very credible reason for needing to start a band: girls flocked to bands. "All these fantastic birds, long hair, made up, false eyelashes and things, crowding round this group of scabby, spotty teenagers," marveled Anderson.[48]

As professional bands changed the culture, the slightly younger cohort found themselves playing covers and filling teen dance halls. "I remember doing a lot of Tamla Motown stuff like 'Knock on Wood,' which we thought was crap," remembered Tony Wilkinson, the sax player in Anderson's band.[49]

The more interesting sounds were found in jazz music, but the first-wave progressive musicians came to that at different speeds. Ian McDonald got a head start. When he was very young, he watched *The Glenn Miller Story* and was captivated by the moment when Miller, played by Jimmy Stewart, rewrites a trumpet part for clarinet.

"I know it sounds corny," McDonald said, years later, "but as a kid, I thought: 'That's what I want. I want to find my sound. I want that moment for myself.'"[50] He found it after seeing an ad in a music paper that read something like "Band Musicians Wanted, 15 Years Old." He was fifteen and a half, and answering the ad got him thrown into the military to play in a band.

"All this stuff was happening in swinging London, and all this rock music was happening, and I wanted to be part of it," he said. Instead, he was in the jungle, teaching himself music theory, learning to play the piano and saxophone. "We did concerts where there was everything from classical overtures to show tunes, Broadway tunes and pop classics," said McDonald.[51] It was not immediately clear how that would play in rock.

THE TWO DISCIPLINES that would create progressive rock were growing in tandem, and nearly in secret. A teenaged Keith Emerson was learning the first discipline when he attended further-education classes at Worthing College. Joining the Worthing Youth Swing Orchestra was an obvious decision, and a revelation. He had not known what he did not know. "He selected a piano chart from a pile and asked me to play it," Emerson said of an instructor. "I'd never seen music like this before. It was full of strange lettering above each of the bars. What was a Gm7?"[52]

Emerson found an ad in *Melody Maker* for a jazz piano course, and each week he would get chord charts in the mail. He would learn the cycles, mail his work back, and open the mail again to find it corrected. When he felt ready, he formed the Keith Emerson Trio. It would have been impossible to do anything else.

"I used to work in a bank for two years, and this was enough to fuck my head up," Emerson would tell an interviewer. "I used to go there every day and I used to listen to all the normals say; 'I'm getting out of here, man, this summer comes, I'm splitting!' And I never used to say a damn thing. . . . I just got out of there and I'm fucking glad that I did."[53]

One morning in the early '60s, at the Organ Center shop in the southern England city of Portsmouth, Keith Emerson arrived with £200 to spend on a keyboard. He had options. But he got distracted by something bigger, more beautiful, and beyond his means. "There it was," he remembers in his autobiography, "resplendent in beautiful shining mahogany—the Hammond L-100 electric organ! I played it." He heard the warm tones, engineered to sound like they came from pipes, but with distinctive warm hums. "That was the sound."[54]

Emerson had noodled around with the Hammond before. The L-100, rolled out in 1961, imitated the sound of a church organ by placing ninety-six metal tone wheels in front of ninety-six electromagnetic pickups. The tone wheels rotated, charging the pickups, generating the sound. Two keyboards shared space with nine "drawbars." Move the bars, change the sound of your notes. Jazz musicians used this feature, as did (somewhat less inspirationally) the nice old ladies who played during the dull sections of ballgames.

Some people could afford to put the cost of a small car into an organ. Emerson couldn't. But he had all the training, years of piano and music lessons. The Royal College of Music had offered him a place, which he had turned down, working instead for a bank, gigging with jazz and rock groups. Emerson contemplated what the Hammond could do for him. Could he quit the bank gig full-time? His father, who had joined him on the shopping trip, broke in—"You've got to have it"—and paid the price difference.[55]

Meanwhile, in Canterbury, the refugees of Mallorca formed a new group, the Wilde Flowers. Wyatt played drums, Hopper played bass, Kevin Ayers was on vocals and guitar, and Hopper's brother Brian played a second guitar. The group eschewed Daevid Allen's dark goofball antics for grounded rock-and-roll music. Debuting in January 1965, the Wilde Flowers had a repertoire that included cover songs like "Johnny B. Goode" and "You Really Got Me," with occasional jazz flourishes inspired by Coltrane and Ellington and Monk.

The noodling behind poems, and the angry looks from confused bookers, were left behind. The new band wrote and played original songs that followed pop formats. "I had not yet come to terms with such bourgeois concepts as keeping time and singing in tune," joked Wyatt. Really, none of the players had.[56]

Ayers, whose long hair and smoldering looks made him seem a natural front man, had a limited and laconic singing voice. After the band's fourth gig, Ayers took flight again—for Mallorca.

Fronted by a new singer, Graham Flight, the band took every chance to strike out. On July 10 the Wilde Flowers, led by Allen and Wyatt, played for a "near empty" Kingsmead Stadium, at the Canterbury Jazz and Folk Festival. Undaunted, the band adopted an idea inspired by jazz and pushed by Hugh Hopper: a "continuous set," with song flowing into song, and no momentum-killing breaks for tuning.

"Originally the idea started by linking together some of the jazz numbers that had similar riffs and patterns," said Brian Hopper. "Then we extended the format to other numbers and eventually more and more of each set." One reason it worked, and one reason it was necessary, was the sort of gigs that the Wilde Flowers got. They played "late into the night, where it seemed natural to let one number flow into another to keep the ravers and dancers going."[57]

The trick was perfectly suited to the gigs. It papered over the lack of success the group was having in getting anyone to cut a deal with them. "We did the experimental-type stuff with Daevid and his friends for years," said Robert Wyatt. "Then we tried pop music and we couldn't really do that properly either, so we had to make up our own sort of music."[58]

On Easter Sunday 1966, Robert Graves blessed the holiday parade. Among the blessed was Wes Brunson, an optometrist from Oklahoma who, like the rest of the instant clique, had come to the island to find himself. As reporter Graham Bennett would tell it, "The trip encouraged Wes to explain to Kevin in great detail how he had been instructed in a vision to serve

God, preferably by using his wealth to broadcast the coming of the New Age."[59]

Daevid Allen had the same vision. He needed money to start a new-age band in England. Right away, he called Hugh Hopper with the offer. "We're going to start a pop group and make a thousand pounds," Allen informed the bass player. "Do you want to come in?"[60]

He did. Together, Allen, Wyatt, Ayers, and Hopper, joined by a Mallorca-scene guitarist named Larry Nowlin, formed Mister Head. The group first played live in August 1966, at the Midsummer Revels gathering in Coombe Springs, joined at last by Mike Ratledge on keyboards. "The harmonic possibilities of the band started to open out," said Wyatt.[61]

"The French like arty things," said Ayers. "What made [us] was an article in *Nouvelle Observateur.* . . . We got written up, I think, 'cause Mike was fucking the journalist, actually. So we got a good review, and that was it. Suddenly France just opened up. We were the darlings of the literary scene there."[62]

The band relocated, too, though Nowlin did not make the final journey back to England. The new five-piece band changed its name to Soft Machine, a tribute to the William Burroughs novel. As close as everyone was to the author—three members of the band had backed up his poetry, and Ratledge had briefly stayed with him—the name change needed his sign-off. Allen was dispatched to get permission from Burroughs. He met him at a street corner in Paddington, cloaked in needless mystery one more time.

"He appeared out of a shopfront, hat pulled over his eyes, looking like a crumpled insurance clerk from the lower east side of Manhattan. When I told him the purpose of our meeting he blinked like an old alligator and drawled, 'Can't see wha not.' When I asked him what he was going to do next he said, 'Ahm gonna get a haircut and disappear!' In fact I never saw him again."[63]

2

THE PSYCHEDELIC BOOM

T he formula was simple: guitar, bass, drums, singer, and organ. In the summer of 1965, Britain was spilling over with that music, the best (or best packaged) piped to Europe and the United States. Kids who had bought the pawned guitars from seamen were playing dance halls, covering American R&B. The Paramounts would rehearse all forty-five minutes of James Brown's *Live at the Apollo*, then re-create it onstage. "Any deviation from the original plan, where I might inject a drum fill, would lead to my getting a small fine," recalled drummer Phil Wainman.[1]

The Moody Blues had an honest-to-God hit in "Go Now," a lush, bleached cover of an orphaned American R&B song. They followed it with a series of clunkers; Decca, their label, kept them on, but with no great expectations.

The music that had brought young Britain into rock and roll, with its pulsating danger, became less dangerous. Louder—just not disruptive. Keith Emerson, who was playing his first gigs with his new organ, discovered at a Marquee Club show in 1965 just how easy it was to tweak the volume. "I couldn't figure out how the same keyboard that I'd just played sounded louder when Manfred played it," Emerson remembered. "A kind roadie tipped me off. He'd seen Manfred turn the Leslie cabinet down just prior to the T-Bones' performance. On the last night, I cranked it up. We went down a storm, and Manfred Mann never spoke to me again."[2]

At one northern France show on the V.I.P.s' 1966 tour, a fight broke out in the audience. Another band might have stopped. The V.I.P.s, though, heard Emerson messing around with the mechanics of his Hammond to make unearthly, violent noise. The band's music was replaced by "air raid sirens" and "machine gun sounds," the products of Emerson's experiments with his poor tortured device. Soon enough, the fight was over.

That was on tour. In some clubs, already, there were all-night raves where bands would roll forward, one after the other—something the Wilde Flowers had discovered at their Canterbury gigs.

And the raves themselves became mainstream on January 30, 1966, the first all-night "happening" at the Marquee Club in London. Progressive rock grew out of the counterculture, but its roots went deeper. In 1966, no obvious design had bands diverging from pop structure. "I think it was a stroke of good fortune that we couldn't work out how to play covers," Roger Waters would say, assessing 1966 gigs by the Pink Floyd Sound. "It forced us to come up with our own direction."[3]

Psychedelia, arriving after Daevid Allen, spread beyond anything he could have dreamed of, with mainstream acts like the Beatles glomming onto it, labels buying anything that sounded like it, and steady work for bands that understood it. Soft Machine and Pink Floyd—which quickly dropped the "Sound"—became mainstays at the Marquee and UFO clubs, the anchors of all-night shows. "I tripped three times at UFO," remembered Pete Townshend, confessing that he kept fearing that Waters would steal his girlfriend while he was "weakened by acid."[4]

"The whole thing about Soft Machine," said Kevin Ayers, "was that it had all these people from middle-class literary, educated backgrounds suddenly going, 'Fuck it, I'm not going to join medical school, I'm not going to become a lawyer or doctor, I'm not going to be a professional.' And this hadn't happened anywhere else in pop."[5]

But the majority of bands in London were still focused on songs and melody. The Syn had done a residency in Cannes—though, as Steve Nardelli remembered, the venue was "expecting some kind of cabaret combo not a full on rock band and we were thrown out after about three weeks for being too loud and blasting the customers away." When they returned to England, firmly established as a Motown cover band, they got an audition at the Marquee Club and played "I'll Keep On Holding On." John Gee, the club's manager, waved them on: "You'll do." Bit by bit, the scene was building.[6]

The Syn had a new guitarist, Peter Banks. He was introduced to the whole band, including guitarist John Painter, even though he was going to replace him. "This was my first introduction to how cold the music business could be." After he got in, he inherited Painter's Rickenbacker. "Not only did I steal his job, I stole his guitar as well."[7]

Chris Squire, the bassist, struck Banks as "talented, vain and selfish, all underlined with an affable, friendly persona."[8]

Emerson joined the V.I.P.s, a band managed by Chris Blackwell, in August 1966, hearing about them in pubs near the Marquee. "We were taking our lead from the likes of Frank Zappa and the Mothers of Invention and Charles Lloyd, contrasting heavily with PP Arnold's black soul approach," he said. "There was never a problem in moulding different ethnic backgrounds together musically."[9]

"'A WHITER SHADE OF PALE' was born during a party at Guy Stevens's house," Keith Reid would remember to a biographer. "There was a large group of us sitting round smoking and joking. During the course of much banter, Guy was trying to tell [his wife] Diane that she had turned very white and he was jumbling up his words." The jumble, as multiple parties remembered it: *You've turned a whiter shade of pale.* Reid had his lyric. "It was much later after . . . when I had written the whole song that I told Guy about my moment of inspiration," he recalled. "He was of course totally unaware that he had said anything that inspired me."[10]

Reid's lyric, three verses that were later cut to two, captured the scene from the party and placed it in an inscrutable new context. "I never understand when people say they don't understand it," Reid would say, decades later. "'We skipped the light fandango.' That's straightforward. 'Turned cartwheels across the floor.' It seems very clear to me." Reid was a fan of French new-wave films and surrealist art, and he'd merely written a lyric that fit into the tradition. "You can draw a line between the narrative fractures and mood of those French films and 'A Whiter Shade of Pale,'" he said.[11]

Mystical lyrics were nothing really new to the charts—not in the spring of 1967. What Procol Harum had, and no other band had, was a classical hook played on a Hammond organ, blown up to cathedral proportions. The hook, a rising C-Em-Am-G figure, was copped from Bach's *Air on a G String.*

More precisely, it was borrowed from the light, jazzy, bass-heavy version performed by Jacques Loussier. Gary Brooker had heard it on a commercial for Hamlet cigars, a little comic scene in which a young man at a laundromat undresses down to his underwear, to the shock of the female clientele. After packing his suit into a washing machine, the man swivels around. He lights a cigar. The women calm and swoon; the Bach chords swell. "Happiness," purrs a narrator, "is a cigar called Hamlet."

"The original Hamlet cigar commercial featuring *Air on a G String* had always been a big favorite of ours," said Brooker. "When the guy lit up the cigar everything just went cool. Anyway, I sat down one day and tried to play 'Air on a G String.'"[12]

Matthew Fisher, who actually played the organ on the track, gave Brooker credit for the hook but not for the interpretation that created the hit. "He says he was trying to play *Air on a G String* sort of like the Jacques Loussier version, because I don't think he ever listened to Bach in its original form," said Fisher. "He was trying to play it and singing along to it, and he sort of got it wrong because he didn't have a record of it at the time, so he was just trying to remember how it went, and it sort of went off in a sort of a different direction. *I* knew *Air on a G String*, so I kind of went along with that, but when I was constructing the solo, I made another reference to another Bach piece—you know, "Sleepers Awake," or whatever you want to call it—so that was a deliberate reference again. It ended up as a mixture of the two, with quite a bit of other stuff, which was neither of them."[13]

The massive, celestial sound was a simple trick that no one else had thought to try. "I just had this little preset on my Hammond organ that had a big churchy sound, and I thought that would sound good in a rock band," recalled Fisher. "It was entirely my idea to compose a set solo and to give the last two bars a satisfying 'shape.'"[14]

Procol Harum's demo ended up with Tony Hall, who was

signing acts for Decca's progressive label Deram. "A Whiter Shade of Pale" was precisely the sort of song Deram had been created for—a loping ballad that didn't sound like a *hit*, precisely, but was impossible to dislodge from the synapses. "We didn't stop playing that demo all night long, until about two in the morning," Hall would remember.[15]

This song would not be debuted on the BBC. No—Hall would take it to Radio London, one of the pirate stations getting past British censors by sequestering itself in a boat off the coast. The pirate radio debut happened on April 17. "A Whiter Shade of Pale" was in shops just a few weeks later. The "big churchy sound" had done its trick—Procol Harum was a sensation. On May 12 the band played its first live gigs at the UFO, then performed for a more select crowd at the Speakeasy. "Hendrix was down at the Speakeasy watching us playing," remembered Brooker, "and he suddenly jumped up onstage when we started 'Morning Dew,' grabbed the bass off our bass player, turned it upside down, and joined in."[16]

London was like that in the spring of 1967. The June 3 issue of *Disc and Music Echo* reported on all the boldface names at the last Procol Harum show at the Speakeasy: "All four Beatles, Georgie Fame, Chris Farlmowe, Cat Stevens, Andrew Loog Oldham, Eric Burdon, Pete Townshend, Roger Daltrey and Denny Cordell." Paul McCartney heard the record at the Speakeasy and pronounced it "the best song ever."[17] He met a girl that night, a photographer named Linda Eastman. Later, he'd give her a copy of "A Whiter Shade of Pale," to remind her of how they found each other.

As the single rose to number one and started a six-week residence atop the charts, Brooker and his bandmates stepped into a Chelsea boutique called Dandy Fashions. The Beatles had beaten them there and "were standing around a harmonium singing

'A Whiter Shade of Pale' the very moment we came in," said
Brooker.[18]

THE WILDE FLOWERS had not found their moment. Soft Machine
would, after a few missteps. Like the Beatles, they booked a residency at the Star-Club in Hamburg. Unlike the Beatles, they
lasted for one night of a three-night booking before being asked
to go back home. The time was exquisite; the Softs got a new
residency in the "Spontaneous Underground," a Saturday series
at the Marquee Club.

In September 1966, the team of Jeffrey and Chandler took
on a new client: a twenty-five-year-old guitar player named
Jimi Hendrix. While Soft Machine recorded, Hendrix built a
live reputation over a string of gigs. A November concert at the
Bag O'Nails drew out the likes of Pete Townshend and John
Lennon—and Ayers. "All the stars were there and I heard serious
comments, you know: 'Shit,' 'Jesus,' 'Damn,' and other words
worse than that," Ayers recalled.[20]

Kevin Ayers found them new management, too, in the persons of Mike Jeffrey and Chas Chandler, respectively the former
manager and bassist of the Animals. The club wanted only Ayers
at first, but a deal was struck to pay the Softs £12 per week.
Inspired by the flop in Hamburg, Ayers wrote a song designed
for the charts—"Love Makes Sweet Music"—but the band found
its biggest audiences at the growing psychedelic shows. "The
music we made then was so amateurish compared to the rest of
mainstream pop and rock 'n' roll," said Ayers. That distinction
was bent into a strength: "You could tell that these people came
from different reference areas."[19]

The psychedelic wave hit everyone at a different angle. The
Softs rode it, headlining more "be-ins" of increasing size and

hype. On April 29, 1967, they joined Pink Floyd, the Move, the Crazy World of Arthur Brown, the Creation, and the Pretty Things in the "14 Hour Technicolor Dream," sponsored by the new *International Times* magazine, which would cover whatever this movement would become. The light show included a beam shining from a miner's helmet, worn by Daevid Allen. The music, increasingly, was anchored by a sound that Ratledge was cranking out of his Lowrey keyboard by running it through a fuzz box. "We couldn't afford a Hammond, which was the authentic article, so I was playing this weedy Lowrey," said Ratledge. "I wanted to approximate the power that Hendrix had. I got sick of guitarists having all the balls."[21]

The Syn evolved from the Motown covers and attempted to write epics, something that involved longer styles of composition and intricate costumes. This trend befuddled Peter Banks, who could not understand why American-style drug rock was catching on. We "ended up doing psychedelic rock operas," said Banks. "We did one about gangsters. We would dress up in gangster attire—one of us had a yellow, double-breasted suite [sic], and Chris had a green one, and there was a white one. We each would act out a part and sing these songs like a musical—like a rock opera. Because we'd always read that Pete Townshend was writing one, which obviously became *Tommy*. So we were determined to be the first band to do one on stage—which we probably were."[22]

Other acts took more naturally to the scene. Steve Howe moved from a series of cover-heavy bands to Tomorrow, whose single "My White Bicycle" paid tribute to a radical ride-sharing program and was easily mistaken for a drug anthem. The gigs went into the night; the atmosphere, Howe remembered, was improving all the time. "Hippie promoters would actually come in and say things like, 'We really liked the show, here's some extra money,' " he said. "It was such a change from the old music biz agents who would just rip you off."[23]

Decades later, Howe would tell the journalist Jim DeRogatis that the style, and the scene, built bands like Yes. "Yes couldn't have played the kind of music it made without having the experience of developing the freedom and total nonconformist approach that came from the psychedelic bands."[24]

More bands were coaxed out of the remnants of the ones who had made it. An agent named Ian Ralfini encouraged Pye Hastings, the left-behind member of the Wilde Flowers, to strike out with something new. "Progressive" had started to mean something—not a set definition, but a sense of scale and newness.

"He said, I want an English progressive band to take to America and get an album out," said Pye Hastings of Ralfini. "If you give me a good album and everything I'll give you whatever you need—a van, clothes, gear—all the things you need to get by on the road. At that time we were still using odds and sods of Soft Machine equipment—amplifiers and so on, because they were in America but they were about to reclaim it. Then the deal came along at the right moment."[25]

And at that moment, Soft Machine was back in France, touring to audiences that were ready for the be-in. In Saint-Tropez, the band extended a simple melody called "We Did It Again" to more than forty minutes. "It was his idea that if you find something boring—a basic Zen concept—then in the end you will find it interesting," Ratledge told band biographer Graham Bennett. "The ear either habituates or forces a change on itself, which is similar in a way to the stuff Terry Riley's doing. Kevin saw it halfway between this spiritual libertarian thing and showing how hip we were."[26]

In August, the band rounded the continent and returned to England. It was stopped at the port of Dover. Immigration had cause to inspect Daevid Allen's work status; Allen knew exactly why. "My name was on their list in a big black book," he said. "Being thrown out of the country was exhilarating, liberating, the best thing that could have happened to me."[27]

"We were lucky," remembered Davy O'List, guitarist for the Nice. "Jimi Hendrix came to one of the gigs and invited us on tour." The "first psychedelic tour" of Britain—forty minutes for Hendrix, seventeen minutes for Pink Floyd, twelve minutes for O'List—turned the Nice into a headliner. "Rondo" killed.

Their album was named *The Thoughts of Emerlist Davjack* after Lee Jackson's habit of carrying around Mao's book.[28] The album couldn't have been less political: the title's profundity was a joke, a portmanteau of the musicians' names, illustrated by the quartet tied together by cling-film.

IN 1967, MIKE PINDER got a call directing him to the Dunlop Tyres factory social club. There, for a steep discount—£300, down from £3,000—he could pick up a mellotron. What Pinder found resembled a keyboard, but each stroke set off a recorded sound from analog tape. The size of the tape was limiting; only seven or eight seconds of sound could play at a go. "I had two lead sides on my own machine: I had duplicated the right-hand side on the left keyboard and primarily had it as an organ," he recalled. "So I had organ on my left hand and strings, flutes or brass on my right hand. I could show them that I was playing every note."[29]

While the Moodies were struggling, singer Denny Laine had left; Justin Hayward, a singer steeped in British folk, stepped in to replace him. Decca assigned them a new producer, Tony Clarke. When the mellotron was hauled in, Clarke was just twenty-five, with more expression as a faceless session musician than as an arranger. "It was an important instrument," he said. "Anybody who was anybody was using one at the time. The Beatles had something like four and even Princess Margaret had one, black with gold bits on it."[30]

For Pinder, the little organ with the BBC orchestra trapped inside it was a godsend. "You get sick of playing piano, piano, piano on everything," he said. Suddenly, he could summon "the ideas that I'd had in my head as a kid": the countermelodies and colors that pianos could never conjure.[31]

"If someone could read music, you could put C above E and know that was the rocket ship taking off," said Graeme Edge. "You could retrieve the sounds by writing it like a musical form. Mike figured out to add horns, strings, bagpipes and all that sort of stuff behind it and turn it into a more natural musical instrument."[32]

Pinder was waiting for a project, and Decca came up with one. The label "wanted to combine an orchestra and a rock'n'roll band to make a demonstration record for a new stereo sound they'd developed on Deram," he said, and its first idea was a rock-and-roll cover of Dvořák's *New World Symphony*.[33]

The band was cool to the idea. So was Clarke. What grabbed him, more than the idea of a straight cover album, was a demo of a Hayward song called "Nights in White Satin." He'd written it before joining the group. The inspiration—seriously—was a set of satin bedsheets. "A girlfriend had given me white satin sheets that were terribly impractical because I had quite a heavy beard growth, and it's terribly unpleasant if you're trying to sleep on satin," Hayward said. "I came home one night after a gig, and sat on the side of the bed, and a lot of these thoughts came out."[34]

The band, ignoring the advice of the studio, hunkered in Decca's Studio One. "When the lights were down or out in the studio you had this massive cinemascope screen effect and years later I actually built a working screen at the far end of the studio," said Clarke. "The projectors were underneath so we could sit and beam stuff onto this screen and it would slowly dissolve into something else."[35]

Instead of fiddling with someone else's symphony, they created their own, with seven tracks corresponding to the times of day. "The Day Begins" led into "Dawn: Dawn is a Feeling," which led eventually into "Nights in White Satin." There was a song about the lunch break, and another pop song, "Tuesday Afternoon."

"I smoked a couple of joints, went out into a field with a guitar and sat there and wrote that song," Hayward said. "It was just about searching for some kind of enlightenment or some kind of religious or psychedelic experience in life. I didn't really mean it to be taken too seriously, but six months later, there it was: Our first single in America. Bang! You never expect to have to analyze these lyrics, or be questioned about them."[36]

According to Clarke, the first cut of the songs came as a surprise to Decca. "I remember arriving late one day at the Monday meeting and all the heads of department were pontificating with serious faces about the recording," said Clarke. "Our managing director was saying 'well, I didn't ask for this,' only to congratulate us a few weeks later. But then the head of classical got up and said: 'I think it's great. It's a brave step.' That was nice of him."[37]

The label went with it. In short order, the band was joining the London Festival Orchestra for a full recording of the song cycle. For the first time, a rock album was written as a single piece, each song flowing into the next, guided by the novelty of strings and brass. "The musicians just about fit into the studio— there were three bow basses and one of them had to stand in the doorway," remembered Clarke. "It was quite an impressive sight. Some of the orchestra had headphones on, all the first violins, which was a first."[38]

Decca released both "Nights in White Satin" and the album *Days of Future Passed* on November 10, 1967. In their roundabout way, the Moody Blues had produced something new: a pop song carried along by an orchestra. In Graeme Edge's wry recollection, the secret was assembling "a bunch of guys who were too stupid to know that we weren't supposed to be able to do it."[39]

BY 1968, THE PSYCHEDELIC boom defined the whole London scene—and the entirety of what rock labels were interested in. The Syn came apart, and both Banks and Squire joined another group: Mabel Greer's Toyshop. The gigging came easily; for songs, Squire penned a new one, with his bass as the lead instrument, called "Beyond and Before." "We would play a lot of the 'happening' London clubs at the time like the UFO, with the liquid lightshows and plenty of people wandering around, wondering what day and what year it was," groused Banks.[40]

In August 1968, Squire introduced Banks to a lithe singer with a reedy voice named Jon Anderson. Banks knew of him, as "one of the characters that were constantly in and out of the Marquee, the La Chasse, and a little pub up the road called the Ship." Recalled Banks, "It was me who came up with the name 'Yes.' Actually, a couple years before the time of the Syn, I had that name floating around. I always liked one-word names and Yes was short and sweet—it looked big on posters. Since it was only three letters, it would get printed bigger."[41]

The band added Bill Bruford, the drummer who had grown up on jazz, and who by this point was exhausted and "bitter" at the scene. His shoes bore the heretical slogan "MOON GO HOME," making fun of the Who's drummer, who otherwise bathed in the praise of critics.[42]

Tony Kaye, who would wait six months before the band could replace his Vox with a Hammond organ, took over on keys.

"Rehearsals could often be chaotic with everyone trying out their own ideas at the same time, almost in a state of musical anarchy," said Banks. "There were terrible days when nothing seemed to gel; my guitar sound went to pieces, Bill would be angry, saying 'Come on, come on,' Chris would be too loud, Jon's ideas would make no sense, and Tony would be noodling on the Hammond—all at top volume for hours. No organization, no discussion, but sometimes some beautiful music would arise out of all this cacophony."[43]

As Yes—Banks's name, not that he got the credit he wanted for it—the band slid right back into the scene. The sets were heavy on covers at first; "we thought we'd get more work that way," said Bruford.[44]

"We stole from everybody," said Banks. A particular highlight, a cover of "Something's Coming" from "West Side Story," replaced the original arrangement's steadily rising string section with a pure 4/4 rock rhythm. "To be honest, we really stole that arrangement from the Buddy Rich Big Band," said Banks.[45]

But the band was also playing with the structures of these covers, turning relatively simple Beatles songs into loud-quiet-loud tests of dynamics. They were writing too; the first original song was a ballad called "Sweetness," but improvisation set more of the tone. "Instead of the drummer just playing the rhythm, Chris and I would set up something and the melody would have a counter rhythm on top," said Bruford. "There would be a couple of rhythms happening at once, and that would be more fun and exciting."[46]

Some elements were consistent—Squire, for example, high up in the mix. But there was a collaboration that pulled the melodies into unexpected directions. "We were all writing in as much as we would each throw bits into each piece of music and change things around," said Banks.[47]

"Harold Land" was born from that technique. In its center

was a cryptic, reaching Jon Anderson lyric about the horror of war. It was treated with care, the singer's vocals floating over Kaye's block chords. On either side was a rampage, Banks and Bruford and Squire all hammering away in changing time signatures. "I didn't realize how liberating it was because I didn't have anything to compare it to," said Bruford.[48]

PROCOL HARUM TOURED "A Whiter Shade of Pale" and returned to the studio with the unenviable task of following it. Reid and Brooker came up with the idea of an epic suite of songs, one track with many parts, with the working title "Magnum Harum," and with pieces pulled in from any idea that meshed, any found sound that could be imbued with meaning. The result was "In Held 'Twas in I," a seventeen-minute track that resembled nothing else in pop music. It consisted of five parts: "Glimpses of Nirvana," "'Twas Tea-Time at the Circus," "In the Autumn of My Madness," "Look to Your Soul," and "Grand Finale."

"You didn't have to take psychedelic drugs for your mind to expand," said Gary Brooker. "'In Held 'Twas in I' started out with talking, then some chanting, followed by some singing. And that was quite mind expanding in itself."[49]

That song anchored *Shine On Brightly*, released in September 1968 to capitalize on the band's American tour. It fell short of expectations, coming in at twenty-four on the *Billboard* charts. Released two months later in Britain, it sold better, but it did not dominate the landscape like "Whiter Shade" had. The people who got it, however, found an urtext worth studying. "In Held," in particular, did not hang together especially well as a suite. But the idea of the suite was worth taking forward.

"*Shine On Brightly* I really think is an incredible album," Pete Townshend told Barry Miles in a 1969 interview about the Who's forthcoming album *Tommy*. "That will be from this point on a very heavy influence for me." The interviewer was curious—why would music as square as Procol's have anything to say to Townshend? "I think that their musical thing now is far more basically strong," he said. "I know it had its roots in such a vague era of music, that's why. Days of cantatas and God knows what, was a very very boring one, and there was only about 4 or 5 pieces of music which lifted their heads above the rest in that era, and so that's all that Procol Harum have got to draw on."[50]

AT THE SAME TIME, hours away from the London scene but heavily informed by it, the members of Genesis had gotten a lucky break. They'd recorded a few songs between classes at Charterhouse School, like the shouty stomper "Hey," and sent around a demo. No one seemed interested, until a slightly older Charterhouse graduate stumbled upon it.

Jonathan King, who at twenty-one had written the worldwide 1965 hit "Everyone's Gone to the Moon," had parlayed that success into a job as a TV host, then as a scout for Decca. He was checking in with friends from Charterhouse when one suggested that he hear what the promising band of teenagers had come up with. "I remembered the dreams and hopes that I had had at Charterhouse two years earlier, and I wanted to be a star, so I thought I might as well listen to it," said King. "I put the tape on and listened to them and thought: Well, they're not so bad, actually."[51]

King changed hats quickly, from skeptic to aspiring Svengali. He paid what Peter Gabriel would call the "mighty sum of £10" to record a more professional demo. "We were still thinking of ourselves as songwriters at this time, but before we knew what was happening, contracts were produced—10 years—and, of course, over a cup of tea and a chat, they were signed willingly," Gabriel remembered. "So there we were, signed up to Jonathan's publishing company, which leased recordings to Decca.

Our parents were pretty horrified when they learned what we'd done, but fortunately we were all minors, so the contract was void. So then we entered a legal contract, supported by parents' signatures, for one year."[52]

The young musicians went back and forth with King over what the band should be. One idea was that Gabriel, Banks, and the others would be a songwriting collective. King saw them as a band and packaged them as such. "The Silent Sun" would be their first single, taken from the studio and treated generously with strings by arranger Arthur Greenslade. It sounded anonymous; it sounded professional.

For the first time, the quavering, confident voice of Peter Gabriel appeared on vinyl, singing sentiments like "Baby, you feel so close" and "Baby, you changed my life." For the first time, the song was reviewed, with no pandering about the age of the composers. "A disc of many facets and great depth, but it might be a bit too complex for the average fan," wrote a reviewer in *NME*.[53]

King was giddy about the band's prospects, and infectious. "Jonathan King told us that we would be on Top of the Pops," said Gabriel, "so we all went out and bought new clothes." The band even had an original idea for outfitting. Other bands would explode with colors. Genesis would wear black and white. They suited up—and went nowhere. There was no "Top of the Pops" performance. There wasn't even a spot on Jonathan King's show. "We were all the way over the top," said Anthony Phillips. "I, probably as much as any of the others, wanted to be a star."[54]

THE NICE WAS PSYCHEDELIC too, with suitably space-cadet lyrics and Hendrix-esque guitar solos by O'List. They leaned into the image, and the association with the underground's most golden god.

"The basic policy of the group is that we're a European group," explained the Nice's lead singer Lee Jackson in a 1969 *International Times* interview. "So we're improvising on European structures. Improvisation can be around any form of music, so we're taking European work. We're not American Negros, so we can't really improvise and feel the way they can."[55]

Despite the slightly weird allergy to syncopation, the live show held. Emerson, still fooling with the Hammond, realized that a flat object, if wedged between the keys, could hold them down, playing notes that grew more and more distorted even as Emerson played another instrument. Emerson used spoons at first, then knives. One Nice roadie, Emerson remembered in his memoir, "had a great collection of German army knives and gave me two Hitler Youth daggers, saying, 'Beats the shit out of the British Boy Scouts. If you're gonna use one, use a serious one.'"[56] The roadie's name was Lemmy Kilmister. Thanks to his advice, Emerson seemed to be murdering his instrument onstage, nightly.

"There's a new group called the Nice—who are," quipped Nick Jones in the September 1967 issue of *Rolling Stone*. "The group is led by organist Keith Emerson who plays like a groovy astronaut orbiting around everything . . . if your eyes are open, you'll soon be digging these guys."[57] *Melody Maker* gave readers lengthy readouts on the band's look—"leather and suede, fringed leather jackets, and trousers that disappear into tight thigh boots"[58]—and pronounced 1968 the "Year of the Nice."[59]

The band took itself seriously. On June 6, after Robert F. Kennedy had been shot, Emerson thought about the allegorical power of the song the band was rehearsing—Leonard Bernstein's "America," from *West Side Story*. "If Bob Dylan, and his counterpart Donovan, could make protest songs, why shouldn't we?" he asked himself. "It could be the first protest instrumental."[60]

In the hands of Emerson, Jackson, Brian Davison, and O'List, "America" lasted six minutes or longer. The first sounds on it: dark organ chords, wailing chorus, muffled gunshots, screams. The last sounds: a three-year-old boy nervously saying, "America is pregnant with promise and anticipation, but is murdered by the hand of the inevitable!" Folded right into the middle of all that was a staccato figure from the fourth movement of Dvořák's *New World Symphony*.

Here was Broadway, here was classical, wrenched into 1968 and given pomp and purpose. On June 26, when the Nice played the Royal Albert Hall, Jackson screamed the "America is pregnant" line—the cue for Emerson to set fire to an American flag.

Emerson decided to write a symphony. It would be called *Ars Longa Vita Brevis*—Latin for "Art is long, life is short," and the motto of Lee Jackson's grammar school. It was built out of pieces collected from here and there: a section of Bach's *Brandenburg Concertos*, a nearly twenty-minute psychedelic freak-out titled "Ars Longa Vita Brevis," and an excellent seven-note hook from Davy O'List's guitar.

But O'List, so key to the old Nice sound, was fired while recording the album after failing to show up for a gig. (At one point, remembered Emerson, O'List had been so out of it that he had started "crumbling a chocolate bar over tobacco in mistake for the real thing."[61] O'List does not dispute this.) The band was more serious now. Seriousness meant a piece with a prelude, four movements, and a coda.

The first sound on *Ars Longa Vita Brevis* would be a minor chord, played by the English Chamber Orchestra. The second sound was a six-note run up Emerson's Hammond. Two more doomy chords from the orchestra. Back to the Hammond. The notes ran together, fast, as the guy in the leather pants raced the men in bow ties.

Emerson took special pleasure in playing so fast. While recording *Ars Longa*, Emerson ducked into the bathroom and overheard two members of the orchestra whining about the indignity of the gig. "I can't believe the tempo they're taking on the Brandenburg," sighed one of them. "It's way too fast."[62] Emerson finished his business, returned to the organ, and cranked up the volume.

The prelude ended after two minutes, rung out by a gong. The first movement, "Awakening," was a nearly four-minute drum solo. Ambitious and totally misguided, it tossed the listener out of the melody into a dreamworld of timpani hits and repetitive rolls. But then came the O'List guitar lick, salvaged even though he'd been fired from the band. The second movement, "Realisation," was a pop song with vocals, and a lyric that Jackson practically spit out about a "life of bliss."

It was more bitter sarcasm than listeners signed up for when buying a "psychedelic" record, but they were in luck. After three minutes, Emerson's organ and keyboard took charge again, playing out the seven-note theme, until he replaced it with the Bach melody in "Acceptance (Brandenburger)." The concerto excerpt was played by organ, bass, and drum—and then, by elements of the orchestra.

To the listener, wondering what the Nice had gotten up to, it was tough to tell where this ended so that the final movement, "Denial," could begin. By the time they sussed it out, the theme had re-emerged; Emerson and his bandmates had tied the song together and completed their symphony.

Immediate Records, the Nice's label in the UK, decided to sell this as a serious work of art—with Keith Emerson as the genius behind it. He wrote his own ultraserious liner notes. "Newton's first law of motion states a body will remain at rest or continue with uniform motion in a straight line unless acted upon by force," he proclaimed in bold white text on black background. "This time the force happened to come from a European source. Ours is an extension of the original Allegro from Brandenburg Concerto No. 3."[63]

"If Bach were alive today," Emerson told *Melody Maker*, "he would be playing like Keith Jarrett."[64]

Davy O'List would stew over this. He saw the band's pretentious later incarnation as evidence that they'd lost their touch. His guitar had once filled out their sound. Jackson couldn't sing "rock," O'List thought, as well as *he* could. "The part of 'Ars Longa' that worked was the part we wrote together," he told me.[65] "The Nice had reached the pinnacle of their success all over the world by the time America was a hit in the charts," he told another interviewer in 2006. "I don't think I missed anything."[66]

But the postguitar sound of the Nice *was* new. When the band played *Ars Longa* live, that ropey first-movement drum solo would get standing ovations. The Nice were playing bigger crowds in further corners of Europe and the States. It's true that "Brandenburger," released as a single, didn't reach the top ten like "America" had. But single sales were mattering less and less; 1968 was the first year that album sales outpaced them in Britain and the United States. Listeners had bought plenty of pop; now they were ready for pomp, played by people who threw knives at Hammond organs.

Ars Longa Vita Brevis became the title of the Nice's second record. The cover portrayed Emerson, O'List, and Jackson as interlocked skeletons with brightly colored organs. To get that photo, the three were injected with mildly radioactive solutions, then X-rayed. When Emerson was photographed, he learned that sometime earlier he had broken two ribs.

"You break ribs playing keyboards?" asked his doctor. "I wouldn't have considered it such a hazardous occupation."

"Depends how you play 'em," said Emerson.[67]

3

A BILLION TIMES THE IMPACT

rom the summer of 1968 to the summer of 1969, a British fan of the new music who couldn't catch live bands could settle for *Colour Me Pop.* The BBC had been booking acts across its other, stodgier shows, but the London scene was cranking out hits and idols faster than the press could cover it. The surplus of new bands, any of which might produce the next *Sgt. Pepper*, would be given thirty minutes each Saturday to prove themselves.

So *Colour Me Pop* debuted on June 14, 1968, with a credit sequence that proudly embraced cliché. A "cool" bass line and drumroll played under psychedelically retouched photos of Jimi Hendrix, Mick Jagger, and Frank Zappa, as if asking who'd be next to join the pantheon. The answer on that first Friday was the increasingly progressive Manfred Mann. Spooky Tooth got slotted in at the end of August; the Nice's set aired on November 16, as their fame was cresting.

That same day, Giles, Giles and Fripp were filming their *Colour Me Pop* debut. Thanks to the lobbying efforts of Peter Giles, they'd finagled a full thirty-minute episode all to themselves, "when people like the Hollies were doing half a program with somebody else."[1] The Saturday night audience would hear eight tracks from an album almost nobody had bought, one of them—the spoken-word fairy tale "Elephant Song"—given its own animation.

It was the last-ever gathering of Giles, Giles and Fripp. After one day of filming, Fripp and Michael Giles stayed up past midnight to figure out what the band needed to break through. Fripp wanted a new vocalist, one he'd already known for years. Greg Lake, a twenty-one-year-old singer and guitarist in the Bournemouth scene, possessed the pipes and star quality that the band had always lacked. "In my circle," Fripp would say, "Greg Lake was considered one of the front-runners for fame."[2]

Lake looked and sounded like a star. He was tall and handsome, full lips and eyes framed by a sharp Roman nose. He had shared a guitar teacher with Fripp but hadn't trained his voice; his lusty, accented croon came naturally, and found drama in every lyric. The two of them bonded when Fripp accompanied Lake as a roadie, on an ill-starred series of southern England gigs.

"We ended up in Ventnor in the Isle of Wight and got to the gig and there was literally no one there," remembered Lake. "No audience. The promoter had booked the show and somehow or another mystically failed to get any people to buy tickets. The band was ready to play, the doors opened, and no one came in. So Robert and I decided that what we would do was just play our guitar lessons. We started playing things like Spanish malagueñas and did duets with them. That's how Robert and I started playing together."[3]

In 1967, Lake's band the Shame released a cover of the Janis Ian song "Too Old to Go 'Way Little Girl." The sixteen-year-old Ian had written a dark advice column to any woman her age: "Now, there is no escaping, and you'd enjoy a raping / just to find out the facts of life."

The Shame fixed all that. The key line became "There's no

denyin' you're gonna end up cryin' "—a better fit for a vocal that told the girl to get past her prudery, Lake drawling out every mention of "sexxx" and "guuuuuys" and "your dirty miiiiiiind." This couldn't have been further from the harmless, cricketer-friendly vocals of Peter Giles.

Fripp made his Solomonic pitch. Lake had to join the band; something had to be sacrificed. Maybe Lake could replace Peter Giles on bass and vocals. Maybe he could replace Fripp on guitar.

Peter Giles didn't see this as a bargain at all. "That thing of Fripp offering to leave is just a ploy, basically," he'd say later. "It would have happened quite naturally. Fripp is very cute with political moves." And Michael Giles was plenty ready to jettison his brother and form a different band. "As much as I love him," he'd remember, "we were never some kind of inseparable brotherhood that had a design on the world."[4]

By November 30, when BBC2 viewers were being introduced to the cheerful insanity of Giles, Giles and Fripp, the rump of that band was already starting to practice with Greg Lake. There were no tears for Peter Giles after hearing Lake tackle songs like "Drop In." The band had traded precious talk-singing for pure swagger. "I couldn't sing like that," Michael Giles pronounced. "Robert couldn't sing at all. Peter couldn't sing like that. None of us had that sound or power."[5]

On January 13, 1969, the new band found rehearsal space in the basement of the Fulham Palace café in London, with— and this was important—plenty of room for a mellotron. And there was the right sort of space and ambience for Peter Sinfield as he fiddled with a few lightbulbs and timed them to flash at key points in the songs and sets. "The basics were there," Fripp wrote in his diary. "Sinfield's lightshows embryonic . . . [he] builds stage lights out of baking foil and plywood."[6]

But it worked. "It's something to this day that I still tell people doing lighting productions," Greg Lake remembered to band biographer Sid Smith. "I say, 'Do we need all these fucking lights up there?' And they say, 'Oh yeah,' because of this reason, and I tell the King Crimson story. One light bulb in the right place is worth 100 varilights going off at the wrong time."[7]

"Most clubs have a light bulb, and that's it—joke lights," Peter Sinfield told me. "So we thought we'd take our own around with us. We have always had a good light show, with the mood changing with the music, doing what a light show should."[8]

Nine days into the Fulham Palace café rehearsals, Sinfield made a second major contribution to the band. It obviously couldn't be called "Giles, Giles and Fripp," given the sudden and unexpected Giles shortage. Sinfield reached into his notebook and pulled out "King Crimson," a term he had come up with to fill in when "Satan" didn't fit a rhyme. "I wanted something that had some power to it, like Led Zeppelin," Sinfield told Paul Stump. "Anything was better than Giles, Giles and Fripp. King Crimson had an arrogance to it."[9]

The name was adopted straightaway. "Invited audience to rehearsals," wrote Fripp on January 27. "Success. This band will be bigger than we anticipated."[10]

At the end of February, King Crimson hopped a train three hours north to Newcastle for their first gigs—seven nights at a three-story venue called Change Is. Every week, the club would switch out a theme—"love" or "fun" or something—and adopt a new one. The week of Crimson's residence, the theme was "horror."

That wasn't preparation enough for Crimson's performance, all riffs and improvisations, Gustav Holst and fairy-dancing lights. When the band returned for its second set, club manager Ron Markham made a special introduction that Fripp found amusing enough to save in his diary. "Ladies and Gentlemen," said Markham, "Giles, Giles and Fripp who for reasons best known to themselves have changed their name to King Crimson, will have a freak-out without the aid of pot, LSD or any other drugs."[11]

AMERICAN AND BRITISH youth music had grown together from the moment the Beatles landed at JFK. In 1969, the two sounds finally started to grow apart. This was the year that the Grateful Dead grafted country and roots sounds into its music on songs like "St. Stephen," presaging the next three decades of their career as a jam band. Jefferson Airplane and Love were recording their own down-to-earth anthems. Bob Dylan, recovered from his motorcycle accident, debuted (and never used again) a completely new vocal timbre for songs like "Lay, Lady, Lay." The Beach Boys, having sequestered all evidence of the *Smile* debacle, covered the folk standard "Cotton Fields" and waxed it as a single. The Bay Area's own Creedence Clearwater Revival became the biggest band in America with three albums of nascent country rock.

The British bands did not go this route. They were helped by the continued growth of specialty labels. Deram kept raking it in from the Moodies and Procol Harum. In 1969 Deram was joined by Harvest, a division of EMI that focused on "progressive" music, and by Chrysalis, started by ambitious promoters Terry Ellis and Chris Wright. Ellis and Wright came straight from the college circuit, booking bands for student unions, seeing a greater and untapped financial potential.

"We got Ten Years After and involved ourselves with bands that we really like and whom we knew were talented, in spite of what everybody else thought," Ellis told *Top Pops and Music Now* in 1969. "Their career built up, not because of any hype, but because the places where we managed to persuade the promoters to book them—they went in, played, and all the kids went potty. That, for us, was the beginning of the 'Underground' scene. We thought we would get the whole organization under one roof."[12]

Harvest ran the same play, from inside the industry. Malcolm Jones, a trainee at EMI, had brought Pink Floyd to the label. His higher-ups had counted their profits. There was money to be made in the "underground" scene, and the best way to collect it was with a microlabel with a crunchy name. The first six months also saw the debut of Deep Purple, the first post–Soft Machine record by Kevin Ayers, and a sizable Pink Floyd hit in *Ummagumma*. "By the end of the year," Jones crowed to a reporter, "75 percent of the album charts will be progressive music."

The bands would be there for it anyway, even if not all of them could write hit records. Hit singles weren't the point; bands that could move albums and sell out British venues were inking deals and being covered intimately by the music press. A&R (artists and repertoire) men pulled promising bands from the school union circuit and from the London clubs, two scenes that overlapped from month to month. None of them had Genesis's connections, but it hardly mattered when A&R men were racing to sell the "underground."

Van der Graaf Generator benefited from the chase. The school union gigs had built a real following for the band, and a smattering of media attention. At the end of 1967, Peter Hammill, Judge Smith, and Nick Pearne recorded a demo for interested parties, with "Sunshine" on one side and an Icelandic myth called "Firebrand" on the other. Within months the demo had ended up with Mercury Records, and the band was being lobbied hard in London clubs. In May 1968, the three bandmates signed a contract as their manager, a fellow student, watched.

"They spent a whole morning giving their life story to John

Sipple, the head of Mercury World Publicity, and also went to Littlehampton for the day to have their photographs taken," reported the *Manchester Independent*. "The Generator bought a new 120 watt amplifier and a Vox guitar which they call Meurglys, after Ganelon's sword in 'Roland,' which is covered with fur so that it looks like a flying squirrel with strings attached."[13]

But that band fell apart a week later. A chance conversation at a bus stop ended up bringing Hugh Banton aboard as an organist. The new band was "discovered" by Tony Stratton-Smith, fresh off his deals with Genesis. Five months after the Mercury signing, a new version of the band recorded a first single: "People You Were Going To" backed by "Firebrand." Mercury, understandably, objected to releasing this single by their artists on some other label.

The parties reached an impasse. Van der Graaf Generator broke up, again. Hammill headed into London's Trident Studios to record a solo album. Sort of. "Having the opportunity to make an album," he told a radio interviewer, "I got everyone from the band together again."[14] Hammill fulfilled his Mercury deal by getting the label to rename and remarket his record as the first VdGG album, then let him free.

The band that couldn't stop collapsing was able to put out *The Aerosol Grey Machine*, a name that Hammill had dreamed up after the drinks at some VdGG gigs kept getting spiked with acid. "Peter joked that I should have an aerosol grey machine which would have the opposite effect to psychedelics and make everything artificially grey," explained Smith.[15]

A cover was mocked up, a grim female hippie tilting her head as she sprayed shades of gray out of a can, obscuring a backdrop of trees and grass. That was scrapped for something more generically psychedelic—not that it mattered.

The album was released in the United States and Europe.

There would be no release in Britain. Mercury's investment was largely squandered—a down payment on a band that sold nearly no records for them. The label had paid for men barely into their twenties to experiment, and to record the songs that had clicked for student unions in the north. All the labels were taking that risk; any group like this could be the next Pink Floyd, couldn't it?

"The sheer adversity faced in order to produce the music fired me and the others up to do the rest of the stuff," Hammill wrote later, when *The Aerosol Grey Machine* was released on compact disc. "It therefore follows that without this there would be nothing. I would not have attitude if I had not had to get through this. I'll be honest with you; there are moments on these recordings when I now sound to myself like a real twenty-year-old, know-it-all, know-nothing prat. I was so. But those moments are blips along the track of attempting to make music; that's nothing I can bring myself to feel embarrassed about."[16]

KING CRIMSON FELL into place during that week at Change Is. Greg Lake and Robert Fripp hadn't spent this much time together since the guitarist had done sporadic roadie work for the singer, years earlier in Bournemouth. Once they became bandmates, Lake tutored Fripp in the ways of stardom.

"When I got to the band," said Lake, "I seem to remember that Robert was dressed in a red maroon pullover, grey flannel trousers, black Oxford shoes—he was dressed to go to grammar school!"[17]

"Greg said we should go into the club and line up the birds," Fripp remembered to one biographer. "He looked on me, somewhat rightly, as an inept puller" and "took it on himself to give me some help in strategy and maneuvers."[18] Lake was an excellent teacher, with ego to spare and share; Fripp did pull birds at the Newcastle shows.

The band returned to London. Lake took his guitarist to Portobello Road, outfitting him with "black magic" gear that would be toned down to a modest hippie jacket. Fripp discovered the reward for his carousing in Newcastle: a ripe case of gonorrhea.

Crimson made its London debut on April 9, 1969, at the Speakeasy, gigging steadily through the spring and folding into the scene. They started talking to the Moody Blues about touring with them—an embryonic band backing up the country's symphonic hit makers. It didn't pan out. "I think they [the Moodies] were terrified," said Michael Giles. "There was a power and an energy coming off Crimson that couldn't be denied."[19]

None of the musicians who popped up at the shows even attempted to deny it. King Crimson settled into a sound and image. Fripp, never comfortable standing up to play guitar, decided at the band's May 14 gig that he would play seated on a stool. "You can't sit down," warned an exasperated Greg Lake. "You'll look like a mushroom!"[20]

Fripp was unmoved. "My considered opinion," he'd tell an audience at a later concert, "was that the mushroom is a fertility symbol in many cultures."[21] So the guitarist sat down, and he won immediate validation from one of the only people whose opinion mattered. Jimi Hendrix was at the show, "jumping up and down," and pronouncing Crimson "the best group in the world."[22]

After the show, Hendrix approached Fripp wearing a white suit with a matching sling on his right arm. "One of the most luminous people I've ever met," remembered Fripp. "And he said to me: Shake my left hand, man, it's closer to my heart."[23]

The Rolling Stones were set to play an outdoor concert at Hyde Park on July 5. King Crimson, just six-odd months into its existence, was booked to support them. On July 3, the Stones' multi-instrumentalist Brian Jones was discovered at the bottom of his pool. There was a moment of panic about whether the show would go forward. The panic subsided and nothing was canceled, as funereal portraits of Jones were placed at either side of the Hyde Park stage. King Crimson would have forty minutes to play to the largest audience they'd ever seen.

"Here's a band that's going to go a long way," promised the announcer. Seven seconds later the band crashed into the first chords of "21st Century Schizoid Man," all majors and sharps in 4/4 time, the entire band swinging like a fist. They played the ascending riff three times, each iteration ending with a higher, more discordant bending of Fripp's guitar strings. The riff ended, and Fripp played flattened C chords as Lake howled Sinfield's lyrics.

With the last line, Lake switched from a howl to a croon— then back to the riff, and to one more verse. After ninety seconds, the band charged into a faster sort of jazz number based on an old Ian McDonald melody that he'd titled "Three Score and Four." The players ran through their solos for three minutes as Michael Giles sweated out a backbeat. Then another crash, another chorus. In just over six minutes it was over, and the crowd was theirs.

King Crimson held the stage for forty minutes at Hyde Park, playing highly structured songs—"The Court of the Crimson King," "Epitaph"—and songs that served to scaffold their incredibly quick solos. Lake didn't even get vocal parts for the last thirteen minutes. The brief "Mantra" consisted largely of a tender McDonald flute melody. "Travel Weary Capricorn" was a showcase for Giles—a song so evocative of basement jazz that the impressions of "Schizoid Man" started to fade.

But the jazz number ended with a strangled-cat solo from

Fripp, as Lake and Giles laid down a thudding beat. This was "Mars," a travel-sized cover of Gustav Holst's piece from *The Planets*. A mellotron carried the melody as the band relentlessly bent the classical piece into a Satanic groove. It ended with air-raid sirens, played by the band's management. And that was the show. "Standing ovation," recorded Fripp in his diary. "Mammoth Success, of importance which will take time to appreciate. We'll look back to see this day in years to come and fully realise its significance."[24]

Sinfield was far less satisfied. The open-air festival setting had thwarted his main live contribution to the band, the light show. The next night, back at the Marquee, Sinfield was in control again, and the band was able to refine the sound it was simultaneously trying to capture in the studio. "They've learnt when to clap," recorded Fripp in the diary.[25]

King Crimson played thirteen gigs at the Marquee in 1969; they played on the night three American astronauts first stepped across the Moon. "I'm sure we'd like to wish them the best of luck,"[26] announced Lake. The band played "Epitaph," and the teenaged Lake's voice hit the walls, with something about "the wall on which the prophets wrote" and "the instruments of death."

By July's end, King Crimson were recording their album. It was the second attempt, after sessions with Moody Blues producer Tony Clarke produced a fat lot of nothing. "Our energy was trying to be transformed into another Moody Blues," complained Michael Giles, "with lots of strumming guitars, one on top of the other, all heavily compressed with no dynamics."[27]

On the second go, the band recorded itself. The record would contain five songs, all but one of them road-tested at most of their shows. "21st Century Schizoid Man" was given a slower burn, starting with half a minute of ambient noise—wind blown through a pipe organ. The stomp of the song was essentially what crowds had been hearing at the Marquee. Lake's vocal had been heavily distorted, though, and he'd reigned it in, ending each verse and chorus on a low note.

The record followed a rhythm, a sprint/rest alternation between pomp and pastoral music. "I Talk to the Wind" twinned Lake's lead vocal—again not showing off his range—with a Michael Giles harmony, cooing over Ian McDonald's flute and some light guitar fills by Fripp. Both "Epitaph" and "The Court of the Crimson King," mainstays of the live shows, were anchored by mellotron samples of orchestras.

Nestled in between was "Moonchild," a largely experimental song. It began with a gentle waltz that evoked George Gershwin's "Summertime," every bar ending on a menacing note. The waltz faded away; the band began a lengthy improvisation, a slow walk through jazz figures that, at one point, involved Fripp quoting the melody from Rodgers and Hammerstein's "Surrey with a Fringe on Top."

The whole job took about two months. Barry Godber, an artist who had met Peter Sinfield when they were boring themselves senseless in the computer industry, was given tapes of the music and asked to paint a cover. He came back with two watercolors that occupied both sides of a gatefold LP sleeve, with no room for a band name or album title.

On the front was a red face, the color of pulp and muscle, screaming as it turned to look at some threat from behind. The inside presented another face, less terrifying at first glance, embedded in a red moon and throwing shapes with his hands like Christ in an icon. The face smiled, revealing a set of white fangs. There they were: the Schizoid Man and the Crimson King.

On October 10, *In the Court of the Crimson King* hit British shops. On October 11, King Crimson played its final city concert at the London College of Printing. The gear was set up, and most of the band was in place. No one could locate Greg Lake. Ian McDonald's girlfriend, Charlotte Bates, was deputized to find him. "We had to go get him in the end," she remembered, "and he was bonking in the changing room. Greg was a great big ego, a big penis on legs."[28]

But none of that interfered with the pivot to America. King Crimson flew across the Atlantic at the end of October, just as EG Records was ramping up their promos. The label approached Pete Townshend about blurbing the album. His praise was so fulsome that the eventual full-page ad, which ran in music magazines on either side of the Atlantic, consisted entirely of Godber's art and of "What Pete Townshend Thinks about King Crimson," which was, in part:

> A friend listening to the album from a room below says, "Is that a new WHO album?" Deeply I'm ashamed that it isn't, but I'm also glad somehow. That kind of intensity is music not Rock. Twenty first century schizoid man is everything multitracked a billion times, and when you listen you get a billion times the impact. Has to be the heaviest riff that has been middle frequencied onto that black vinyl disc since Mahlers' [sic] 8th.[29]

Thus King Crimson was flogged to the masses as its members flew to America's East Coast. "We'll lose money on our way across from the east coast to the West," Fripp told *Beat Instrumental* in an oddly honest pretour interview. "As soon as you call yourself a rock band, for instance, you limit yourself."[30]

The tour wore them down, and quickly. "It's all that hanging about in hotels and airports, backstage—it's a strange place," Michael Giles would recall. "I used to think of it, and still do, like it's the lions coming into the circus through those tunneled cages and then let loose and they've got to perform and then they're taken away again."[31]

The "circus" dragged on through November, taking Crimson from Boston to Chicago to Detroit to Florida. Band members included speed or marijuana in their diets, depending on whether work or travel was the order of the day. Giles was talking about turning Crimson into a studio band. Fripp was ignoring him.

The band played five nights in a row at the Whisky a Go Go and were panned by the *LA Times* as "artists, shrewd manipulators of myriad rock and other techniques" who happened to be "boring almost beyond description."[32]

Giles and McDonald were fraying, pining for their girl-friends. For the first and not the last time, the US was rending King Crimson apart. "We were blowing audiences' minds," said McDonald, "and the thing was turning into this monster that was growing and maybe at the time I wasn't equipped to deal with it." Fripp said, "My stomach disappeared. King Crimson was everything to me. To keep the band together, I offered to leave instead but Ian said that the band was more me than them."[33]

"King Crimson will probably be condemned by some for pompousness, but that criticism isn't really valid," argued John Morthland in *Rolling Stone*. "They have combined aspects of many musical forms to create a surreal work of force and originality. Besides which they're good musicians." There was one caveat. "How effectively this music can be on stage is, admittedly, a big question. The answer is probably not too well."[34]

The review ran weeks after King Crimson had effectively ceased to exist as a live band. They wouldn't appear on stage again for more than a year.

"That band died during the recording of the first album," Fripp would tell an interviewer a few years later. "It had gathered such a momentum that the impetus of the corpse twitched on until it finally fell over in San Francisco in December 1969. It was just down the road in a small motel just off Sunset Strip when Ian and Mike decided to leave. They leapt about the hotel in fits of excitement and glee that they had snuffed this burden of responsibility. I envied them considerably because I couldn't do the same."[35]

THE MUSIC PRESS caught on slowly to King Crimson's problems. Fripp had long established himself as the band leader, the scientist revealing his equations in loping interviews. Lake was the voice of the band. By the end of 1969, the "underground" and the official scene had been altered completely by the mere presence and terrifying success of Fripp and company. Bill Bruford, then the drummer for Yes, saw the band perform at 4:30 a.m. one night, and left obsessed. Steve Hackett, a guitarist who would later join Genesis, saw one of the London gigs and marveled at the presentation.

"Yes and King Crimson were very much rival bands," said Yes guitarist Peter Banks. "When King Crimson came around, and we saw them perform, we were absolutely stunned. I remember Bill saying, 'I want to join that band,' which of course he later did."[36]

And Yes was having a good year. The band had signed to Atlantic, and in the spring they had recorded an album of six original songs and two covers. They didn't really sound like King Crimson, or try to. Chris Squire's bass was mixed far louder than Greg Lake's, chugging the rhythm of "Beyond and Before," rendering the Beatles' "Every Little Thing" into a nearly unrecognizable jam. Anderson's lyrics carried none of Sinfield's mysticism; they were quirky, but grounded. There was no opacity to them. When Anderson got dark, as on the war ballad "Harold Land," he told a literal story of a veteran who lost all sense of reality while on the front.

In the Court made Yes's sound seem several evolutionary cycles behind. "It kind of blew our thunder completely," groused Peter Banks. "Also, their album did very well, in contrast to ours, which didn't."[37]

King Crimson was, at that very moment, in a state of collapse—as was the Nice. Keith Emerson's band had just recorded its second symphony, one that moved further away from rock structure than the old *Ars Longa Vita Brevis* had. Nineteen minutes long, entirely instrumental, it was arranged for an orchestra and would be played live by one. Emerson's ambitions were larger than the band could support. After one rehearsal, Emerson and Davison retreated to the Speakeasy, and the keyboard player's suggestions turned the meeting into "a 'fuck you,' 'fuck you, too' kind of conversation."[38]

Emerson sought out new talent, starting with Lake. He met him first in the dressing room after a San Francisco band showcase, when Crimson was at its most fractious. Emerson would remember Lake "majestically enthroned in the only overstuffed tatty armchair of his band's dressing room, snapping fingers at the nearest subject to light his cigarettes," and had a first conversation that consisted of Lake lecturing on "the clarity of sound" and why "some of the notes you play seem blurred."[39]

The keyboard player was undeterred. Over the long Christmas holidays, he met again with Lake at the bassist's cottage. "He was still indecisive," Emerson would remember, "almost evasive about discussing King Crimson's future, centering discussions around what I was doing and how I could do it better."[40]

Weeks later, at 3 a.m., Lake rang up Emerson with an offer. "Listen, I've been thinking. We should get the band together."

Emerson trekked back to Lake's house, ready to cut the deal over a bottle of red.

"You've got to work with professionals," explained Lake to the star who'd spent nearly three times as long in the music industry. "That's the key word—'Professionals,' and the reason The Nice fell apart bad management."

"Hold on a second," said Emerson. "The Nice fell apart because of their changing artistic attitudes. It's got nothing to do with set-ups. I happen to think that Tony Stratton-Smith is a very fine, very fair manager."

"Maybe he was okay for The Nice," shrugged Lake. "We have to move on."[41]

Lake suggested the management of EG Records, carrying straight on from King Crimson. This wasn't the only thing he copied from his old band. He cut a deal with Fripp—a sort of kick-starter for the music he would make with his new, genius partner. "The actual phrase used by Greg was 'for my art,'" said Fripp.[42]

"Robert had asked me if I wanted to continue the group under the name of King Crimson," Lake would say, "and I think I would have done had it been just one of the two of Ian and Mike who had left."[43]

Fripp didn't have that choice. The band still had a deal, and a burgeoning audience won over by 1969's best album. "King Crimson was too important to let die," thought Fripp.[44]

His band—and it was quickly becoming, by default and intent, *his* band—only lacked material. "Cat Food" was a dada rumination on fast-food culture that had been cobbled together on the chemically enhanced bus ride between the Detroit and Chicago gigs. Lake stayed on to provide vocals. Fripp had been a fan of Keith Tippett, a freestyle pianist, and invited him into the band. The King Crimson sound changed completely, to the disquiet of the other players. "Without the piano it might have actually done something," said Peter Giles. "Fair enough. Fripp stuck to his guns, even though the guns were pointing in the wrong direction."[45]

That direction was set not just by Fripp, but by the prodigal McDonald and Giles. Back in England after the tour, as they hammered out songs for the second album, Fripp and Sinfield had visited McDonald with some unfinished tracks. "My feeling at the time," remembered the multi-instrumentalist, "was that they were trying to get free ideas and I just kept my mouth shut."[46]

Fripp never agreed with that. "If half of the most exciting band of the year leave as it takes off," he asked an interviewer, rhetorically, "which they later acknowledge as a mistake, how could they be trusted/relied upon again?"[47]

Soon, McDonald was collaborating with Giles on an album of their own, taking with them some of the melodies they'd written for King Crimson. "Some people have likened it to middle-period Beatles," Giles told an interviewer who'd heard the new album. "Fine by me, because that's what we wanted to get, the sort of music which doesn't come from technique but which works on a warmer level."[48]

McDonald and Giles had taken melodies with them, starting with a side-long suite that became "Birdman." Fripp "had hoped that this would be the centerpiece of the second Crimson album." A brief, sweet, and lilting ballad became "Flight of the Ibis." The lyrics were pure sentimentality.[49]

The same melody had ended up with Fripp and Sinfield, and in the light-show poet's hands it became a story of blissful roadie seduction.

The album's cover art was gatefold, a photo of the bandmates and their current girlfriends traipsing through a garden, colors touched up to psychedelic standards. This was cheerful, an increasingly stark contrast to the goings-on in Fripp's studios. The sophomore King Crimson album, *In the Wake of Poseidon*, was filled out by revisions of material that the old band had worked in concert. "The Devil's Triangle," which closed the record, came about after the band was prevented from putting that cover of Holst's "Mars" on vinyl. The new song sounded like Holst's music trampled by demons, the melody oozing from a mellotron. The song closed with a sample of the old band's harmonies from *In the Court of the Crimson King*.[50]

Fripp faced a challenge. He was open and available to the press; the press was avidly interested in whatever King Crimson did. Yet the quality of the new music was impossible to spin. The band stopped touring; indeed, it wouldn't tour again until more than a year after the American run ended.

Sinfield was more confident, sure that inspiration would come again, remembering what had risen from the bones of Giles, Giles and Fripp. "Within a year of its release and demission, somebody had stirred a cauldron, pointed a bone, painted a throne, and crowned a king," said the lyricist to Fripp. "You'll work it out."[51]

But with what band? The *Poseidon* sessions were filled out when saxophonist Mel Collins was brought in, and—eventually—when singer Gordon Haskell agreed to take the place of Greg Lake. Haskell had been friends with Fripp since the Bournemouth days, when the two of them sat next to each other in class. "Robert got me started," Haskell said later. "He played me Django Reinhardt, but I preferred American music. Looking back, Robert was drawn to European music, and I was my father's son; he was American-Greek."[52]

The differences between the singer and the guitarist had only widened since. Haskell had clocked time on the London scene, playing for a while with the Fleur de Lys and recording a strings-drenched solo album—*Sail in My Boat*—that he later condemned as juvenilia. "I was easily manipulated," he would later admit.[53] Haskell's inborn mistrust of the music machine synced up quite well with Fripp's. But Haskell originally turned down the offer to join King Crimson. The band was too weird.

When he relented, the band found new ways to make him skeptical. "They took 12 hours to get a drum sound and it was still shite," Haskell remembered. "You know, Otis Redding's band took two minutes to get a drum sound and that was perfect. Fripp and Sinfield didn't know what they were looking for."[54]

Not on drums, not in any way—at least not in Haskell's opinion, shared by others being asked to remake the band. Trombonist Nick Evans was disturbed to see how "our parts were added in small sections, maybe four or eight bars at a time" and placed like ink strokes across the tracks as Fripp required them.[55]

And the choices really were Fripp's to make. After McDonald and Giles quit, and Lake followed, what had been a 22.5 percent royalty share for Fripp became 60 percent. He was an impresario now, even if his new singer was utterly unmoved by Keith Tippett and couldn't understand what the point was, musically, of the pianist's fingerings on songs like "Cat Food."

"That sounds just like a cat walking across a piano," Haskell told Fripp.

"Yeah," said the impresario, "but Keith knows what he's doing. A cat doesn't."

"Yes," sighed Haskell, "but it sounds the same!"[56]

Haskell stuck with the band. *Poseidon* was done, and the "Cat Food" single would feed the press and public attention. The new King Crimson would have time to congeal—and to war internally. After one row, Fripp snapped at Haskell to remind him of who had the most to gain from being in this band. "How many hits have you had, then?"[57]

The singer just steamed. "It's got to sound 'innovative,'" Haskell would carp to an interviewer decades later. "They shouldn't have used drums—they should have used my dick."[58]

Haskell was angrier than Fripp knew. "I can honestly say I always felt the same as a slave, as I was and have always been intuitive," Haskell would remember. "I knew we were slaves in a fascist country intuitively, but failed to articulate it—so I continually was self-effacing when I should have been a warrior and stood my ground. I was so unbelievably pleasant. Stupid, really. And I ought to have ripped a few heads off."[59]

Fripp and Haskell were bound to combust eventually. The singer didn't know what Fripp was playing at. Fripp, in talks with the band and the press, broadcast the confidence of complete control. "The ideal size for a band would be 15 people because you could then have the musicians who could interpret any song you wanted to play, but that is impossible," Fripp told *Music Now*'s Tony Norman. "The Beatles had it down to an art. When you heard one of their songs for the first time, your interest was immediately aroused. But then with things like *Sgt. Pepper* you can hear them three years later and still be hearing something new. That is what we are trying to do. We want our albums to last."[60]

Haskell simply didn't hear that in the music. "Indoor Games" had the structure of a pop song but elements that spun it sideways. The trumpet that drove most of the melody ended each bar on a jarring up note. The conclusion blended this sound with a raining synthesized effect. "They were all such pricks," Haskell would say. "No studio experience at all. I had spent three years in studios, with superb musicians, world class."[61]

But in the studio, confronted with "Indoor Games," Haskell

was tasked with a simple tune wedded to an abstruse Sinfield lyric. He never stopped struggling with it. He couldn't take it seriously. "I was in a booth on my own with the lyric sheet in front of me and the lyric ended with 'Hey Ho.' When I saw the line come up I thought 'I don't know how to sing this.' I thought this was fucking insane so I just went 'Hey Ho!' Who says 'Hey Ho?'" So he burst out laughing. "It was the worst thing I'd ever heard up to that point and there I was actually doing it."[62] On the track, the context happily removed, Haskell's spite sounded rather jovial. The cackle stayed in.

Outside the studio, Fripp put a positive spin on things. "Cirkus," a song with the structure and lyrics of a Renaissance ballad and the tones of a horror film, had terribly challenged the new singer. "Gordon Haskell is struggling heroically to be a singer in a context where such endeavor is a functional impossibility," Fripp explained. "An accompaniment which declines to accompany, and lyrics sufficient to set the psyches of strong men flapping."[63]

Even that nicety suggested that Haskell couldn't stay. The breaking point came when the band rehearsed "classic" Crimson songs—material that was a year old, or less, but remnants of an entirely different band. Haskell's wry, adenoidal voice could simply not wave and soar the way Greg Lake's could. He wanted "Schizoid Man" shifted down, into his range.

"I'm not going on stage and making a cunt of myself," he snapped.

"Do you want to leave?" asked an exasperated Fripp.

"I do," said Haskell, in his telling of the story. "I'm not going to go onstage and sing something I don't believe in. It's bullshit."

Haskell remembered storming out; he remembered Fripp telling him, "You'll still get your royalties."[64] Then he remembered seeing the whole dispute in the music press.

"He knew how to grab a headline," groused Haskell. "It must have been the first thing he did that night of the row, and after promising to pay me my share of *Lizard*—clearly a blatant lie, as I have never received a penny. Typical fascist behavior. He struck me as an utter buffoon."

The *Lizard* incarnation of King Crimson would never play live. Haskell would never forget the darkness of the tryst. He and Fripp would meet again, on fair and friendly terms; he would get another crack at a solo album, *It Is and It Isn't*, approved by Ahmet Ertegun himself after a spontaneous performance in the Atlantic guru's hotel room. "Excitement, vindication, proof of my sanity," Haskell remembered.

He would move on, recording the sort of soulful music he had wanted—the antithesis of Crimson. "The King Crimson weapon is musical fascism, made by fascists, designed by fascists to dehumanize, to strip mankind of his dignity and soul," he said later. "It's pure Tavistock Institute material, financed by the Rothschild Zionists and promoted by two poncy public school boys with connections to the city of London."[65]

That—well, not all of it, but some of it—was what kept the world interested in Fripp. Even as the latest iteration of his band was rending itself apart, the guitarist was giving more interviews about King Crimson's philosophy. "Some people say our music is pretentious," he told *Music Now*. "I would say the music is arrogant. It is presumptuous to hold an opinion, but on the other hand it is better to be like that and hold an opinion than to have no opinion at all. If you record that opinion then your music is arrogant. But I am right in thinking that pretentious means trying to be something you are not. Well, I wonder what we have tried to be that we are not."[66]

At the close of 1970, the question was bound up with optimism. King Crimson was now largely Fripp's project, partly

Sinfield's project. It was, definitively, falling out of the cosmos. Other "progressive" bands, celebrated by the same music press, were filling the black sky. Sinfield would hear Fripp repeat a theory he'd come up with—the parable of the "good fairy": A positive spirit flitted from band to band, acting as muse just long enough to produce some great work. When the work was complete, the muse moved on.

"You don't have to believe in God, but a musician believes in music as if it was a God," Fripp would say, in one telling of the theory. "One would have to say with that band that something took place outside of the band, and the words I'd use would be that *music leant over and took us into its confidence*. Music played that band for a short period of time. In King Crimson, we called this our 'Good Fairy.' We knew it had nothing to do with us. And yet, despite the foibles, weaknesses, animosities, and limitations of the members of that remarkable group, something exceptional occurred. Despite the people."[67]

4

MOOG MEN

he supergroup needed a name. Neither Greg Lake nor Keith Emerson appreciated the term—"supergroup"—or its associations. They had not yet played a note in public, and already they'd been categorized, branded, oversold, their union announced in the front of the April 4, 1970, issue of *New Musical Express.*

But they *were* ambitious. Emerson had wanted to bring on Mitch Mitchell, Jimi Hendrix's drummer. Mitchell, in the process of bombing the audition by talking about the bodyguards he needed, suggested that Hendrix himself might want to join. Emerson didn't buy it. Hendrix had been telling people that he wanted to work exclusively with other black musicians. It was a hell of a story, though; more press buzz followed. "I think what appealed to and amused them more than anything," recalled Emerson, "was that ELP would have been HELP."[1]

"ELP," for Emerson, Lake & Palmer—that was Emerson's preferred name for the band. They'd hired Carl Palmer, a supernova drummer for Atomic Rooster, who'd been deeply bored with that group. "I realized that the first album was trash, but

I thought I must give it longer," Palmer told *Sounds*. "So I did, but a couple of weeks later Greg called up and suggested I had a blow with them."[2]

Yet after the group was formed, after EG management agreed to take them on, Lake continued to fight the name. "We should have a group name, one that is marketable," he told Emerson. "One name that personifies, exemplifies all the individual energies of this band." He pitched "Triton," then "Sea Horse." Emerson didn't budge, to Lake's great frustration. "Why should your name come first?" griped Lake.[3]

Lake never came up with a workable alternative; ELP it was. Emerson was ready to flog the band in the music press, bringing around reporters who'd been helpful promoting the Nice. Palmer did his part.

Lake joined Emerson for an afternoon meeting at the A & R Club in London with Richard Green, an *NME* writer who had flowed forth with praise for Emerson's old band. The talent showed up. The journalist didn't. It took half an hour for Emerson to spot Green at the wrong end of the bar, three sheets to the wind.

"Now, let me see," said Green, digging out a battered notebook. "You two are getting a 'supergroup' together?"

Lake, who'd been ready to leave, eyed Green contemptuously. "We don't like the 'supergroup' take," he said.

"What do you like?" asked Green.

"Well, for one, we like punctuality and accuracy."

A few questions later, Lake was out. Emerson did what he could to salvage the promo but knew, as he would write years later, that "a bad seed had been sown and its spores would blow." The rock press's impression of ELP had calcified. The band would "have to contend with the media's general disaffection for the group's entire career."[4]

He was overstating the problem. For the first few years, into the mid-1970s, ELP was an object of obsession by the music press. They became, in the words of one critic, the band that took "rock to college." King Crimson had worked Holst into its stage show; ELP would experiment with classical themes, with studio technology, with the most outré stage antics anyone had yet tried, and then reveal the process for the waiting press.

This was where the Moog came in. Emerson was still with the Nice when, as he told it, a record store owner in Soho pulled out a copy of *Switched-On Bach*. The Nice had turned Bach's *Brandenburg* Concerto no. 3 into a tight rock song, "Brandenburger," with Emerson battering out the melody on his Hammond. The clerk assumed that Emerson would want to see what Walter Carlos, an electronic musician who would later become Wendy, had done with the same song.

Emerson contemplated the cover. A Bach-a-like (not Walter Carlos himself) stood in front of a box of mysterious technology, occupying the desk of a well-appointed study. "What is *that*?" he asked. "That's the Moog synthesizer," said the clerk.[5]

The clerk spun the record. Carlos's keyboards, processed in a fashion Emerson could not recognize, made up the entirety of the track. There were no drums, no acoustic sounds to breed familiarity. But there was a song. Emerson had plenty to think about. "Some other tracks sounded almost comical," he'd say, "like a load of elephants farting counterpoint with whoopee cushions in accompaniment. I became more interested in how the effects had been achieved with electronics, rather than air forced through a tiny space."[6]

But he remained interested in what the Moog could do. After ELP had recorded "Take a Pebble" and "Knife Edge," pieces that allowed the musicians to show off their skills in extended solos, Emerson entered the studio to hear Lake "strumming away to what sounded like a Country and Western tune in three-four."[7]

The song was "Lucky Man," a simple ballad with fantastical lyrics that Lake had written as a teenager. The verse, just a
repeating G-D pattern, told the story of a wealthy man with
"white horses" and a "gold covered mattress" who died on the
battlefield, pointlessly. "No money could save him," sang Lake.
The chorus was a croon over sorrowful minor A and E chords.

"There seemed to be an awful lot of strumming at the end,"
thought Emerson. He spotted a toy in the studio—a Moog synthesizer. Eddy Offord, the producer who'd been elbowed aside a
bit by Lake, joined Emerson in trying to untangle the machine.
They grabbed the cables (the cover of *Switched-On Bach* had
shown no such cables) and jack plugs and started sticking them
into holes in the hopes of something strange and beautiful coming out. "The portomento knob seemed to be a load of fun
during the level check," said Emerson. "You could 'slur' notes.
I made a mental note to use the effect when they ran the tape."[8]

Lake and Offord played back "Lucky Man," and Emerson
went to work on the knobs. His Moog did not appear on the
track until the final chorus. At first, it was a low hum, an under-
layment for the rest of the song. As Lake's multitracked vocals
sang out, the Moog started rising, then suddenly slurring; the
tune hit the ceiling, then fell back down, rising and falling as
the knob twisted.

Emerson figured he would need another take. "I thought it
was the most mediocre solo I'd ever played," he remembered.[9]
Here he was, a virtuoso who slipped incredibly delicate figures
into fast rock songs, and here was a solo that meandered around
the track.

The solo stayed. Lake and Offord adored it. Shortly thereafter, a Moog arrived at the studio with a note from Robert Moog
himself: "I understand that you want to tour with your instrument. As an experiment, we have built a pre-set box that will
enable you to have up to eight different sounds."[10]

The touring machine, while more portable than the one in the studio, was a monolith. "It was prone to tuning shifts if the surrounding temperature deviated more than 10 degrees either way," said Emerson. "I had a frequency counter built in with a digital readout,so that I could immediately reference the situation of all three oscillators whilst playing in performance, but it required more than dexterity to utilize. Playing away with my right hand while tuning the Moog with my left was something I'd have to get used to during the next six years."[11]

He adapted quickly. ELP made its live debut on August 23, 1970, a Sunday night, at the Plymouth Guildhall. The full spectacle was reserved for the next weekend, night four of the five-day Isle of Wight Festival. "Most bands, you get a chance to develop a bit before you get really thrust in the public arena," Lake would say. "ELP was sort of instantly out there."[12]

The band would play in the evening, Moog onstage, a row of cannons hazardously close to the bank of photographers. "Take a Pebble" was the only original in the set; the band concentrated on classical covers, starting with "Pictures at an Exhibition" and continuing with songs played frequently by the Nice. "The sound we were making left the stage and kept going," said Emerson. "There was no ambiance and no feedback from an audience that appeared to be having one huge picnic breaking down the perimeter fences."[13]

"Emerson is one of the few experimentalists who makes rock usage of electronics work for him and not the other way round," wrote Chris Welch in *Melody Maker*. "He controlled his £3,000 worth of Moog Synthesizer with cunning skill and produced effective if expensive bleeps, howls and rhythmic squeaks. The applause was almost as deafening as the cannonade which blew the spectacles off a man sitting in the firing line."[14]

"Today we believe in getting the audience to an even bigger better orgasmic peak than ever before," Emerson told *Sounds* after the Isle of Wight. "To get tighter and tighter. As it is, the ESP of the group is amazing. Carl blows my head off some nights because he knows what I'm going to do four bars ahead."[15]

Emerson, Lake & Palmer hit the shelves in October. King Crimson's debut album had peaked at number five in the UK charts, and it made the top twenty in the US. Lake's new band came in at number four in the UK and number eighteen in the US.

ON THE LAST DAY of 1970, the British High Court received a writ that confirmed what Beatles fans had known all year: the Beatles were breaking up. Paul McCartney was suing to dissolve the band—or, as the killer legalese termed it, the "partnership business carried on by the plaintiff and the defendants under the name of The Beatles & Co."

None of the Beatles would revisit the psychedelic pop or conceptual suites they had popularized at the end of the 1960s. That would be left to the progressives, which was lucky; the success of ELP helped along two waves of bands. The first had gotten their starts in the London scene and evolved with it. The second had developed outside of London, in but not of the milieu, finding their way to deals with Charisma or Harvest or Island. Within the UK, the record industry was signing and promoting any "progressive" band with an audience.

Yes was the immediate beneficiary. The band parted with Peter Banks in April 1970, after a gig at the Luton College of Technology that the guitarist would remember as not particularly great. The task fell to Jon Anderson, confronting Banks in the dressing room as Chris Squire watched.

"I think it would be better for you and the band, if you left," said Anderson.

Banks boiled over. "Don't give me any fucking reasons!!!" he snapped, packing his gear in a huff.[16]

It was rotten timing for a tantrum; Banks had no other ride back to London. He endured the 30-mile return trip, then found other gigs, but did not stop stewing about Yes. Critics gave him no credit for the sound of the band. Squire and Anderson couldn't summon a kind word about him. Said Squire of Banks, "He made a bad business decision—not to show the same enthusiasm as everyone else around *Time and a Word*. He was not a very happy participant in the *Time and a Word* album. We were going in slightly different directions than the one he wanted to go in. . . . No one in Yes has ever been kicked out."[17]

Anderson blew off one question about the firing by telling a journalist that Banks was "more interested in his clothes" than in Yes. Banks would remember the insult for decades. "It was a really cruel, childish thing to say," he wrote in his memoirs.[18]

And Banks's replacement was being courted with great warmth. Guitarist Steve Howe had left Tomorrow, which had never built on the success of "My White Bicycle," and had been playing with a five-piece psychedelic combo called Bodast. They couldn't get a deal. Yes already had one. As Howe remembered it, Squire pitched him over the phone with tales of Yes's success. "It's real big-time," Howe remembered Squire saying. "We've got loads of bucks to buy new equipment and a record deal and everything."[19]

The band never hesitated to tell journalists: Howe was a natural, a major step up, the savior of the band. "I feel ten years younger," said Bill Bruford.[20] Howe was a soul mate, a rock musician who was happiest when he strayed from the norms of rock. "I was one of those people who dug in and said, 'I'm not going to play blues,'" Howe would say.[21] "I liked to play jazzy bits, like in 'Perpetual Change,' which Peter had been doing also," said Howe. "I'll give Peter his credit: He was utilizing different styles. But I felt, 'Aye, yeah, I can replace Peter.'"[22]

Over the summer, under Eddy Offord at Advision Studios, the band started to lay down tracks for its third album. "All our new songs tend to last for at least ten minutes," Anderson told an interviewer. "At the beginning we were consciously trying to do something different, now we work out new arrangements because we enjoy it."[23]

The new compositions started off simpler than the songs written with Banks. "Yours Is No Disgrace" started with simple block chords—E, A, E, A, D, A—in sync with a bass line and a drumbeat from Bruford. It sounded like the start of a TV show, because it sort of was. "We just changed the chords and moved everything around," Howe admitted years later. "Our idea was orchestral: We're going to start with something, and then we're going to play a theme, then we're going to stop, then we're going to sing, and then we're going to play more music."[24]

The song became a suite; the thud-thud-thud intro segued into a Chris Squire bass run, which segued into Anderson's lyrics (ninety seconds into the song) over Kaye's keyboard atmospherics. It was typical Anderson dream factory material. Only later did the song clearly become about the Vietnam War. "My idea was a soldier crawling out of the mud, not wanting to be there, and if he was going to be dead tomorrow, why not rape and plunder and kill and fornicate? It's not his disgrace, it's the evil bastards that put him there."[25]

The songs on *The Yes Album* were grounded, based on recognizable musical forms: four long suites broken up by short pieces. "Clap," a Howe solo piece written upon the birth of his first son, was plunked in as one of the tasters. (It had been recorded on July 17, 1970, at Howe's first appearance with the band. Banks could only seethe.) Howe supplied a section of an unused Bodast song, "Nether Street," for a layered piece to be titled "Starship

Trooper." In Yes's hands, Howe's sliding G–E-flat–C melody was titled "Wurm" and piled high with Tony Kaye's keyboards.

The whole record was like that. "We were always looking for a couple of lines to go against each other, a bit of counterpoint," Bill Bruford would tell an interviewer. "That was all a very art school-classical-art rock type thing. Counterpoint was unknown in rock, there was no such thing as that. To have contrapuntal lines like that . . . that was considered all very tricky. But bear in mind nobody wrote music at this point."[26]

The "Your Move" section of "I've Seen All Good People," which would become the only single from the album, began with Squire, Howe, and Anderson singing together, an a cappella preview of the song's vocal hook. Then came Howe, plucking and strumming a twelve-string laud, an earthier and more classical sound than had appeared in any Yes song before that. The structure built from that—Bruford hitting his bass drum for a "heartbeat" effect as Anderson sang his transcendental vocal at the higher end of his range.

"Every time I would think 'cause his time is time in time with your time,' I was trying to say that I will do anything that is required of me to reach God," Anderson explained to one interviewer. "I think that whoever is listening to it should feel the same thing, that they are in tune and in time with God."[27]

The song ended with block chords from Kaye's Hammond organ; this, according to Anderson, was meant to symbolize that "religion as it stands is subsequently destroyed and there is hope for real understanding."[28]

Exactly halfway through the piece came the straightforward show-off rock of "I've Seen All Good People." It was the mysticism twinned with rock dynamics, colored by improvisation, that Yes had always put into its live shows. In February 1971, when the record hit shops, Atlantic bought full-page ads in *Mel-*

ody Maker and the *New Musical Express*. Michael Tait, the band's tour engineer, took it upon himself to slap posters up in London record shops.

It worked. So did the band's relentless touring, which started in the summer of 1970 and continued through the summer of 1971, as Yes snaked its way across the United States.

"We can use our instruments theatrically and incorporate asides, exits, dramatis personae," said Bruford. "The day of playing chords is over now. Formulated music is finished. Now the bass player might be playing a drum line. You can use good lighting to create a theatrical effect and make the whole thing more dramatic."[29]

Yes were innovators, but not alone. Hawkwind, a band that started as a coalition of buskers—street musicians—but made a quick pivot to psychedelic rock, brought in a light show that spun around a blue-painted, six-foot-tall Aphrodite named Stacia. Arthur Brown, the surrealist who'd created so much of the scene, had assembled a new band—unimaginatively, the Crazy World of Arthur Brown—and had been playing in Paris. He found audiences ready to lose themselves with or without much new stage drama.

"It was strange," Brown told one weekly, in an understatement. "The biggest mistake we made with that band was calling it the New Crazy World, because people came along expecting the fire act, and of course we weren't doing it," he said.[30]

AS THEIR FIRST ALBUM climbed the charts, Emerson, Lake & Palmer wondered whether they could continue to exist. Lake was wound down. At the band's third gig, Emerson insisted that the crowd needed an encore of "Nutrocker." Palmer went along merrily, but Emerson noticed his bassist moping through the instrumental. When the song ended, the bass thunked down to the floor, its player beelining for the green room. Emerson followed him with a bottle of red wine and smashed it on a radiator. "You fucking cunt!" he screamed. "You fucking unprofessional cunt! Don't you ever show me up like that again!"[31]

The incident "cleared the air," for the rest of the tour. Yes played through its 1970 gigs in Europe and returned to the UK.

"I'm getting much more inspired by contemporary music than the classics now," Emerson told Palmer.[32] The keyboard player had remained obsessed with the Argentine composer Alberto Ginastera's Piano Concerto no. 1, which he'd first heard at the "Switched-On Symphony" concert, a recital of classic music on electronic instruments. "I wanted to be able to get that kind of sound from the instruments I was using," he told a researcher years later. "I had also always wanted to write atonally, although I wasn't sure what that was."[33]

Palmer gave Emerson his opportunity. One day in early 1971, Palmer played Emerson a thundering drum pattern and asked him for the time signature. "It's either 10/8 or 5/4," Emerson speculated. He ran through an ostinato, a repetitive, self-contained melody, that he'd been playing around with. It fit like a dream. Weeks later, Emerson called Lake over to his home to see what he had.

"I've been working on this piece since Carl played me a rather obscure drum pattern," said Emerson. "I've got this image of us creating a vast 'sheet of sound' that defies conventional structures. There doesn't appear to be one set time signature or key signature but the total effect played by the three of us could be very prolific."

Lake wasn't following. Emerson sat down to play the ostinato and looked back up to see his singer "staring blankly" at him. "I think if you want to play that kind of music, you should play it on your solo album," said Lake.

"But I want us to play it," beseeched Emerson. "I know it sounds complicated, but it'll have a tremendous effect with all three of us playing it together."

"I'm really not interested in that sort of thing," said Lake. He headed for the door. Emerson picked up the phone and dialed John Gaydon at EG to tell him that the band was "finished." All sides settled for a meeting, where spleens could be vented in full.[34]

"It's just not commercial," said Lake.

"Was the unison line in '20th Century Schizoid Man' commercial?" asked Emerson. "No! But it was King Crimson's biggest hit."

"But that had a song!"

"What's to say that this piece shouldn't go into a song?"

"By the time you've got through playing all that esoteric rubbish you won't have a fuckin' audience," said Lake.[35]

The two of them kept squabbling, until Gaydon suggested they head to Advision to record what they had; it was too late to cancel the studio time anyway. In the studio, learning the music at their own pace, the band congealed again. The 10/8 pattern with the melodic figure became "Eruption," the first movement in what was to be the "Tarkus" suite.

"When I suggested anything a bit freaky then, people were a bit funny," Palmer would tell *Sounds*. "I had a 10/8 riff when I was sixteen which people didn't want to know about because they thought it was too hard. And of course, that 10/8 riff is applied to 'Tarkus.' I was labeled as a rock and roll drummer and I couldn't get out of it. With Rooster I got out of it a bit and with ELP I am fulfilled."[36]

"Tarkus," according to Emerson, was written in only six days "because there was an awful lot of inspiration and one idea triggered another idea."[37] The ideas ended up chasing each other, section upon section, in a musical suite that filled half of the eponymous *Tarkus* LP. Emerson's 10/8 pattern became the overture for a science fiction tale of allegorical monsters warring for the future. A musical section—always driving on that 10/8 drum line—would be snapped short, and a pop melody and Lake lyric would tell the story.

The rest of the album came together just as smoothly, if less bombastically. Side two was a song cycle that traveled through some of the same musical territory, just with more humor—in "Jeremy Bender" a song about a transvestite, in "Are You Ready, Eddy?" a rockabilly tribute to the band's producer, Eddy Offord.

The real heft was on side one, and artist William Neal designed a gatefold cover illustrating the battle that listeners were supposed to be transported away by. "Tarkus" became a creature from some lost Godzilla film, half armadillo and half tank.

It "was simply a doodle created from a fusion of ideas," Neal explained years later. "I had produced a gun belt made up of piano keys, which somehow led to WW1 armoury, nobody liked the idea, but the little armadillo remained on the layout pad." But it played with ELP, who let Neal hear the album on acetate, and the band collaborated with the artist in fleshing out the story and the name. "Tarkus" was a combination of "a condition of deep spiritual debasement" (the "Tartarus") and of the word "carcass." The name of the album was spelled out in painted bones.[38]

It hit shops on June 14, 1971, shooting straight to number one, refusing to vacate the charts for seventeen more weeks. The UK press embraced the album, which was promoted by a single that julienned two of the pop sections of the title track. American reviewers, meanwhile, expressed confusion at what the Brits had inflicted upon them. "*Tarkus* records the failure of three performers to become creators," wrote David Lubin in *Rolling Stone*. "Regardless of how fast and how many styles they can play, Emerson, Lake and Palmer will continue turning out mediocrity like *Tarkus* until they discover what, if anything, it is that they must say on their own and for themselves."[39]

But the Americans were showing up to the shows anyway. The supergroup label was taken seriously; each member of the band was suddenly talking in the most rosy terms about what they accomplished together. "I'm sure people think Carl and I are shivering in Keith's shadow and hate it," Lake told *Sounds*. "That's their problem. And I know there are people whose minds are so closed they can't think of anything but Keith with the Nice and keep saying he's doing the same things. That's rubbish. We never control our act. What Keith does on stage are just ideas he's had on the spur of the moment that have stuck. I don't want to do explosive things to get attention. You've got to work as honestly as you can, and that's exactly what we do. If you do something else people know you're putting on a false front. They're not stupid."[40]

COMPETITORS STARTED TO FLOW into the charts. Island signed Curved Air, which offered something no progressive group had: smoldering sex appeal. Sonja Kristina, an aspiring folkie and member of the West End cast of *Hair*, roamed the stage in high-heeled boots and shimmering tops, black hair tumbling over her shoulders. Island printed ten thousand copies of the first-ever picture disc, which ringed the vinyl with sixteen female figures, holding hands as if gathering strength for a Busby Berkeley performance. The buyer who put the record on the turntable could watch, accompanied by the substance of his choice, as the image blurred into a hypnotic pattern.

"Some of the so-called Heads and some of the people in the business, especially those companies we'd turned down before signing with Warners, said it was all a hype," Kristina told an American interviewer. "But it wasn't conceived as that."[41]

What made it progressive? The picture disc spun, and keyboard player Francis Monkman let loose a glissando, then a minor-key boogie-woogie, played under a scaling guitar riff. Kristina's voice swooshed in, double-tracked, singing a melody that was as sideways from pop as the rest of the track. The album raced across the styles, taking a little Jefferson Airplane here ("Propositions") and a little folk there ("Blind Man"). The highlight, as critics soon decided, was seven and a half instrumental minutes—driven by violin, quoting baroque melodies—titled "Vivaldi."

"I think Vivaldi's a terrific piece," Monkman told an interviewer. "There's not a progression that couldn't have been written in 1700, and yet at the same time it couldn't have been written anytime before the late 1960s."[42]

Deram signed Egg, an experimental group that grew out of a psychedelic band called Uriel. They had formed it in college, fronted at the time by a dervish guitarist named Steve Hillage. When he left, Egg slimmed down to Dave Stewart on keyboards, Clive Brooks on bass, and Mont Campbell on drums—no guitarist, none necessary. Their first single—their only single—was called "Seven Is a Jolly Good Time" because its chorus was played in 7/4 time.

"[Deram was] a classical music company trying to redeem their mistake in turning down the Beatles by signing up anyone and everyone, including us," said Campbell. "A very expensive strategy, and they soon went out of business. They understood nothing about pop/rock except that it made a lot more money than classical music! We celebrated being signed by going out and buying a transit van, a Hammond L-100, and a WEM PA. Total cost: £2,000."[43]

From Genesis to Revelation had flopped, but Genesis had been signed anew, by Charisma, and headed to Trident Studios to record a set of progressive songs. Jonathan King was out too; their new producer was John Anthony, who had manned the studio for the first two Van der Graaf records. The result was *Trespass*, an ambitious suite of lengthy numbers that showed off Gabriel's storytelling and, for the first time, a mellotron. Banks had purchased it from Robert Fripp himself.

"Was that the one actually used on *In the Court of the Crimson King*?" asked Banks. "Oh yes, yes!" said Fripp, with a smile. That was Banks's recollection anyway. "He must have had about three or four of them there and I'm sure he was trying to sell them all with the same spiel."[44]

Trespass didn't ignite the charts—it didn't flop either—but that wasn't the group's problem anymore. Anthony Phillips was out. "He didn't like the road, felt too nervous playing in front of people, and he thought that playing the same numbers over and over again, night after night, was causing it to stagnate," Gabriel explained to *ZigZag*.[45]

The band was hunting for a guitarist. It stumbled across an ad:

> *Imaginative guitarist/writer seeks involvement with receptive musicians, determined to strive beyond existing stagnant music forms.*

An audition was arranged with Steve Hackett. "We had the feeling that he also had the personality to become a band member rather than a hired hand," said Gabriel.[46]

"Having listened to other groups like Family, Fairport Convention and Procol Harum—and obviously to what *Sgt. Pepper's Lonely Hearts Club Band* and *Pet Sounds* suggested—we realized that there were no rules, that we could go somewhere else if we wanted to," recalled Tony Banks. "And so we went to orchestrated strings. We had a 25-minute piece that never got recorded, but bits and pieces got pillaged later on. . . . The music was all long and weird. That sort of approach interested me most because I felt the pop style had been pretty well covered."[47]

In August 1971, Genesis headed into Trident Studios to record the first album with Collins on drums and Hackett on guitar. "The Fountain of Salmacis" was the first real mellotron song. "I had a chord sequence which became very much a Genesis trademark, where we would be in E minor and go to the chords C and D, often keeping the bass note down on E," Tony Banks would say. "Taking this little sequence and then adding the Mellotron sounded really good and made me realize that you could take what was almost a classical piece and make it sound very exciting."[48]

The album was blurbed in ads by Keith Emerson. "People are a lot more swayed than one thinks," said Gabriel. "They think 'if Keith Emerson likes them, they must be good.' I know it influences people because I am as bad."[49]

When it appeared in 1971, *Nursery Cryme* established Genesis at last. The group graduated from university halls to larger venues, touring Italy and France. In the summer of 1972, Genesis played the Reading Festival, for which the band members were each paid £175. (Curved Air, a larger draw, took in £1,000.) And by that point they were in and out of Island Studios, recording what would be their breakout album, *Foxtrot*.

The previous two records had begun with recognizable-enough sounds. *Trespass* kicked off with "Looking for Someone," and the first thing a listener heard was Peter Gabriel's voice twinned with Tony Banks's block keyboard chords. *Nursery Cryme* showed off Hackett's versatility on the twelve-string guitar, as he plucked his way through "The Musical Box." *Foxtrot* started in outworld, on the mellotron, Banks alternating between B-major-7/F-sharp and C-sharp/F-sharp, then careening into a melody from out of a Hammer horror film.

"On the old Mellotron Mark 2 there were these two chords that sounded really good on that instrument," Banks explained. "There are some chords you can't play on that instrument because they'd be so out of tune."[50] The result, as Steve Hackett would later call it, was "an aircraft hangar type of rumble ideally suited to spacecraft impersonation."[51]

Banks's melody lasted ninety full seconds, ending abruptly, as producer David Hitchcock stitched in the main groove of the song. It started quietly, but the elements grew louder with each bar—a sort of Morse code drum fill and bass line and guitar riff, another heavenly mellotron melody, and finally, after two full minutes, a lyric about an Earth emptied of its people. "Has life again destroyed life?" sang Gabriel.

The tone was set. On "Time Table," Gabriel put the listener at a gathering of proud medieval knights and asked why "we suffer each race to believe that no race has been grander." That ran into "Get 'Em Out by Friday," an allegory about Brits being shunted into council homes that imagined "Styx Enterprises" and "United Blacksprings International" profiting as humans were degraded and exiled. A public service announcement, from "Genetic Control," announced a "four foot restriction on humanoid height," the better for packing more people into less space.

Tasters—all preparing the listener for the longest and darkest song Genesis would ever write. Side two of *Foxtrot* was devoted to "Supper's Ready," a multisection suite of music that stretched to nearly twenty-three minutes. "Mike and Phil created a 9/8 riff," Banks would recall, "but I didn't want to be tied to the time signature, so I just took it as a 4/4 thing and played right against their riff, starting off with cheeky little major tunes, almost a pastiche, and then slowly making it more and more sinister and unsettling, so you're not quite sure where it's going to go."

The song kept building, kept changing form. "I brought in the really big chords again," said Banks, finally going back out of the minor key to an E major chord, which created this very serene, simple chord sequence, a strong, uplifting moment. "It's like the angels have arrived, the heavens have opened. And it had taken about 20 minutes to reach this point: that was what was so great about it."[52]

It was Gabriel, fittingly, who gave the song a hook that elevated the menace while adding a dash of self-parody. As the 9/8 riff thundered, Gabriel recited the number of the beast. "There is a line in Revelations which says 'this supper of the mighty one,'" Gabriel explained to one reporter. "Anyway there are very straightforward levels at which you can take the lyrics if you want."[53]

"When Pete suddenly started singing over it—666—I thought, 'Oh shit, he's doing it again, he's singing on my best bit,'" said Banks, "but I have to say this time it only took me about 10 seconds to think 'This sounds fantastic, it's so strong.'"[54]

It came across even stronger, and stranger, when the band took it to the stage. Since the first tour, Gabriel had been wearing simple full-body costumes and filling time between songs with short, absurd stories. "The storytelling had emerged as a means of filling in the gaps when we had thirty-six strings being tuned by people who weren't very good at tuning them," he explained, "and during long debates about which strings were in or out of tune. It was out of pure necessity, because during those moments everyone looks at the singer to fill in the gaps."[55]

Paul Whitehead's cover for *Foxtrot*—the third of Genesis's gatefold covers, and the third by the artist—was rather literal.

The first thing a prospective buyer would see was a shapely female figure in a red dress, with the head of a fox. "It contains aberrations from a human situation which are so slight as to be absolutely bizarre," wrote a reviewer for *Sounds*. "Gruesome heads are seen on perplexed horsemen and as the hunt arrives at the sea there stands the beautiful lady with the fox's head—and hence the title of the album."[56]

The people crowding into Genesis shows got to see Gabriel in the exact same getup. "It was a shock, this apparition coming towards me in a fox's head and a dress," Banks remembered. "I thought 'Christ!' but carried on playing . . . and the audience loved it. Even more importantly a picture of him in this bloody fox's head was on the front page of *Melody Maker* the following week. Hey, this is interesting. Because we knew we had difficult music to get across, and with no TV, no national press, no singles, what do you do? You need something more than just music to attract a bigger audience."[57]

"The word Elgar comes to mind for some reason," joked Hackett. Elgar on acid perhaps. "We weren't on acid, we weren't on drugs; we were on beer and wine and Earl Grey."[58]

IT TOOK TIME, and some gimmickry, for the musical establishment to consider the ambitions of the progressives. In the summer of 1970, the producers of the BBC's Proms, its annual celebration of classical music, allowed one night of experimental music that did not fit the straitjacket. Soft Machine would be allowed to play—news that titillated a press corps that was reserving its biggest rock headlines for the deaths of ill-behaving young stars. It hardly mattered that the Royal Albert Hall had been playing host to other bands, or that it had even hosted the Softs at their reunion show, a year earlier. The move needed to be explained.

"For most, this must have conjured up visions of wild young men in outrageous clothes playing, very loudly and very badly, the latest Top 20 hits," reported Richard Williams in *Radio Times*. Not to worry: "The Soft Machine is one of the most unusual groups in pop music," with music "as far from Top of the Pops as Chopin is from a Vaudeville Act," wrote Williams.[59]

"I hope that introducing pop music into the Proms will be a popular move," said Sir William Glock, the BBC's controller of music, in a sheepish interview with the *Daily Mail*. In the same interview, Glock reassured the conservative paper, and its readers, that pop groups shouldn't be backed by orchestras.[60]

"I don't suppose the powers that be at the BBC knew what they were getting at all," Robert Wyatt told an interviewer. The band showed up, and according to Wyatt, "Before our bit, I went out the back for a quick fag, and then the doorman didn't want to let me back in."

"I've got to play in there," Wyatt remembered saying.

"You must be kidding," said the doorman. "They only have proper music in there."[61]

That night, they had Soft Machine. The band had just released *Third*, a double album consisting of four side-long, improvisational-sounding pieces. At the Proms, Soft Machine played three-quarters of the album, starting on a misstep. "Out-Bloody-Rageous" was supposed to begin with an electronic sample, leading into a bass line from Hugh Hopper. The fuzz box didn't work. The ambient noise was followed by stop-start clatter, until the rest of the band rushed in.

Neither reviewers nor audience members complained about the sound. The rest of Soft Machine's set, shortened versions of the album tracks "Facelift" and "Esther's Nose Job," smoothed away some of the experimentation. On the record, "Facelift" was a blending of two live performances, ending as the tape was

sped and slowed; played live, it was a tour of quiet-loud dynamics, nudged along by Hopper's subtle bass lines.

The performance stopped cold before midnight, as every
Proms concert was required to do. The reviews were glowing in
the pop press, recounting the predictable tale of the most daring
group in progressive rock and how it had failed to prove the snobs
right. "In those days the Royal Albert Hall was a terrible place
to play because it wasn't designed for live music," said Hopper.
"It wasn't a bad performance, considering it was very artificial."[62]

TARKUS WAS NOT SUPPOSED to be ELP's second public statement.
The band had done something even more ambitious: it had
adapted, played live, and recorded Modest Mussorgsky's 1874
suite *Pictures at an Exhibition*. Emerson had heard *Pictures* played
in full years earlier, when he was still with the Nice, and he'd
kept the piano sheet music. After ELP recorded its first album,
he took it to the band. "I wanted to use it sort of as an educa-
tional piece, exposing our audiences to this great work of classical music," he said.[63]

They set to cutting up the source material. Mussorgsky had
written a ten-part suite, with five "promenade" interludes, all
based on paintings by the late painter Viktor Hartmann. Emerson excised most of that, leaving the main promenade themes
but adapting only four of the "pictures": "The Gnome," "The
Old Castle, "The Hut of Baba Yaga," and "The Great Gates of
Kiev." On December 9, 1970, ELP debuted the new arrangement at London's Lyceum Theatre, a former opera house in the
West End. That recording, meant for film, simply wasn't releas-
able. "The film and everything was so bad, and the soundtrack
on the film was so bad that we just had to re-record it," Palmer
explained.[64]

That left the official recording for March 26, 1971, after most of *Tarkus* had been set down. Emerson introduced the piece to an audience at Newcastle City Hall—"We're going to give you 'Pictures at an Exhibition'!"—and when the cheers subsided, he sat behind a pipe organ to play the "Promenade" processional. After a few bars, the full organ rattled the room.

Then came the drums. Palmer banged out the introduction to "The Gnome," joined by Emerson, then by Lake, who was running his bass through Emerson's Moog. The melody was all Mussorgsky's, until Emerson introduced his own arabesque on the Moog. Back to "Promenade," now handed over to Lake, who added lyrics about "endless years" and "tears as dry as stone."

There was no time to settle—Emerson re-emerged with a flurry of Moog noises, interrupted by Lake, picking out a new song called "The Sage" on his acoustic guitar. Back to Emerson, who introduced "The Old Castle" by yanking the ribbon controller from the Moog. "I got so many freaky sounds out of a Hammond organ—sounds which weren't thought up by the people that made the thing—that I wanted to go further," Emerson later told reporter Penny Valentine. "For me the Moog was the only answer."[65]

It was dizzying. "Blues Variation," another new composition, was the only musical moment that bopped along like the Nice or Atomic Rooster. When the band got to "The Hut of Baba Yaga," Emerson treated it like he'd treated "America" and "Rondo," wrenching the melody out and splattering it with glissandos. "The Great Gates of Kiev" became a six-and-a-half-minute workout, starting off close to the melody, but at the midpoint breaking back into the "Promenade" melody.

Emerson had found a way to evoke the rising-fourth, falling-third theme through buzzing synthesizer feedback. Above the clatter rose one more Lake lyric—another meander through some grand, meaningful-sounding themes. "Day is night!" howled Lake, as the band let the song drop and explode with feedback.

That was the piece. After a suitable wait, ELP returned with another sort of classical adaptation. They covered "Nutrocker," a rock version of Tchaikovsky's suite, as made famous in a one-hit wonder by B. Bumble and the Stingers.

The March recording went to Eddy Offord's studio and was mixed for an eventual November release. The band remained on tour, no longer playing "Pictures," instead playing sets of maybe seven songs that were anchored by "Tarkus." From June to November they toured the US, and on September 1 they played in New York's Gaelic Park. Robert Moog himself showed up, to finally meet the man who had turned his machine into a concert set piece.

"There were 10,000 kids standing on a soccer field and here's Keith Emerson sticking knives in a Leslie cabinet," Moog remembered a decade later. "A New York musician who had bought some of my equipment was there and he was in complete shock. He said, 'This is the end of the world.'"[66]

Reporters ran to their stashes of superlatives. "The theatrical aspects of ELP's concert moves them out of the class of ordinary rock musicians," wrote Jody Breslaw in *Sounds*, after covering the Gaelic Park show. "The syntheses which can be said to have succeeded in the fullest sense, opening new possibilities for the future, are those for which the label 'rock' no longer applies."[67]

A few months later, when ELP returned to the UK, another *Sounds* critic praised the band's new cohesion. "There's no sound or sight quite like it, when Keith Emerson disappears from stage twenty yards into the audience, shouting at them with a machine gun pattern on the ribbon keyboard of his moog."

The rapture continued when the album finally hit. "A perfect showcase for their musical flamboyancy" (*New Musical Express*). "One of the finest British group albums of the year" (*Melody Maker*). "One to convert nonbelievers" (*Record Mirror*).

"Before ELP played 'Pictures at an Exhibition,' classical music was only reserved for the elite, for clever people, for the intelligentsia," said Lake in a 2012 interview. "It wasn't for your ordinary people on the street. They would never be really exposed to or in touch with classical music. Now, you get classical music on your cell phone. You get classical music at sports events. You get the Three Tenors playing rock 'n' roll arenas. All this was partly due to ELP's first brave move to play 'Pictures at an Exhibition' at a rock 'n' roll show. It's something that I take quite a lot of pride in."[69]

And at the time, at the end of 1971, it was just accepted wisdom that ELP had taken pop where it always needed to go.

5

A HIGHER ART FORM

T ony Kaye's relationship with Yes came to a sad and graceless end. At the end of July 1971, on the strength of the *Yes Album*'s success, the band closed out a tour with a gig at the Crystal Palace Bowl. Elton John was the headliner, and years later Yes would recall how he burst into the VIP area looking in vain for a "naked man." And then things got awkward.

The reasons for jettisoning Kaye were simple. The first was puerile. "Tony liked to drink and he enjoyed the company of women," Squire told the journalist Chris Welch. "The problems arose when Tony and Steve were sharing a bedroom which they did in those early days of touring and staying at Holiday Inns."[1] The second reason was a sense that Yes could do better than a keyboard player who anchored songs with mammoth block chords.

Kaye would be replaced by Rick Wakeman, twenty-two years old and reportedly bored with the more traditionally song-focused Strawbs. That band had just opened for Yes in Hull. "Everything was wrong," Wakeman recalled. "Every band then had a lead singer who was 6'7" who hadn't washed for three years, forty-eight stacks of Marshall amps for the guitar player and the bass player." Here was a band led by a tenor, with a bass player who played like a guitarist, and "drummer who mics up his kit—unheard of, in 1970."[2] The band was watching Wakeman, from the rafters. "We saw this guy with five keyboards onstage, and we said: That's the guy," said Jon Anderson. "Listen to what he does, and what he would do with Steve."[3]

Squire dismissed Kaye and lobbied Wakeman in person, at one point treading into Wakeman's yard and negotiating through the keyboarder's curtains. It worked; it had to work. "Tony Kaye was mostly playing B-3 and not much else, and not wanting to do much else," said Eddy Offord.[4]

"Steve had very much established himself as a guitar star," said Squire, "and when it came to deciding on who was gonna stay and who was gonna go, I suppose that's when Steve stayed and Tony went."[5]

It was the second purification of the band in less than a year, the second Lego switcheroo of an original player for someone more talented. Tony Kaye, who would re-join the group several times, sued in 2002 on the grounds that he had quit over internal band issues and wasn't properly paid.[6] "As soon as they found someone with a better organ he got booted out," Bill Bruford said of Kaye, years later. "And so you got a bigger and better organ, and eventually we got Rick Wakeman with it. But there was no big change for the drummer, it just got bigger, a bigger band and more scope but all mostly emanating from the keyboards which were a combination of Mellotrons and organs followed by synthesizers."[7]

Hendrix drummer Bruford was lucky. As he half-reasoned, half-joked to Welch, "If Mitch Mitchell had become available, I probably would have been history."[8]

There was no more need to worry. Wakeman completed the

Yes lineup, and his hiring was front-page news in Britain's music magazines. He'd been with the Strawbs only a year, appearing live with the band and on two records. Songs like "Sheep" and "I'll Carry On Beside You" had established him as a daring player, layering multiple keyboards and bargaining time for running, skipping solos.

The press had gotten to know him, all 6 foot 3 of him, bantering and riffing about how he played. He came off like a younger, stranger Keith Emerson—more mystical and more at home in a pub. "It seems almost impossible," wrote Penny Valentine in *Sounds*, "despite the band's acceptance of the possibility, that Yes will do anything but rise to even greater heights from now on in."[9]

"Up to the age of 13 or 14 I was totally immersed playing classical music," Wakeman told *Sounds*, in one of many awed pieces about his technique. "Until I heard a Springfields record. On that, someone bent a guitar note. I realized that you couldn't do that on a piano, and a whole new world opened up to me."[10]

The first sound on *The Yes Album* had been the unified stomp of Howe, Squire, and Bruford. The first sound on *Fragile*, the record the band started recording with Wakeman, was sui generis—a piano, played backward, a single note ending with the single plug of Howe's acoustic guitar. "What we did was turn the tape over and record the piano forward, and stop at exactly the right time so it coincided with the first note of Steve's guitar," Offord would recall, crediting Jon Anderson with the idea. "It all kind of blended together. It was a physical tape manipulation, rather than putting it into the sampler and hitting the button."[11]

This was the start of "Roundabout," eight and a half minutes of hooks alternating with rhythmic looseness. In a cut-down form it would be Yes's first hit single; on the album, it raced from theme to theme in a manner unlike anything Yes had tried before. The intro gave way to a nimble, jarring melody with Squire's 8/8 bass line high in the mix. Near the three-minute mark, everything paused in midair; another melody had begun, the first to really show off Wakeman. Then Wakeman played a rapid run down the keys, the lake's water flowing in the form of notes.

The song changed again, to harder rock, bass and guitar playing ominous and syncopated triplets. Then, at 4:57, there was a return of a loping, babbling-brook keyboard figure and the reprise of Howe's gentle picking. The intro theme, played on Howe's acoustic guitar, came back at the very close of the song, but instead of ending on an up note, it shattered on a major chord—a Picardy third. Yes had just closed a major pop single with the sort of flourish previously and familiarly reserved for classical music.

Everything about *Fragile* screamed, We are virtuosos. "Roundabout" was followed by "Cans and Brahms," the first of five solo pieces on the record, one for each member. Wakeman, the new arrival, played a quick cover of the third movement of Brahms's Symphony no. 4 in E Minor, op. 98: Allegro Giocoso. It ended quickly, and the record spun on to ninety seconds of overdubbed Anderson harmonies called "We Have Heaven." Then to another suite: "South Side of the Sky," anchored by an out-of-nowhere Wakeman piano solo.

Fragile's second side began with the album's only concise pop song. "Long Distance Runaround" began with the beguiling harmony of Howe's guitar and Wakeman's keyboard playing nearly identical sounds—harmonics for Howe, soft tones for the star keyboarder. Squire's bass rolled in, and he and Wakeman played in 5/4 time as the rest of the band played in 4/4. It was disorienting, which matched well with an Anderson lyric about (in his words) "how religion had seemed to confuse me totally."[12]

"Long Distance Runaround" segued into "The Fish," Squire's solo piece, which led to "Mood for a Day," a flamenco guitar composition inspired by Howe's affection for Sabicas and for Carlos Montoya.

And that led to "Heart of the Sunrise." It started with a rumble, a 6/8 bass line from Squire and a drumroll from Bruford. Then came Wakeman, with a horror-film keyboard melody in 3/4. Back to the ascending riff, joined by Howe's guitar. The melody suddenly changed, to a 4/4 beat, with the original riff being phased in slowly by the mix. Then a dropout, to a melody that Anderson had written on his acoustic guitar. The themes repeated, announced at various intervals on keyboards, by what the band came to call "Rick-recapitulation." Critics would quickly point out how much this—the riff, at least—sounded like King Crimson. "I always thought the riff was influenced by '21st Century Schizoid Man,' but I suppose we got away with it," shrugged Howe.[13]

They did. *Fragile* was an instant hit. "South Side of the Sky," according to a review in *Rolling Stone*, put "everything they've got into a wide-ranging and most impressive package which demonstrates that progressive (remember progressive rock?) doesn't mean sterile and that complex isn't the same thing as inaccessible."[14] Even at that point, early in 1972, "progressive" was a pejorative. *Rolling Stone* preferred to compare this music to the best of the Kinks.[15] But it was no use to pretend Yes wasn't "progressive," as *Fragile* also introduced most of the record-buying public to the artist Roger Dean.

Yes had narrowly missed working with Dean years earlier. Atlantic Records had discovered Dean, then twenty-five and recently out of architecture school, before the band's debut album. Dean had scored a job designing the discotheque at Ronnie Scott's Jazz Club in Soho, the venue where the Who would debut *Tommy*. Disco-goers were greeted by a kind of landscape,

seats designed in topographical shapes and filled with foam.
"The fire brigade who inspected the club were very concerned
about the amount of foam we had used," Dean later told Chris
Welch. And yet, when a fire finally came, "the foam furniture
wasn't touched, but the murals were burnt off the walls."[16]

There was no such risk in the album cover racket. Dean
established himself quickly, painting alien landscapes that beck-
oned the listener and promised an unpredictable danger. The
Osibisa afro-fusion band ~~Osibasa~~ got a yellow-brown portrait of a
doomed planet being patrolled by an insect. The acid rocker
Billy Cox got a portrayal of a man on a horse being pursued—or
accompanied—by insectoid airplanes.

"It really came as a surprise to me at first that people were
liking the drawings for their own sake," Dean told an interviewer in 1972. "I really had to teach myself to draw when I
started doing this stuff. Most of them were done towards an
end rather than being ends in themselves, to show [that] things
I'd designed but couldn't possibly construct because it was too
expensive could fit into some sort of scheme."[17]

The art, at first, wasn't really identified with any kind of
sound. "If you take a piece of music and put it as a soundtrack to
a piece of film of a bird eating seeds, of a volcano erupting, of a
dogfight in the air, of a little girl blowing seeds off a dandelion
clock, it would probably fit all those things," Dean shrugged.
"So I don't think that side of it is really important. You could
fit an amazing number of different visual images to almost any
piece of music and it wouldn't jar."[18]

Dean approached the Yes job literally, having heard the title
but not much of the music. Given very little time to create, he
disappeared inside his studio and emerged with two icons. The
album's title was given a science fiction weight, now represented
by a planet hanging in space and punched through with holes,

being circumnavigated by a wooden ship. The band's name was displayed in transparent bubble letters, linked as if drawn in one strike. "We went into the New York office, we banged our hands on the table," said Howe. "*Work this record.* We felt it could break us, and it did."[19]

"It was all a fairly natural progression," said Bruford, "and you just waited every week to see if the keyboard player would turn up with something new. And indeed he did, and then he surrounded himself with four or five instruments, and that was extraordinary, but then he got a monophonic synthesizer, then a polyphonic, and so on and so forth. In a way percussionists were looked on to do something similar by producing gongs, percussion racks, perhaps even xylophones and little percussion instruments and whatever. It was an expansive time."[20]

"I'm never sure that the things I've written are going to last any kind of time, so much music seems a momentary thing," Jon Anderson told *Sounds* at the end of 1971. "We were only talking the other day about the possibility of rock music—in the next 10 years—really developing into a higher art form. Building up the same way classical music did into huge works that last and stand the test of time. Rock musicians will make music that will last a hell of a lot longer in the future."[21]

PETER BANKS DID NOT want for work after Yes. He quickly joined Blodwyn Pig, a more straightforward rock group than Yes—another one that had just seen off its guitarist. Mick Abrahams had played with the first iteration of Jethro Tull, gotten bored, and left to join something louder. When he got bored again, he moved right on, freeing up the job for Banks. "It was just getting too noisy," Abrahams told one journalist. "Towards the end, there were too many different ideas in Blodwyn Pig."[22]

Blodwyn Pig never recorded a new album; both Banks and Abrahams started new bands. They watched as Yes and Jethro Tull achieved real greatness. Banks was full of praise for the new Yes. Abrahams wondered whether rock was tumbling down a rabbit hole. "Rock music isn't and never has meant to be an intellectual exercise," Abrahams said at the end of 1971. "There are performers who adopt a very cynical attitude and they would never dream of thinking of themselves as entertainers. I think in a lot of ways rock is going the same way as jazz did. Jazz was a happy music originally until a few people started intellectualizing it and after that the musicians thought to themselves, 'yeah, we're on to a good thing here,' and started playing up to it."[23]

He wasn't wrong. Yes and ELP and Genesis were able to sustain what they'd built. So was Jethro Tull; so was a clutch of other bands being signed to labels where ambitious music was encouraged and quickly released. Hawkwind had played at the Isle of Wight, just like ELP; just like ELP, they had gussied up the show with special effects. Dik Mik, the band's engineer, had brought on a ring modulator to create drones that could be pitched at the audience. It was revolting, but didn't stop Hawkwind from winning over the press.

"Can you imagine 400 people together and the force field given off by each—it could really be unbelievable," guitarist Dave Brock told *Sounds*, in an early story about their ambitions. "You can force people to go into trances, and tell them what to do; it's mass hypnotism, and you're really setting yourself up as God. . . . Dikmik's hustling for a Moog, and some quite incredible things could happen when we get that—it could stretch people's minds. The sound waves we produce are ruining us, and some of the sounds we produce are beyond registering on the metre."[24]

Hawkwind's stage show only grew more psychedelic and

ornate. So did the music. At the end of 1971 the band released *In Search of Space*, six songs making up a vaguely connected concept album. It was far more rudimentary than contemporary "progressive" music; the band never pretended otherwise. The point of the music was the groove, a concussive, writhing thing created by Brock's guitar, Nik Turner's saxophone, and the bass lines of Robert Anderson—replaced in August 1971 by Lemmy Kilmister, Keith Emerson's old roadie.

"Here was Hawkwind at Powis Square with no bass player," remembered Kilmister, "and somebody was running around asking, 'Who plays bass?' Dikmik, seeing his opportunity to have a full-time partner in speed, pointed at me and said, 'He does.' 'Bastard!' I hissed at him, because I'd never played bass in my life."[25]

All of this undergirded the megalomaniacal lyrics of Robert Calvert, who was happy to explain his ambitions. In 1972, as the band toured *In Search of Space*, Calvert excitedly told *NME* of the song suite that was in the offing. "It doesn't have a plot like a traditional opera," he explained, "but *is* an opera nevertheless in the way it presents a situation. It concerns dreams people might have if they were suspended in animation in deep space. Whereas our last album concerned a journey into space, this is more about actually being there. On stage it'll be a totally theatrical event, with dancers, mime and a new way of using light techniques which will cover the whole audience. Hopefully we want to get together the best-ever light show ever put on the road. And it won't just be complementing the music but actually part of it. The guy operating the lights will be playing them, if you like, just as the others play their instruments."[26]

That was exactly how Hawkwind played. Years after the Summer of Love, after the hippies had vanished, the band was creating "be-ins" out of endless songs composed of riffs piled atop riffs. "They don't say 'me,'" said Kilmister of the band's faithful audience. "They shout 'us.' It's a growth of a collective conscious."[27]

Jethro Tull's live reputation was growing too, though there were no pyrotechnics, no instruments of sonic torture. There was dancing, but it was Ian Anderson doing it. When *Creem* magazine sent reporter John Ingham to explain Tull to American readers, he described Anderson as "Leonard Bernstein on Speed." This was a compliment. "Many of his actions are contrived," wrote Ingham. "Playing on one foot, and hitting himself on the head to end a riff, for example, but the way he crouches back, arm swirling and flying into the air, and then surges up to the mike stand has a vitality and excitement missing from nearly all current groups."[28]

The band had been in a bit of a holding pattern since it broke out at the end of the 1960s. In early 1970, it retreated to the suboptimal recording conditions of what Anderson would call a "badly acoustically treated church building that sounded really quite horrible."[29]

They were nasty sessions, marked by false starts and failures of confidence in what had just been recorded. Toward the end, Anderson personally called Terry Ellis at Chrysalis, begging him for a rescue mission. "I'm not happy with the band," Anderson said, according to Ellis. "They're not playing well. They're not playing what I want them to play."[30]

Anderson was simply establishing himself as the singular force in the band. *Aqualung*, he would later explain, was the record where he "started to make more of an effort to write songs that were not the kind of songs other people were writing."[31]

From the first track, the title track, this was a record that listeners and critics could overanalyze. It started with a six-note riff in G minor, then an Anderson lyric—the listener could only surmise—about the creature on the album's cover. This was a heavy metal song, seesawing between G minor and D major, until one minute in, when the riff disappeared and a distorted Anderson vocal trilled over an acoustic guitar. A whole new song cracked through, Martin Barre ripping through a guitar solo that, during recording, was visually accompanied by "Jimmy Page waving" Martin on.[32] But at 5:08, another sharp shock: the folk melody sliced by the prodigal six-note riff. The song was a small epic, seemingly the start of a concept album. In the second track, "Cross-Eyed Mary," the eponymous "poor man's rich girl" was being watched "through the railings" by Aqualung.

Yet this would be Aqualung's final appearance on his eponymous record. The vinyl spun on with longer, multisection rock tracks—"Locomotive Breath," "My God"—alternating with short songs composed on Anderson's acoustic guitar. "My God" had been the album's working title, and a metaphor-stuffed song titled "Hymn 43" ("his cross was rather bloody, and he could hardly roll his stone") was the only radio single.

The album, rough as the recording had made it, did everything Anderson had hoped it could. Jethro Tull broke out and toured America. Anderson, who'd always been noticed for his stage presence, started being covered as an actual musical genius. He rejected it at every turn. "Most of the songs on the record have nothing to do with the others. So it could not possibly be a concept album," he explained.[33] Was "My God" some statement about the power of the creator, or the effects of his absence? According to Anderson, it was "really a lament for God that he has to try and be so many different things to different people!"[34]

The culture beseeched Anderson to be deep. He decided to have fun with that. "We'll give them the mother of all concept albums next time!" he remembered thinking. "So we did the completely over-the-top spoof concept album."[35]

That would be *Thick as a Brick*, released in 1972, featuring one track that ran over forty minutes and occupied both sides of a disc. One track, but not one song. Anderson, who had now firmly taken the songwriting reins, composed thirteen identifiable pop melodies, stylistically similar to what had been on the previous few records. There *was* a theme this time—a pastoral guitar tune that opened and closed the album, as Anderson sung the titular insult.

But the overarching pomp of the record was, as Anderson promised, a piss-take. He insisted at first that the album was taken directly from the writings of a young savant who'd been punished for his individuality. His "story" was told on the album cover, a faux newspaper that folded out into a serviceable-looking broadsheet. The ruse initially fooled *Melody Maker*, whose correspondent Chris Welch described the album as "based on an impressive poem by one Gerald Bostock," and rated the source material as "one of those poems that fixes one with a penetrating gaze and snaps somewhat bitterly."[36]

Anderson abandoned the ruse quickly, before the album was released or fans could truly get lost in the mythos. It hardly mattered, with multiple papers asking whether the codpiece-wearing auteur had created "Tully's *Tommy*." On the road, the new music was folded into an epic-length rock show, a service for the growing Tull cult.

"The opening night of their first British tour in a year at Portsmouth was the best rehearsed and most cleverly executed show staged for a rock band," wrote Welch, the *Melody Maker* reporter. "Their performance came somewhere between the musical excellence of Yes and the inventive audacity of the Mothers of Invention. Many groups have tried a little stage 'business' but few have succeeded in pulling it off so well." Tull was doing it with a "barrage of pre-recorded tapes, startling use of stage props, lights, and dynamics that in turn baffled, amused and finally delighted a crowd who responded by roaring great cheers of approval."

And Anderson was still joking around about the swollen ambitions. "Ian was moved to apologize for the discomfort caused to patrons glued to their seats for a show that eventually lasted nearly three hours," reported Welch. "'It's a bit like Ben Hur,' he admitted solicitously." Later in the show, John Evan "began a berserk imitation of his leader, only to be led gently back to the organ and put firmly in his place."[37]

This was more pantomime than "progressive," which was how Anderson wanted it. "We did see the slightly annoying spaghetti noodling of long, drawn-out instrumental passages, and we did kind of spoof that," he would say years later. "There are some rambling, free jazz moments . . . that were more of a piss-take on some of the bands that were rapidly disappearing up their own arses."[38]

"Jethro Tull may think they are making art, which is something that isn't of much use in the twentieth century in the first place," wrote Dave Marsh in *Creem*, "but it looks from here as though they are only making an ultra-sophisticated lounge music for the post-lunar space age."[39]

"It will undoubtedly impress an awful lot of dull minds with the superficial grandiloquence of its scope," wrote John Swenson in *Crawdaddy!* "Jethro Tull ought to think about coming down from the clouds to do their next one."[40]

But what if the listeners were in the clouds? *Thick as a Brick*, a forty-three-minute song cycle based on a nonexistent poem and written to be performed in its entirety, went straight to number one in the United States. It stayed there for two weeks, dislodged only by the arrival of the new Rolling Stones album.

ON MARCH 27, 1972, Yes ended thirty-two stops in the United States with a show in Boston. They had "broken" in America at last, and it had been exhausting at the level of the soul. Bill

Bruford was nearly ready to quit the group. He gave *Melody Maker* a tour diary from New York, reporting on how Americans "believe that anything British is 'better' in music," and describing the band's conquest of the States as a run through a sensory deprivation tank. "The musicians are pumped with antibiotics and kept closed off from America in the capsule's womb-like interior," he wrote. "The walls of the pod may be hotel walls, aeroplane walls, or walls of roadies and managers. There is nothing at all to say that I haven't got it muddled up, and in fact we fly to gigs in a Holiday Inn and check into a United Airlines DC9 to stay the night."[41]

But the gigs were coming off perfectly. The Boston show started with Stravinsky's *Firebird Suite*, an idea of Jon's, some time-marking music while the band emerged from backstage and set up. As the strings subsided, the band tore into "Roundabout," which was only then finishing its residence in the top ten.

King Crimson was marking time backstage. They'd been duct-taped together to tour their latest record, *Islands*, an intermittently beautiful and atonal suite of songs that had not sold well and featured the final Crimson lyrics of Peter Sinfield. As a *Melody Maker* reporter listened, Robert Fripp described Yes's true role in the ecosystem: "As you know, Yes started their band, their original band, with Pete Banks and Tony Kaye, just as Crimson had established itself. Yes attended our first gig at the Speakeasy in '68. When they saw that we were playing exactly what they had set out to accomplish it blew their heads and they never actually recovered you see. Yes is a very good band, mind you. We had Jon Anderson sing on our 'Lizard' album and they asked me to perform on one of theirs but I declined."[42]

Right in time to squelch the awkwardness, Anderson bounded off stage with a sunny quote: "That was a really fine set by King Crimson, wasn't it?"[43]

Melody Maker's write-up focused on the "internecine warfare" anyway. After the Boston concert, Yes received a gold record for $1 million sales of *Fragile*. They showed up, they collected the prize, and they left. Fripp was left alone to talk to reporters, waxing philosophical again. "You have no idea how it pains me to have to force my ideas on other people," he said to one reporter. "They couldn't play their parts without careful instruction. The arrangements were difficult for them to begin with. How can they be expected to embellish on it properly? But I don't delude myself in thinking that I am King Crimson. King Crimson is merely a way of doing things."[44]

What the press didn't know was that the dour-sounding Fripp had, through all the misery, made a sale. It was true that Yes had tried to hire him, but he had an eye on Yes's talent too. When he got a moment with Bruford, the drummer evoked the harsh judgments Fripp had delivered on Yes and asked how he—Bruford—had measured up. "Well, what do you say?" Bruford asked Fripp. "I think you are about ready now," said Fripp, according to Bruford.[45] And he nearly was.

In 1972, after returning to England and enjoying a respite, the band walked back into Advision to top *Fragile*. Pop structures had been abandoned completely. *Fragile* had begun with roughly forty seconds of distorted piano and plucked guitar. "Close to the Edge," the first song on the eponymous album, would begin with forty seconds of nature sounds. This was Jon Anderson's idea. "It took about a thousand tracks to make that opening!" said Eddy Offord.[46]

Of course it did; Yes was composing in the studio, splicing together what it had. According to Wakeman, the loop tape for the bird sounds was "forty feet long," sprawling across and around the room. "We couldn't play any of the tunes all the way through because nobody knew what they were," Bruford said. "They were being invented in the studio."[47]

Rich inventions, though; the band that had come together

for *Fragile* had learned to layer disparate melodies over disparate melodies. "We don't play 12-bars and we are quite envious of other groups who do," Howe told Welch. "We'd love to ramble away on a 12-bar but it would be too easy and not fair on the audience."[48]

"Close to the Edge" continued from the nature sounds to a clanging showcase of Wakeman's, Bruford's, Howe's, and Squire's playing, like four solos stacked atop each other, culminating every few bars in a single chord joined by a wordless Anderson yowl.

"The rest of the band gave him such a hard time about his lyrics," Eddy Offord remembered. "They'd all say to him, 'Jon, your fucking lyrics don't make any sense at all! What is this river, mountain stuff—it's absolutely meaningless drivel!' And he'd say, 'Look, when I'm writing lyrics I use words like colors. I use words for the sounding of the words, not the actual meaning.'"[49]

The lyrics were added to Bruford's irritations. "What does 'Total Mass Retain' mean?" asked Bruford during one session, in full view of reporter Chris Welch.

"What's wrong with 'Total Mass Retain?'" retorted Anderson. "I had to think of something quickly."

"Why not call it 'Puke'?" said Bruford.[50]

The lyrics made complete sense to Anderson. "Total Mass Retain," for example, was a deep metaphor for the subjects barely explored on the previous album. "It's got this deep sad feeling for the mass rape of our planet," he explained, "for the evilness which creates the wars, and there's no answers to all these things. It's common sense in knowing what's right and what's wrong."[51]

The song built with every measure, every section. Eight minutes in, the main melody—or what seemed to be the main melody—faded, replaced by a soft mantra titled "I Get Up, I Get Down." Wakeman played single notes in 4/4 time. Howe's guitar let off some ambient buzzes, sounding a lot like Robert Fripp's. At 12:09, Wakeman switched to a church organ, a sound that blasted around whatever room the record was being played in. Anderson returned, then Wakeman took over again. For the better part of a minute, the Yes sound was replaced by the music a British listener might have heard in church. Suddenly, at 13:56, Wakeman's Moog sliced right through the sound. "We destroy the church organ through the Moog," Anderson explained. "This leads to another organ solo rejoicing in the fact that you can turn your back on churches and find it within yourself to be your own church."[52]

This was an ambitious record, and Yes knew it. It could have only been written and composed by *this* band, not by the Yes that had included Peter Banks or Tony Kaye. "They didn't leave," Anderson told *Rolling Stone* during the sessions. "We decided to get someone else. It doesn't help them to say that. We've always said that Tony decided to leave the band, because it'd get him a better situation. The truth is that we blew them out because they weren't really into what we were trying to get together. Peter was a bit lazy, that's why. He liked his clothes a bit more than his music. Tony had a marvelous mind, he was a great guy to talk to, but he didn't have so many ideas. He wasn't willing to expand himself."[53]

The rest of Yes was willing, though Bruford was reaching his limit. "Alternative takes and optional instrumentations began to sprout like mold around the edge of the control room, on short bits of brown two-inch recording tape," he'd recall. At one point, after the band agreed to use one take of one of the many sections, they discovered it missing—the cleaning lady had disposed of it. They scrambled, though, and they found it, and anyway they owed her more than she'd taken. "Since we were there all night, she had to sort of clean around us, and would frequently be asked for her opinion on this or that, since none of us were in any fit state to decide."[54]

Bruford was done. He would take up Fripp on his offer; he would quit Yes, delivering half his royalties on *Close to the Edge*, and gifting some drums to his replacement. For the first time, the band was losing someone whom everyone considered a real talent. "You can't just get up and leave the restaurant without paying the bill," Brian Lane told Bruford.[55] That was how Yes thought about music? Bruford would take the pay cut.

YES HAD BROKEN OUT, so who was next? Progressive bands, as the music papers persisted in calling them, absolutely dominated the rock charts and the tour circuit. And they all seemed to have produced epics. Van der Graaf Generator had closed 1971 with *Pawn Hearts*, a cycle consisting of three songs. "A Plague of Lighthouse Keepers," which closed the record, stretched over the entire second side. Robert Fripp played on the second movement. The record's cover, by frequent Genesis artist Paul Whitehead, portrayed some of Peter Hammill's intellectual and cultural heroes floating in space.

Van der Graaf was less driving, less guitar focused, than most of the bands it shared billings and label space with. Those tendencies led to more experimentation, and more downright other-worldliness. "I got the transistors organized and suddenly found myself in a completely new world of bass playing," David Jackson told *Melody Maker*. "Put harmonics through the transistors and there's an infinite total range, especially with the wah-wah."[56]

And then there were the lyrics. "A Plague of Lighthouse Keepers" contained ten distinct sections, written by different members of the band but assembled in the studio and given ambitious, inscrutable lyrics by Hammill. It was, he explained, "just the story of a lighthouse keeper" that happened to be an allegory about how to rationalize the fact that people die and the individual cannot save them. "In the end . . . well, it doesn't really have an end," Hammill told *Sounds*. "It's really up to you to decide" (ellipsis in original).[57]

arrogant   If this came off as ~~pretentious~~, that was fine; that required more from the audience. "I suppose it could be melodramatic," Hammill told *Sounds* reporter Steve Peacock, who had been critical of the record, "but melodrama is like pretention really isn't it? It's in the eye of the beholder, it's not a quality conception, it's just how one feels about something. I can see what you mean, but it was just something I had to do. . . . Unless you approach it in the right frame of mind—which actually is no frame of mind—it won't mean anything to you. You can't relate to it on any normal level."[58]

All of the concept songs seemed to evolve in the same way, and out of the same ambition. Artists had the arrogance to write massive compositions. Audiences had the patience to listen. Studios had the capability to stitch them together. David Hitchcock, who had produced the side-long apocalyptic poem "Supper's Ready" for Genesis, recalled "sticking together loops of tape that went around the room," by hand.[59]

Labels had the audacity to sell it, all of it. Ever since Soft Machine had broken out, music journalists had argued that a "Canterbury scene" was producing a crop of baroque, strange progressive bands. This was true, insofar as the components of the Wilde Flowers became the Softs and Caravan, and as neither band engaged in the mysticism of some of the London groups. "The people who played at Canterbury made this particular noise and had a particular brain pattern," speculated Caravan's Richard Sinclair.[60] "We were certainly not driven to be a commercial pop band, that's for sure."[61]

Caravan had been well reviewed, and it inspired the occasional story that asked, then answered, why it was not the next big thing. In 1972, a reporter for *Disc and Music Echo* followed Caravan to a gig to explain why it lacked "that unfathomable quality that inspires young men to roll up their shirt sleeves and young ladies into orgasmic relief."[62]

Caravan did not have that; it offered, instead, the purest distillation of the Canterbury Sound. The band's own contribution to the epic-rock canon was "Nine Feet Underground," nearly twenty-three minutes of music that closed the album *In the Land of Grey and Pink.* "Dave was really bursting with music and really needed to get this composition out," Sinclair explained, "so he wrote twenty minutes' worth. . . . I like writing heaps and heaps of music that changes key and changes time."[63]

Lots of bands did. Gentle Giant had burst out in 1970, distinguishing themselves from the rest of the progressives by weaving Renaissance musical themes into their music. They opened for Yes; they delighted the music press with records that defied easy categorization. In 1972, they spent a summer backing Black Sabbath on a tour of the US—eighteen gigs, from the Deep South to the Midwest to California. They would play only fourteen of them, but this was not because the audiences rebelled. "We weren't precious about our music," singer Derek Shulman said. "We'd get over by being entertaining on stage. The fans that came out to see Black Sabbath and Gentle Giant and the Eagles and whoever else were quite open to it. Music, as a culture, was quite new. It wasn't narrowly cast."[64]

The exception came at the Hollywood Bowl, the biggest show of the tour. There was only a small cell of hecklers, but they were armed, and a cherry bomb hit the stage and exploded. Phil Shulman, the multi-instrumentalist behind much of the band's sound, called the audience "cunts." That did it. "The booing that went up was spectacular," remembered Derek Shulman. "Funny enough, that same show we were so whacked out that Tony Iommi literally fell flat out, on his face."[65]

The rest of the American tour dates were scrapped, for the usual reasons of rock excess. In Britain, progressive bands could still contemplate breakout success and feel slighted when it failed to arrive. Egg, a boldly experimental group, struggled to capitalize on its success with "Seven Is a Jolly Good Time." "We're fed up with the colleges," keyboard player Dave Stewart told *Melody Maker*. "That's where the money was, but it ain't now. Students are very conditioned, concerned more with maintaining their cool than with listening. It really seems to pervade student life. They're very concerned with liking the right things. The pressure on them to go to a gig is not 'Do I like the band?' but 'Is everyone else going?' or even 'Am I expressing my social liberation by going?' "[66]

In that same interview, the members of Egg—who would soon bolt for more successful bands—explained that an audience had always been there, out of reach. "Zappa has talked about electronic chamber music," said Mont Campbell, the band's multi-instrumentalist, "and I think we're in that category. It's an orchestral thing, in that each instrument is playing its own written lines, independently. The music is getting more complicated, in order to explore the integration of the various parts, rather than just complicated ideas for their own sake."[67]

Dave Stewart agreed: complicated music was the next wave. "The Soft Machine were very popular, but the only new thing they did was with time signatures—and it got very repetitive, not an organic part of the music. It was a fetal stage, if you like, and I don't think there's been anybody in rock who's really been concerned with developing the time side."[68]

BILL BRUFORD WAS GONE, but Yes had an album to tour and sell. *Close to the Edge* dropped in September 1972; the band canceled a few gigs in the US but was otherwise able to hew to a schedule that had it playing sold-out arenas. It took only a little while for Alan White, a journeyman drummer who had played on John Lennon's albums, to get caught up on Bruford's material. "I had to adapt to Yes's music, but I think they also had to adapt to me," White told a reporter for *Sounds*.[69] "I knew the band wanted a drummer with a little bit more weight than Bill anyway. I was more of a rock 'n' roll player."[70]

Jon Anderson, as soon as Howe joined, had talked about making a double album. "We'd made the decision that all the music we'd ever write for the band would be for stage, not for radio," says Jon Anderson.[71] Their music became more virtuoso, more ambitious, more spiritual, with even denser transcendental lyrics. Yes's long pieces were just that—pieces, not jamming, with the audience welcoming the ambition.

Wakeman, on his own, was trying the limits. While on the band's US tour, he happened to grab a copy of the book *The Private Life of Henry VIII* at the Richmond airport. "I wanted to do an album without vocals because I can't sing," he told *Sounds*'s Penny Valentine. "I can't write lyrics either. Dirty poems yes, lyrics no." But then he delved into the book. When "I started reading about Catherine of Aragon . . . this first theme I'd laid down earlier came into my head. It sounds daft but it really was a surge of excitement, because I'd found a concept which was what I'd always needed but hadn't realised."[72]

Wakeman's solo album *The Six Wives of Henry VIII* was released on A&M at the start of 1973. The cover suggested a messing-with-the-classics ethos in the mold of Wendy Carlos— the titular wives arrayed in a grand room, their husband looking on, as Wakeman shambled past them in jeans and sneakers. "Catherine of Aragon," which kicked off the record, started with Wakeman's piano melody and let it be bent by his trunkfuls of equipment, which included two mini-Moogs, two mellotrons, a

Hammond, and an ARP synthesizer. On other tracks, Wakeman ran his fingers over a harpsichord and over the church organ at St. Giles-without-Cripplegate.

It was a hit, moving right into the top ten and being reviewed favorably across the British press. The timing was perfect, because the reporters who had built up progressive music were about to take down the first idol. Jethro Tull put out *A Passion Play* in July. They had played the test-your-patience game before, with *Thick as a Brick*, but they'd been "taking the piss" out of the whole "concept album" trend.

Who told the same forty-minute joke *twice*? *A Passion Play* jigged its way over the line from camp to aggrandizement, with a Joycean retelling of . . . well, of a passion play. "Son of Kings make the ever-dying sign," sang Anderson, "cross your fingers in the sky for those about to BE." The liner notes credited the music to a troupe of fictional actors ("John Tetrad was born in Birmingham and spent his early life in the engineering trade before embarking on a theatrical career as 'Willie' in *Pass Me a Pippin*.") and advised that "latecomers may be asked to wait until a suitable break in the performance."[73]

Critics went after *A Passion Play* like a piñata made up to look like Hitler. "I cannot recall an album by a British rock band that has given me more pain to endure," groaned Chris Welch, one of the most sympathetic prog embeds, reviewing the LP for *Melody Maker*. "I am left with the feeling of never wanting to hear another British rock group album again. I don't want to hear arrangements, Moog synthesizers, electric guitars, or bloody clever lyrics for as long as the polar caps are frozen: if this is where ten years of 'progression' have taken us then it's time to go backwards."[74]

The band was crushed. "That was the front page!" remembered Ian Anderson. "Our manager, Terry Ellis, hatched a plan for the next issue. He planted a story: 'Jethro Tull Quit!' It was a bit of a joke between him and *Melody Maker* editor Ray Shulman, that we'd quit because of the bad review. That was on the front page! I remember the day I walked down on the street and saw that issue, and I thought: *What the fuck is this about?*"[75]

Yes never thought about scaling back. They wanted to reach transcendence, not radio. "We're close to the edge of spiritual awareness within the framework of the group, making music," Jon Anderson told the *New Musical Express*. "We have this long song, which we felt could hold a listener's ear for the whole length, rather than just a track here and there that they like."[76]

The band debated whether to record their next album—which would be *Tales from Topographic Oceans*—in the country (for inspiration) or in the city (for convenience). The compromise: they booked London's Morgan Studios and made it *look* like the country. The drum kit was plunked inside of a picket fence, facing a cardboard cow. Rick Wakeman's keyboards were balanced on hay bales, near potted plants. When Anderson decided that white tiles would enhance the acoustics, gaffers put up a bathroom wall. "About halfway through the album," producer Eddy Offord would tell Chris Welch, "the cow was covered in graffiti and all the plants had died. That just kind of sums up the whole album."[77]

Offord put on a braver face for the contemporary press, inviting an *NME* writer to hear the work in progress. "You cannot turn on creativity at the turn of a studio clock," he proclaimed. "No one would have asked Picasso to start work at 2 o'clock and paint a masterpiece by five." The interviewer bought it. "Yes," he wrote, "sounded gutsier than I've ever heard them before."[78]

Everything was hyperambitious. "We got Slinkys, put mikes on them, and threw them down stairs," said Steve Howe in a

2009 BBC interview. "If you put a lot of reverb on it, it sounds great. . . . It's a nice kind of insanity."[79] The gatefold cover, Roger Dean's fourth for the band, smashed together wonders from all over the planet. Here was a rock from Stonehenge; there were the plains of Nazca; over in the back was the temple at Chichen Itza.

"I was accompanying the band to Japan," Dean recalled, "and the wives and girlfriends put whatever dope they had into a cake, which nobody knew about. On the flight, Jon served us slices of the cake. And so, from Alaska to Tokyo, I was talking for hour after hour after hour about this book I was working on about landscapes. I talked his ear off about the religious-spiritual significance of them, of ley lines, of dragon lines, while all the while the most beautiful landscapes of Siberia were passing underneath us."[80]

Inside the sleeve was Anderson's spiritual schematic for the album. "Leafing through Paramhansa [*sic*] Yoganda's *Autobiography of a Yogi*," he wrote, "I got caught up in the lengthy footnote on page 83." He had thought deeply, then taken his ideas into the studio, and then the band had composed on the spot, standing or sitting amid the cows.

"The Revealing Science of God (Dance of the Dawn)" started with thirty seconds of soft sounds meant to evoke lapping waves. Then came Steve Howe's guitar, playing sustained, single notes, imitating whale song. Wakeman—who would claim to have hated every minute of this—arrived on an organ and quickly dominated the mix. The rest of the band arrived one by one, until every instrument was engaged. Alan White frantically hit his cymbals. Chris Squire plunked the bass, faster and faster. At 3:33, Wakeman bent a note on the synthesizer and the song transformed into 4/4 pop. The band bore a load, moved it slowly in one direction, snapped back quickly, and moved again. You could listen, but you couldn't relax. For twenty minutes, the experiment came off.

Yet there were sixty more minutes to go. There were detours, like the vaguely Eastern drum pattern and whining Howe guitar lines that dominated the beginning and middle of part 3: "The Ancient (Giants under the Sun)". But the band scattered hooks in every song. The vocal-and-organ duet in "Ritual (Nous Sommes du Soleil)" sounds like Funkadelic. It would show up three decades later as the key sample in De La Soul's "The Grind Date" on the eponymous album.

The record went gold in the UK from advance sales alone— seventy-five thousand copies. Yes sold out everywhere, but audiences at the *Tales* shows were given a warning: there would be no seating after the performance had started. You grabbed your place for the show, and you were locked in to a piece of music longer than almost any individual baroque symphony.

"Already the piece is being applauded as a masterpiece of contemporary music," wrote Tony Palmer in the *Observer*, "classical in structure, mystical in realization." But in concert, he continued, "the players themselves appeared confused as to what was expected of them, the lead singer being unsure whether each section should be described as, for example, the second movement or the second side of the record."[81]

The band planned to play it all. Wakeman went along for a few shows, until the November 1973 gig at the Manchester Free Trade Hall. "There were a couple of pieces where I hadn't got much to do," Wakeman would recall, "and it was all a bit dull."[82]

During every show, a keyboard tech reclined underneath Wakeman's Hammond organ, ready to fix broken hammers or ribbons and to "continually hand me my alcoholic beverages."[83] That night in Manchester, the tech asked the bored Wakeman what he wanted to eat after the show. Wakeman, the lone carnivore in Yes, ordered the curry.

"Half the audience were in narcotic rapture on some far-off planet," Wakeman wrote in his 2008 memoir, "and the other half were asleep, bored shitless."[84]

Wakeman kept on at the keyboards, adding gossamer organ melodies and ambient passages to the songs. And then, about thirty minutes later, his tech started handing up "little foil trays" of curry: chicken vindaloo, rice pilaf, some papadums, bhindi bhaji, Bombay aloo, and a stuffed paratha. Wakeman began placing them on top of his keyboards. "I still didn't have a lot to do," he wrote, "so I thought I might as well tuck in."[85] The food was obscured by the instrument stacks, further obscured by Wakeman's cape, but the aroma danced over to Yes's lead singer, Jon Anderson. He took a good look at the culinary insult. *Shrug.* Papadum in hand, he returned to his microphone to sing his next part.

But as the tour went on, Yes dropped the third section of the album from the show, then the second. Soon, Wakeman vented to reporters about the band's screwup. "*Tales from Topographic Oceans* is like a woman's padded bra," he told one interviewer. "The cover looks good . . . but when you peel off the padding there's not a lot there."[86]

The band had gone along with the live edits and tolerated Rick's behavior. "Rick had a problem with the song that featured him, and the basic improvisational content of side two," explained Steve Howe.[87] "We started to take two out, three out, and it was a great disappointment to me. The group's got a right to do what the hell it likes. We can't be guided by our audience."

At the next shows, Yes started dropping sections of the suite. "We could tell the audience wasn't reacting," said Anderson.[88] By the end, they were only playing the energetic first and fourth sections, then switching over to the hits. They rented a 63-foot-high balloon with the Yes logo, hoping it would follow them around the country. They scrapped it when the balloon and their bus nearly crashed.

"One of the members of the band got misled by his friends," said Howe, "but *Tales* is possibly one of the masterworks of Yes. I was one of the guys who never said anything bad about the album. We were behind it. We were the guys that built it."[89]

Wakeman would never agree. *Tales*, he would say, was too loping, too ~~pretentiou~~s, too unplanned—boring, pompous, obese music. But him? He was going to write concept albums based on classic British themes. *The Six Wives of Henry VIII* had gone gold everywhere, eventually selling fifteen million copies. His second experiment, *Journey to the Centre of the Earth*, was recorded during a pause in the *Tales* tour, and it went to number one in the UK just as he was parting ways with Yes.

British audiences weren't done with pomp. Wakeman's excess was just more relatable than Yes's excess. *Journey*, a four-part compression of the Jules Verne story, was recorded live with the London Symphony Orchestra, which beefed up Wakeman's twelve keyboards—three of them mellotrons. (It was a busy 1974 for the orchestra; they would later guest on the Mahavishnu Orchestra's *Apocalypse*.) There are no strange time signatures. This is pop music. And Wakeman's timing was perfect, putting him at the center of British music fandom just as Keith Emerson was taking a few years off.

"Hopefully, my music will develop in the way Yes would have developed," Wakeman told Chris Welch. "In fact *Journey* is how I would have liked Yes to have gone."[90]

6

HAMMERS AND BELLS

In the spring of 1973, progressive artists released two of the biggest-selling albums in the history of pop music. March brought Pink Floyd's *Dark Side of the Moon*. May brought *Tubular Bells*. The first record sold roughly fifteen million copies; the second sold about seventeen million. They did not depart the best-seller charts until, respectively, 1978 and 1988. The people behind them remained demigods on the music scene for the rest of the decade. The labels that had stuck by them became fabulously rich. There might be no Virgin Empire, no Virgin Airlines—much less Virgin spacecraft—had Mike Oldfield not attacked a leftover bell with a spare hammer.

And there would have been less solace for outcast teenagers, had Pink Floyd not decided to craft a concept album. The origins of *Dark Side* were in discussions that bassist Roger Waters had with band members about the "pressures and preoccupations that divert us from our potential for positive action."[1] He would write a song cycle about madness; it would bring together elements that the band had been kicking around but be woven into one piece, played live.

It would not be about the moon—not literally. The band behind "Interstellar Overdrive" and "Set the Controls for the Heart of the Sun" was not making a space-rock album, and Waters blanched when the theory was raised. "None of it had anything to do with that. I don't know what's wrong with people." By his admission, he took "the enormous risk of being truly banal about a lot of it, in order that the ideas should be expressed as simply and plainly as possible."[2]

The lyrical content was simple. Nothing else was. Pink Floyd began playing the suite (temporarily retitled *Eclipse*, so as not to conflict with a contemporary album by the band Medicine Head) in January 1972, bringing with them a quadraphonic sound system and a twenty-eight-channel mixing desk. The concert began with the taped sound of a heartbeat, cascading into other carefully "found" noise, like a clanging cash machine, and then into the slow groove of the studiously banal "Breathe."

The piece took a while to sink in with people. It was daring, and difficult; the tape loops malfunctioned during the first performance, forcing the band to regroup with a different set. But *Dark Side* came together over the course of 1972. In the hands of producer Alan Parsons, the album drifted away from Pink Floyd's norms and into a sound that was simultaneously otherworldly and radio ready. On tour, the lengthy "Us and Them" had been anchored by an organ solo. On the record, this was replaced by a saxophone. The song "Time" was given an intro of clanging clocks that was recorded when Parsons went "to an antique clock shop and recorded a horologist's delight of chimes, ticks, and alarms."[3]

KEVIN AYERS WAS THRIVING without Soft Machine. The band had sprinted away from his style of cracked pop music; his new backing band, the Whole World, could play exactly what he wanted. The bassist, Mike Oldfield, was a young and curious savant.

One day, Oldfield grew fascinated with "We Did It Again." It was the song that repeated without regard for time, the song that the Softs had once stretched to forty minutes as a crowd tripped on. "Why do you keep going round and round?" Oldfield asked Ayers. "Why not?" Ayers asked. "That's what you're supposed to do. It's a thing that just repeats. Like the seasons, they repeat. Clocks do that. They're supposed to do that."[4]

Oldfield took note. If he was going to compose for himself, he would begin with a repetitive riff. In the same mood, he played around with the Farfisa organ that Ayers sometimes played on stage. "I fiddled around for a few minutes on the Farfisa," he remembered, "and came up with a riff I liked. I thought of it as one bar in 7/8 time and one bar in 8/8 or 4/4; I wanted to make it different from 16/8 so I thought I'd drop a sixteenth beat. I probably chose the key A minor because it is the easiest key to play on the keyboard."[5]

It was not the music that Ayers might have come up with. Ayers had broken up the Whole World out of boredom and disarray. "I got more and more drunk and despairing," said Ayers, "and the gigs got worse."[6]

Two French horns, two flutes, a trombone, two violins, a cello, a double bass, and the Whole World. "The thing that always upset me about performing was the idea of 'entertaining' people," he told an interviewer. "It's like that when I go to a movie; I think 'why I am sitting here, letting someone else live my life for me?' That's why this trance thing would be good. As a musician, I'd simply be useful to the audience, creating a method for people to release their energies. It would be a very communal thing."[7]

Ayers's bandmates, including Oldfield and keyboard player

David Bedford, were stranded. "I had taken my demos to loads of record companies," said Oldfield, "but they all looked at me as if I was mad. They said, because there were no vocals, no words, no drums or anything, that it was not marketable."[8]

At twenty-two, the bassist was basically stranded and done with the band. "The last tour was a very drunken affair," he remembered.[9] Oldfield recalled being "desperate enough to go to the Soviet Union to become a state musician," and he had nearly done that. But "almost at the moment that I decided to call the embassy to say, 'I want to go live in Moscow,'" he related, a representative from Caroline Records rang him at his apartment.

Caroline had been founded by an entrepreneur just about Oldfield's age: Richard Branson. In the summer of 1972, Branson bought a mansion located in Shipton-on-Cherwell in Oxfordshire and transformed it into a studio where bands could hang out and record. "I was looking at *Country Life* magazine one day while waiting to see Richard," said Tom Newman. "I spotted this house in Oxfordshire in its own grounds. It just looked beautiful and it was thirty thousand quid."[10]

Branson brought Oldfield to his office, and offered to record at the manor. Oldfield rattled off the instruments he'd need. "A good acoustic guitar, a Spanish guitar, a Farfisa organ, a Fender precision bass, a good Fender amplifier, glockenspiel, a mandolin, a mellotron, a triangle, a Gibson guitar . . . oh, and some chimes of course. What are chimes? Tubular bells." Branson paid for it all. The engineer would be Tom Newman, who, unbeknownst to his benefactors, had no idea what he was doing.[11]

"I tried to live up to my claim that I was the world's gift to the recording industry," said Newman. "I read up all the back copies of 'Studio News' in order to find out what I was talking about . . . and I put the studio together with a soldering iron in one hand and a text book in the other."[12]

So Oldfield's scrappy crew started recording the suite that was tentatively known as "Opus One." But there was no pomp or pretense. "I'm not the world's greatest pianist," said Oldfield. "My timing wandered all over the place. So all that first day's work had to be done again the next day with a metronome running to keep me in time."[13]

The second day saw an improvement. "I had this organ chord which I wanted to slowly slide into another chord," said Oldfield. "It would be simple now, but the only way we could do it then was to record the first chord on a tape loop, then put that onto this great big machine with a huge speed control dial on it, and as the engineer turned the dial, the chord went up in pitch. Once we got that sound, Tom was completely converted."[14]

"We had this huge champagne bottle, a jeroboam or something," said Oldfield. "Someone would go down to the pub to have it filled with draught Guinness, and we would drink that while we were overdubbing. At the time I was smoking cigarillos, little cigars. The engineers would be furious with me, as all my ash would fall down into the faders and between the knobs."[15]

Oldfield's twiddling built toward an epic track, enough to fill side one with all of the melodies that had been kicking around in Oldfield's head and apartment. New melodies and riffs were written on the spot; the bass line at the end of part one came together, said Oldfield, after "a few swigs of the Jameson bottle."[16]

"They were complete melodies in themselves," said Newman, "with intros and fade-outs or ends. I liked them very much and was a little nonplussed when Mike strung them all together."[17]

Yet the songs made more sense as part of a single piece. Toward the end of the sessions for part one, Oldfield remembered that a set of bells had been left in the studio from John Cale's time in the mansion. "When I tried playing the bells, they didn't sound very impressive," he remembered. "So I asked if anyone had a bigger hammer. Someone found one, but it still didn't do it. 'Anybody got a really big hammer?' I asked, so someone went out to the garage and got a massive hammer." Hammer in hand, Oldfield "walloped a bell and made a huge dent in it, and it made this amazing sound."[18]

"I was quite rebellious, so I said, 'You want lyrics? I'll give you lyrics!' There was a big wine cellar at The Manor, so I went down there one night—it was flooded with a foot of water— and found this bottle of Jameson whiskey. I drank half of it and ordered the engineer to take me to the studio. I screamed my brains out for ten minutes and I couldn't speak a single sentence for two weeks."[19]

They mixed away, five hundred or so separate pieces of music to get into sixteen tracks—all by hand. And they seemed to be finished, until they played back the piece and heard their edits memorialized by audible, jarring clicks. "Simon started to cut them out physically," said Oldfield, "and join the tape together with sticky tape. Then, when we played it through, instead of a 'click' sound, there was a 'thunk' sound."[20] Oldfield and New- man came up with a Gordian knot sort of solution: they cut the transitions. Instead of easy segues or fades, the music would skip from section to section.

They were done. The album was taken to a trade fair in Cannes, where Richard Branson himself played the life-changing album and was greeted with advice that Oldfield would never follow: "It needs vocals, it needs lyrics."[21]

Duly panicked, Virgin went back to work on its star. "One night I found Richard and Tom Newman in the studio trying to remix the album," Oldfield said. "There was nothing I could do about it. I didn't know what the hell they were up to. As it turned out, they gave up after a day and left it as it was."[22] It was up to the artist and the label to sell the thing.

MEANWHILE, A NEW VERSION of King Crimson was taking a stage in Frankfurt's Zoom Club. It was October 13, 1972, half a year since the last iteration of the band had played the *Islands* tracks on tour with Yes. There would be nothing from *Islands*—nothing from any King Crimson album before.

Instead, there was Bill Bruford, taking his place behind a drum kit and then jangling a set of bells. The only other noise was coming from Jamie Muir, a percussionist who'd been expelled from the Edinburgh College of Art and found homes in experimental free-jazz bands across Great Britain. "I had been hearing of Jamie Muir for several years with remarkable frequency," Robert Fripp would tell *Rolling Stone*. "I knew it was inevitable that one day I would work with him."[23]

Shortly thereafter, the percussionist was on stage, rapping out an Eastern rhythm on a xylophone. This was the start of "Larks' Tongues in Aspic (Part I)," a name that Muir had come up with. Fripp had played him a section of the piece and asked him what it sounded like. "Why, larks' tongues in aspic," Muir had said. "What else?"[24] He'd compared the sound to tiny delicacies trapped in gelatin. This, the band all agreed, was brilliant.

"I was very much more an instrumental style of musician rather than being song-based," Muir explained to a biographer, "and there weren't many other bands that I would have been any good in."[25] He preferred "sheets of tin rattling and ripping, piles of crockery breaking" to the norms of songwriting.

The Zoom Club crowd heard the results. There was no *song* to hang on to for the first minute of the new King Crimson's set. Not until the arrival of a violin, in the hands of new hire

David Cross, playing a clipped, ascending, melody. The tension built, joined by a few spare riffs from Fripp. Then the whole song exploded, with new bassist, John Wetton, joining in on a six-note battering of noise from Fripp and Bruford and Muir and Cross.

The new Crimson had recaptured something of the first band, but abandoned the usual structures of songs. Half of the Zoom Club show revealed the tracks the band had been working on in rehearsals over the summer. Half of it consisted of total improvisation.

Fripp was thrilled. "The Zoom club was amazing—all those little bums and tits all tightly concealed within denims and blouses, eager to break free their confining clasp," he told *Sounds*. "I didn't think it possible again that I'd have the energy to take on the fairly enormous task of being involved with King Crimson. But then of course I wasn't as well tuned in to cosmic energy as I am now."[26]

There were two more nights at the Zoom Club, then a stop in Bremen, and then King Crimson spent November and December aggressively touring the UK. They returned to the studio in January 1973 to cut *Larks' Tongues in Aspic*, an album bookended by the eponymous tracks, all informed by the improvisations worked out on stage. The concerts had been exactly the same: the first title track, followed by the sweet, Wetton-sung ballad "Book of Saturday," then three more songs that skittered around the edges of pop but quickly raced elsewhere.

The album and the concerts culminated with part two of the title track, a genuinely terrifying piece. The song started with Fripp playing flatted electric guitar chords in 11/8 time (theme 1). Bruford came in on the second measure, hitting a cymbal on the downbeat, and the scales went higher and higher until—*swoop*, at 0:45, everything fell away and a softer, less unsettling violin-and-bass-driven melody (theme 2) arrived, courtesy of Cross and Wetton. The pattern repeated, but the second appearance of the violin was accompanied by the distorted voices of laughing gremlins. At 3:40 a new, slower 6/8 melody (theme 3) began. At 4:00, Cross started subjecting the violin to what sounded like torture on the rack. Its death rattle continued until the return of theme 2, and at 5:55 a Bruford drumroll inaugurated a full forty seconds of soft noise, ending with a final, minor Fripp chord.

"Some of the sounds Jamie got on that!" Wetton marveled to *Sounds*. "He used a glass rod through a thundersheet, pulling his hands along it to get the friction. It sounds like a bloody helicopter."[27]

The five-member Crimson completed two tours, as Muir's interest gradually frayed. The improvisation was sort of the problem. "I had a lot of equipment," he'd recall, and "with King Crimson the drum roadie would start to complain bitterly and get shirty because of the problems of setting it up and putting it back down again."[28] These petty concerns made a poor match with Muir's spiritual interests. After two tours, he informed the band and EG that he was out, and that he would decamp to a Buddhist monastery in Scotland.

Yet this didn't alter the mode King Crimson had gotten into. Before the tours even started, Fripp sat with Brian Eno at his studio in London and started running his guitar through tapes. The two men opened a bottle of wine, then Fripp got to work with effects pedals, playing along to some wordless Eno music. The producer fed the Fripp sounds through his reel-to-reel Revox A77 tape machines, looping hypnotically, bouncing the sound between playback heads. "He did all the clever stuff, for sure, but the sound that he was hearing was routed through my machinery," Eno would tell *Mojo*'s Andy Gill, decades later. "That kind of got me into the idea of the studio, not as a place for reproducing music but as a place for changing it, or re-creating it from scratch."[29]

After Muir left Crimson, before Fripp had to lower himself
to the hotel-bus-plane-hotel grind of a new tour, the guitarist trekked back to Eno's studio. They recorded more music,
using the same techniques. When he gave interviews, Fripp
insisted that the Eno tapes were changing music in a way no
lumbering rock band could. "It's the most expressive thing
I've done," Fripp told *Guitar Player* magazine. "It's all guitar,
but 'The Heavenly Music Corporation' is recorded so there's
a build-up of guitars, so that though there's only two guitars
playing, because of the manner in which it's recorded, in one
place it sounds like fifty guitars."[30]

"The Heavenly Music Corporation" ended up running to
twenty-one minutes, taking up the entire first side of an album
called *(No Pussyfooting)*. The second side was devoted to "Swas-
tika Girls," composed in exactly the same way, and with a
slightly busier guitar part from Fripp. There were no lyrics, no
singles, nothing identified with hairy rock and roll. In another
interview promoting the album, Fripp insisted that the cover
would portray its creators "in a state of undress," ideally "as an
invitation to all those ladies in the future who'd like to help us
develop even further."

"We're both incorrigible womanizers," Fripp told *NME*,
"both wonderful examples of young Taurian virility." The music
paper illustrated these quotes with a cartoon of a fuzzy, unsmil-
ing Fripp stripped down to his underwear. But he wasn't truly
joking, and he wasn't out of place. The experimental musician as
sex symbol; it was real, and the record buyers and concertgoers
were proving it.[31]

ON MAY 25, 1973, *Tubular Bells* dropped into the record shops.
The cover, designed by Trevor Key after an idea that Oldfield
had had when crossing two bones, was spare and unforgettable:

a twisting, sci-fi bell floating across a cloudy sky. Virgin was releasing Gong's latest album on the same day, *Flying Teapot*, a slab of glistening psychedelia with a cartoonish cover by Daevid Allen himself.

Four days later, *Top Gear* host John Peel spun a song from Annette Funicello's greatest-hits album, then asked his listeners to steady themselves for the first part of Oldfield's "rather remarkable" album. He had not exactly stumbled across it in a shop. Branson had given him the hard sell, playing the album after treating Peel to dinner.[32]

And luckily for him, luckily for Virgin, Peel heard everything that the rival labels and the snobs in Cannes had not. Peel rattled off all the instruments credited to Oldfield—"taped motorwave amplifier organ chord, mandolin-like guitar, fuzz guitar"—and then listeners heard it: the minor-key piano theme, the gateway into neo-orchestral music that could not have been further from the *Mickey Mouse Club*. Twenty minutes later, the song faded and Peel returned. "I've been introducing *Top Gear* for nearly six years now," he said, "but I think that is certainly one of the most impressive LPs I've had the chance to play on the radio."[33]

Branson was thrilled, and even more thrilled when Peel doubled down with a review of the album in *Listener*. This was a host with no time and many sharp words for "progressive rock," yet he couldn't get enough of Oldfield. "In twenty years' time," wrote Peel, "I'm ready to bet you a few shillings that Yes and ELP will have vanished from the memory of all but the most stubborn and that the Gary Glitters and Sweets of no lasting value will be regarded as representing the true sound of the 1970s. Having said that, I'm going to tell you about a new recording of such strength, energy, and real beauty that to me it represents the first breakthrough into history that any musician regarded primarily as a rock musician has made."[34]

Peel had ushered in a phenomenon. There had been so many

ways for Virgin to fail, but Oldfield's record was going to be a sensation. Oldfield's album, the "breakthrough into history," soared to number one. It was everything the composer had asked for, so Branson asked him for a little more. *Tubular Bells* needed to be played live; Oldfield needed to write a score.

This was no easy task, considering that Oldfield had stitched the music together from years of juvenilia and weeks of in-studio experiments. "I'd been quite happy doing my thing with Kevin Ayers, standing at the back next to the drummer, or getting blind drunk and going wild," he thought. "It took ages to write it all out in multistave form. Eventually someone came in and helped me write out the parts."[35]

Yet this, at least, distracted the newly minted genius from the incipient nightmare of the live show. "I felt awful," Oldfield remembered thinking. "I thought it was all going to go horribly wrong."[36]

Branson's star was ready to bolt, after all of that prep, on the day that a crowd at the Queen Elizabeth Hall was supposed to witness history. The mogul invited Oldfield on a London ride-along in his Bentley.

Branson knew his artist. "I'll get out here and walk home," said Branson. "You just keep driving and the car's yours."

"Come off it!" said Oldfield. "It was your wedding present!"

"All you have to do is then drive it round to the Queen Elizabeth Hall and go up onstage tonight," said Branson.

Oldfield took the deal. Branson would never stop congratulating himself for solving the crisis so easily. "If he was successful," Branson would later write of Oldfield, "I would be able to pick up any car I wanted."[37]

The show may have been destined for success. Peel wasn't alone in worshipping the album; in *Sounds*, Steve Peacock praised it above all the other Virgin releases, and above anything coming out of rival labels, for inspiring "the same kind of feeling as I had when I first heard bands like Pink Floyd and Soft Machine."[38]

But onstage, Oldfield could hear only the bum notes. "Without the benefit of the huge hammer," he remembered, "the compressors and microphones, they just went 'dink' instead of that fantastic sound we had on the album." He fretted throughout the concert, and when it ended, silence enveloped the hall. And then the silence was replaced by a standing ovation. "They clapped and cheered and whistled, they just went totally bananas, they were in rapture. I was just sitting there with a huge question mark over my head, thinking to myself, 'You liked that? You actually enjoyed it?' "[39]

"Even the band applauded him," Branson would write in his memoirs. "He was a new star. That night we sold hundreds of copies of *Tubular Bells*."[40]

Still, Oldfield didn't buy it. He'd been in agony on stage. Why was the piece played as one whole, with no break? Because he wanted to race through it as quickly as possible. When Branson tried to congratulate his star, he found a sullen and unbelieving artist who wanted to flee, convinced that he'd blown it. "We were faced with the nightmare of a #1 artist who would not be interviewed, who would not play in public—who just wanted to compose," Branson told an interviewer later.[41]

The album sold, and sold, yet Oldfield bristled at promoting it. He sat for an "agonizing" interview with *Melody Maker*'s Karl Dallas, puzzling for twenty minutes over "why" he'd written the album, because a journalist wanted to know. What was the right answer? "I did things because that's what I did," the genius thought.

Oldfield groped for a way out. He performed *Tubular Bells* live again, for the BBC, with the Softs' Mike Ratledge on keyboards, but he wanted out. "The whole bubble about fame had burst in my mind." The Bentley, the legendary Bentley he'd been given to save Virgin, was "clapped out" and not worth repairing. "If you pressed too hard on the floor on the passenger side, your foot would go straight through."[42]

So Oldfield fled west. He spotted a house for sale near England's border with Wales, with a "beautiful view" of the Black Mountains. Before even going inside, Oldfield called Branson and asked for permission to spend £12,000 and buy the house—"The Beacon," it was called. Permission was granted.

All Branson wanted, anyway, was another hit from his shooting star. Oldfield, who'd paid little attention to details or contract negotiations when he signed with Virgin, jawed with Branson about the equipment he might need. "There was this organ that David Bedford used to have in Kevin Ayers and the Whole World," he remembered saying. "A Farfisa? Not a Continental, a Professional Two or something." The next weekend, back at Beacon, Oldfield looked out his window, onto the vista that was meant to clear his mind, and there was Branson, "staggering up from the car park at the bottom of the hill, actually carrying this monstrous, ugly Farfisa organ."[43]

Oldfield was left to stew, and compose, and think about what he really wanted in his music.

AT THE SAME TIME, another veteran of the Kevin Ayers circle, another artist regularly consulted by the music press for visions of rock future, had been forced into the same position. Robert Wyatt, the drummer for Soft Machine, had left that band in 1971. "I was the only lout in the group, and I think they found my loutishness tiresome," Wyatt said years later.[44]

Wyatt went on to found a more song-focused outfit called Matching Mole, its name being a piss-take on the French translation of "soft machine"—*machine molle*. "There wasn't any theory there," said Wyatt, "except everybody just played what they knew that might go with what everybody else was doing."[45]

Matching Mole instantly found a following and bridged the gap between the Canterbury scene and the experimentation of the London bands. Robert Fripp had produced the band's second record; Brian Eno had come into the studio to add some synthesized textures. All expectations were that the band would record a third record, or that Wyatt would record a second solo record, until June 1, 1973. "Lady June," June Campbell Cramer, was throwing a party for Gong's Gilli Smyth, who, like Oldfield, was about to release a record with Virgin. Cramer had gotten to know the Softs in their bohemian Spanish days.

Reunited in a flat outside Paddington, Kevin Ayers and Robert Wyatt reverted to type. "God. I really was too drunk to know," Wyatt remembered when a documentarian asked him to recall what happened. "I certainly wouldn't have the courage to climb out of a fourth floor window." However he did it, Wyatt fell from the window and woke up in a hospital to be told that he would never walk again. The fall had broken his spine. "It'll probably knock 10 years off your life, 20 if you smoke," said the doctor, according to Wyatt.[46]

It was too horrible to believe: one of the most inventive and exciting drummers in British rock could no longer play the drums. Pink Floyd's Nick Mason learned of the accident the very day that he received a postcard from Wyatt, asking him to produce his next solo project. Mason sprang into action, helping to organize a benefit concert for Wyatt at the Rainbow Theatre in November 1973.

And then the two of them went to work. "The idea, basically, was just to make a nice record," Wyatt told an interviewer, "not to explain what a terrible time I was having."[47] Just six months after being paralyzed, Wyatt was in the studio recording songs that, out of necessity and style, were more ambient and vocal than anything he'd done before. In July 1974, the buyer who took *Rock Bottom* home and put it on a record player heard barely any drums at all. "Sea Song" opened the record with the sound of a clipped metronome, woozy organs, and Wyatt's nervous, warm words, which had as much or as little meaning as the listener wanted from them.

Virgin signed Wyatt and advertised the album with a composite image of the singer's half-smiling face superimposed on a garden gnome. The ad copy listed the personnel, including Mike Oldfield on guitar, and ended with some of the change-your-life verbiage that was becoming essential to the Virgin pitch. "In Robert Wyatt's opinion, *Rock Bottom* is the finest album of his entire career. And there's nothing Virgin can say to improve on that. So, temporarily suppressing our euphoria, we leave the rest to you."[48]

The Mason-produced album was released in July, to wide acclaim, and very little pity. Two months later, Wyatt released a pop single of a song that sounded nothing like the record. Backed by roughly the same band, Wyatt covered the Neil Diamond hit "I'm a Believer," a faithful and affecting version of the song that veered into the unknown only when Fred Frith added an avant-garde viola solo to the second refrain. It was backed by "Memories," the pop song that the Wilde Flowers had written to great success, for other people.

"There was a bit of a misunderstanding with the avant-garde rock scene, because I think I was sort of swimming the wrong way, really," Wyatt would explain. "A lot of the rock thing came out of people who'd started out doing covers of versions of the English scene and the American scene, the Beatles and Dylan and so on, and then got more and more involved in instrumental virtuosity and esoteric ideas. I was really going the other way. I was brought up with esoteric ideas and modern European music and Stockhausen, Webern, avant-garde poets, and all the kind of avant-garde thing in the '50s, before pop music—the beat poets, the avant-garde painters at the time, and so on. To me, the amazing thing was to discover the absolute beauty of Ray Charles singing a country and western song or something like that. So my actual journey of discovery was I discovered the beauty of simple, popular music."[49]

After years in the spotlight, Wyatt would experience a first: a hit single that got him on *Top of the Pops*. In September 1974, the whole band arrived at the BBC to complete the ritual of syncing their movements to a track of their rump shaker as an audience of teens danced and nodded along. There was a hiccup. Wyatt would be making his return to live performance in a wheelchair. The BBC was hesitant about showing that, until the musicians lobbied, hard. "The director was eventually shamed into giving way," said Mason, "and a good time was had by all."[50]

On the day, there was Wyatt in a robe, eyes sometimes fluttering closed as he bobbed his head and held the mike. There was Frith, re-creating his viola solo. And there was a young guitarist named Andy Summers, filling out the set. "I really had this dilemma about being a drummer, which is really a social act," Wyatt would tell *Melody Maker*. "You have to be in a group. I really wanted to do notes. Actual notes. And I'd always sung songs. So not being able to play drums anymore, not being in a group anymore, absolutely got me out of my dilemma."[51]

IN SEPTEMBER 1974, *Melody Maker* gathered the musicians it had been covering for a virtual symposium. The subject was stark enough to lead readers to a set conclusion: Was British rock "facing disaster?"

The answer was yes. "I don't feel there is anything new

happening of any consequence," said Greg Lake. "It seems to be the same bands doing the same things in the same places." There was, he said, no new Jethro Tull, no new Led Zeppelin.[52]

Robert Wyatt was more optimistic, largely because he didn't see a need to defend "British rock" as a monolith. "In my own circle I can't really see the woods for the trees," he said, "and two of my favorite trees are Fred Frith and Hugh Hopper, who continue to write beautiful tunes."[53]

Wyatt, by necessity and by choice, had retreated from the grind. Lake had not. "There are no new sensational musicians coming along," Lake explained. He was excited about ZZ Top, a band out of Texas: "For years they've been surrounded by cows and farms down there." Other bands were new, but not exciting. "In New York there's a fuss about the New York Dolls, and they're okay—in Max's Kansas City. But they're not going to appeal on a world level."[54]

ELP did appeal on a world level. The band had spent much of the year touring *Brain Salad Surgery*, the most ambitious album in a career that had hardly been humble. Its cover was a jarring horror show, a two-piece work of art by a Swiss fan of the band named H. R. Giger. The record was contained in a white-hued painting of a woman, eyes closed, buried under some combination of dreadlocks and insectoid tubes. This small sleeve was shipped inside a cutout sleeve, the painting visible inside a circle framed by what seemed to be a sarcophagus decorated with a skull.

And the name of the album? A sex joke, basically. "When we were on tour, we would check into a hotel or restaurant and ask the desk clerk or maître d' if they had any Brain Salad," tour manager Stewart Young told *Circus* magazine. "They always said no, they didn't. We just couldn't seem to get any!"[55]

Side one began with "Jerusalem," the Anglican church hymn based on William Blake's poem, given the full Emerson organ treatment. "It's just a fantastic lyric," Lake would explain. "*Bring me my bow of burning gold / Bring me my arrows of desire.* It's worth playing the whole song to get that lyric."[56]

The album continued with an adaptation of the fourth movement of Alberto Ginastera's Piano Concerto no. 1, which Lake had retitled "Tocatta." (According to Lake, Ginastera himself had heard the arrangement and pronounced it "Diabolico!")[57] Lake was next, with an original composition called "Still . . . You Turn Me On," and a lyric that he would never explain: "Every day a little sadder, a little madder, someone get me a ladder."

Side one ended with "Benny the Bouncer," a trifle of the sort that had appeared on *Trilogy*—with one difference: Peter Sinfield, no longer part of the reformed King Crimson, was collaborating on lyrics. "It worked in King Crimson," Lake told *Melody Maker*. "Of all the musicians, he's the one closest to me. He's the only one I could write lyrics with and he writes exactly the lyrics that I want."[58]

Sinfield's influence was all over side two, a suite called "Karn Evil," broken into three "impressions" and four parts. The album cover finally made sense: This was an epic about a dystopian future ruled over cruelly by a computer, whose name was an ominous deconstruction of the word "Carnival." "Karn Evil is a place," Emerson told *Circus*. "Everything is heading for that place unless something is done about it."[59]

The emotional apex of the song, and the part that would send audiences roaring when they heard it, was sung from Karn's perspective. "Karn Evil 9: 1st Impression, Pt. 2" began with a seemingly random assortment of Moog sounds, joined by Lake's vocal: "Welcome back my friends to the show that never ends."

The song built, and built, until the band broke into three simultaneous displays of skill. From February 1973 to August 1974, ELP played 145 live shows, and the full power of the "Karn

Evil" suite revealed itself. This was the tour that cemented ELP as one of the biggest live acts on the planet, behind only the Rolling Stones and the Who, capable of entertaining a third of a million people at the outdoor California Jam.

A fan showing up for that tour would find the band at the biggest venue in his city, with a stage show that included more than two hundred pieces of equipment. According to a *New York Times* story on the phenomenon, the show required "thirteen keyboard units" for Keith Emerson, including a "brand new prototype Moog synthesizer"; a $5,000 Persian rug "for bass player Greg Lake to stand on while playing"; and a stainless steel drum kit, topped off by an "old church bell from the Stepney district of London," surrounded by Chinese gongs.[60] The kit could rotate 360 degrees while Carl Palmer pounded out the solos in "Tarkus." The cost of this: $25,000.

The 1973–74 tour did not start with a *Brain Salad Surgery* track. Keith Emerson's Moog was the first sound of the set, playing deafening notes, pitches that rose fast and fell faster. This, knew Rob McDonnell and everybody else in the audience, was the opening of the Aaron Copland cover "Hoedown." It was ELP's first song for practical reasons. "You could get away with it by just sort of really screwing the instrument just totally up and just freak out with it,"[61] Emerson would explain. The one sure thing was the space-invader noise you'd get when turning it on.

All of the songs were played on one of the biggest sound systems yet built. ELP's sound designer, Bill Hough, assembled a 28,000-watt surround-sound system, controlled by a three-tiered mixing desk. (The three mixing boards, by themselves, weighed 285 pounds.) If you could put up with a little echo, a little delay, you were getting the same concussive sound waves in any part of the venue. You just had to live near a stadium that could handle it.

"In a lot of venues we played it was kind of impractical," Emerson remembered, "because we were blocking fire exits."[62] The first thing many people would see upon entering the stadium was a projection screen, 156 feet in diameter, that would display disturbing skull/erotica imagery from Giger under two sixty-foot proscenium arches that held a hundred spotlights.

Times were good for the supergroups. Yes, minus Wakeman, approached the burly Vangelis, who had hardly stopped working since Aphrodite's Child split up. It wouldn't work; Vangelis did not want to tour, much less jump on a caravan that flitted around the world. So, Yes recruited the Swiss-born experimental keyboard player Patrick Moraz and produced *Relayer*, with some songs as ambitious as anything on *Tales from Topographic Oceans*. "The Gates of Delirium" interpreted scenes from *War and Peace* over an entire LP side, with keyboard parts that sounded, at times, like rubies falling on the ground.

"To tell you the truth I was having nightmares beforehand," Moraz told *Melody Maker*, as the band took the album on tour. "In 'The Gates of Delirium' there are 17 changes of keyboard in the first 22 bars. Of course the audience doesn't notice, but you have to think like a computer. Now I'm past that stage, and it's become second nature, and I can put in the most expression possible."[63]

WAKEMAN, MEANWHILE, PERFORMED *The Myths and Legends of King Arthur and the Knights of the Round Table* outdoors, at Wembley Arena with a full cast acting out his drama. The concept-cum-play ended with a fight sequence for "The Last Battle," which would send knights clambering around a stage. Problem: The stage couldn't be deiced before the show. So he hired skaters instead of dancers. "Lancelot," wearing a dummy horse on his torso, glided back and forth across the ice to battle a similarly attired "Black Knight," as Wakeman commanded the action behind his tripartite wall of keyboards.

Wakeman's departure from Yes made that band look a little less colorful and helped his own paradoxical celebrity shine even brighter. Here was a classically trained Englishman, a savant, writing pieces from the sorts of epic themes that had inspired the great composers, while at the same time bragging about his conquests at the pub. At the end of 1974, Wakeman gave the *New Musical Express* a tour of the "beers of the world," with some extra details about how Yes had drained liquor cabinets in every time zone. "On our rider for the tour of America—for the seven of us—we had twelve six-packs of Budweiser, two bottles of tequila, two bottles of scotch, two bottles of brandy, a bottle of grenadine, and a bottle of orange juice to mix Tequila Sunrises," he boasted. "This is apart from all the ordinary lagers and other beers you get. And on the very first gig we had to send out for more at half time."[64]

It was on to the beers. Young's Special was deemed a "a very good bitter." Watneys Special was "the kind of beer that I was actually weaned on," while Ruddles County was "bloody 'orrible." Ind Coope's Double Diamond "had the sweetness and the glorioso of wandering through a forest on a spring day with the sight of those first leaves and the gentle tweeting of birds." Wakeman's only warning was that the beer "does make you fart."[65]

Wakeman's former bandmates were occasionally asked what had happened to the guy. They obliged with theories. "His humor was ours completely—Python and everything," Steve Howe told one reporter. "Drinking wasn't disallowed in Yes. It's never been disallowed. What I'm saying is . . . Rick did take things to extremes. He doesn't have any trouble holding it but during the recording of *Topographic Oceans* he started to realize that none of us wanted to indulge. Everybody has fun. Everybody has vices. But when they're talking to me, if they're not talking honestly, constructively and creatively then they can sod off for all I'm concerned."[66]

This was the Rick Wakeman that starred in *Lisztomania*. Ken Russell had just directed *Tommy*, the hit adaptation of the Who's quasi-plotless rock opera. The natural follow-up was an impressionist biopic about Franz Liszt, the pianist who had made European audiences lose control and applaud after every piece. Wasn't he the true ancestor of the sexualized rock star? And if it was 1975 and you were looking for a keyboard player, how could you not choose Wakeman? Russell gave him control of the entire soundtrack.

"Liszt was a bit of a rock and roller at heart," said Wakeman in a *Creem* interview, "but he was a bit of a puritan on his sounds. I just had to update the guy's music to fit his image." He wrote a score to accompany scenes in which Liszt (played by Roger Daltrey) rode a hippo-sized rubber penis and a gigantism-afflicted Nazi slaughtered Hasidic Jews with a guitar/machine gun, the victims dropping gold on the ground as they fell. "I think the sun shines out of Ken Russell's asshole," said Wakeman.[67]

The movie was basically unwatchable, not that that meant Russell had *failed*. His vision of rock excess and brain-dead rock fandom is bleak and cruelly cynical. In his world, pompous music is produced by men with monster egos and unresolved sexual hang-ups. Wakeman, who appeared on some promotional posters, got one of the strangest cameos. (And we can't forget Ringo Starr, who played the pope.) At the start of the film's third act, Richard Wagner summons Liszt to his lair, over to an operating table surrounded by "Hammer Horror" electric poles. "We need a superman," cries Wagner. "Such virtue will never be born of woman, Franz! Such a creature must be—created!"

He turns the levers. "They do say music is the gay science, Franz! My music, and my philosophy, will give him—life!"

Wagner's machinery emits beeps and fart noises as his sheet music is fed into it. Thus arises Siegfried—Rick Wakeman, painted in silver and dressed to look exactly like the Marvel Comics version of Thor. He stands up, his 6-foot-3-inch height elevated by golden boots with elevator heels. He drains a stein of beer before Wagner commands him to "go forth!" Wakeman/Siegfried trudges out of the laboratory. He stops at a fireplace, grabs his crotch, and urinates all over the flames.

"Who's going to follow *him*?" laughs Daltrey-as-Liszt. Wagner, chagrined, puts Siegfried back on the operating table. The experiment is over.

But the big bands and stars kept getting second chances. Jethro Tull recovered fitfully from the backlash to *A Passion Play*. "People seemed to object to the fact that they actually had to listen to it more than once," Ian Anderson grumbled to a biographer. "We had to come back with an album that was a bit more to the point, less pompous and overbearing than 'Passion Play' had been, so it was just a bunch of songs."[68]

That album, *War Child*, was supposed to be ambitious in a whole new way. Imagining a dramatic film, a concept album growing across the formats and the senses, Anderson met with choreographers and directors. He had Monty Python's John Cleese on board to punch up the humor of the script. But the project floundered, and Anderson's band put the songs together for a less ambitious LP.

"I remember starting to write an opera when I was at the Royal Academy," Tull's orchestra arranger David Palmer recalled later, to convey just how disappointed Anderson was. "I hadn't got far past Mozart's operas, let alone Wagner, Verdi and the other lot. I was a mile out, but I still desperately wanted to do it, to keep moving onwards. And I'm sure that was the motivation behind Ian wanting to write that film."[69]

Anderson's disappointment acted like some sacrifice to the fickle gods. "Bungle in the Jungle," the leadoff single, became an American top forty hit. In the US and in Britain, the album won back the nattering classes. "The critics have had their way," wrote Chris Charlesworth in *Melody Maker*, "the Passion Play has been forgotten, and Jethro Tull are once again playing the kind of music that won them their hard-earned reputation as brilliant showmen."[70] In another issue, the paper asked whether Tull had become the biggest band in the world again. They had shed some pretention without trading away any of their massiveness.

Hawkwind were finally downsizing a part of their spectacle. They were on tour in Canada, crossing the border from Windsor to Detroit, when customs nabbed Lemmy Kilmister's supply of amphetamine sulfate. The bassist spent five days in jail, and the band bailed him out and fired him. Undeterred, Kilmister promised to create a band of his own—one he could not be junked from for something as petty as a drug bust. "They'll be the dirtiest rock and roll band in the world," Kilmister told *Sounds*. "If we moved in next door your lawn would die."[71]

A few weeks later, Kilmister started putting together a band that he wanted to call Bastard. The commercial downsides of that name were made clear to him, so he borrowed a portmanteau from one of his more propulsive Hawkwind songs: Motörhead.

Hatfield and the North grew out of another impulse: pure experimentation. Formed by veterans of Caravan and other Canterbury groups, it debuted with a self-titled 1974 song cycle of absurdist jazz fusion. After another year, and another album, cofounder Richard Sinclair moved on. The music, he decided, was ambitious but frigid. "The band wrote songs that their structure wasn't so interesting to me," Sinclair said. "I want songs to have more outside references. I wanted to have more interaction when we played live. In those days, the music was so loud and noisy. We weren't performing music that we came up [with] together live. It was all about playing the music correctly. It wasn't about really enjoying it; it was about how you played it."[72]

IN THE SUMMER of 1974, *Melody Maker* reporter Karl Dallas was granted an on-location interview with Mike Oldfield. The composer continued to detest interviews—nothing personal, according to Virgin, just the attitude of an individualist genius. *Tubular Bells* had blown up internationally without his intervention, thanks in large part to the use of that Farfisa organ in the trailer and on the soundtrack of *The Exorcist*. Oldfield knew nothing about the movie, but he had finished *Hergest Ridge*, and Virgin was banking on another hit, so he would grant a conversation in his new habitat.

Dallas asked about the album title, and what it meant. "I dunno," said Oldfield. "It's a nice hill. It looks different from whatever direction you look. And it has all sorts of associations with old Welsh legends. You find it in the Mabinogion. There's iron age relics right on the very top." The reporter followed up, asking Oldfield whether the new record, with eight distinct sections, had been inspired by the setting, or programmed according to the rhythms of this bucolic countryside. "There's no program," said Oldfield. That was all he said.[73]

Everyone associated with Oldfield's work got fresh attention—but the people granting it seemed unsure of what they had. Ayers found himself being promoted heavily by Island, packaged into a world-conquering rock star mold that did not fit him at all. "They thought that it would be a kind of launch for me as a megastar," Ayers recalled, ruefully, in 2008. "They dressed me in silk suits and silver shoes and stuff like that, but I obviously wasn't going to be that, and so I was dropped."[74]

Island Records even assembled Ayers in a supergroup—a onetime, one-show collaboration with John Cale, German singer-songwriter Nico, and Brian Eno. The most sarcastic acronym was the one most used: ACNE. "Personally, I would never have put that together," Ayers said. "Given the choice, they were not the people I would have chosen to do a concert with, because of the dissimilarity of our work and what we did. The only thing we really had in common was being on the same record company, and being from the same era, and being associated with the so-called underground."[75]

Oldfield, meanwhile, had hardly warmed to a role as the next great composer. When the reviews for *Hergest Ridge* came out, he felt justified: critics who had sucked up to him before were raring to pan him. The problems started with the cover, which paid tribute to Oldfield's new pastoral surroundings and to the plane he was learning to fly with his earnings. The music was structured just the same as the megahit had been: one long track split across two LP sides. It zigged where *Tubular Bells* had zagged. Instead of hammer-pounding brass, there was a jingling of sleigh bells.

"The textures of a lot of rock music and the textures of a city street, they're really a similar sort of feel," Oldfield told Dallas in another interview. "Lots of confusion and lots of nasty over-tones; things going bang, crash, car doors, horns. . . . *Hergest Ridge*, on the other hand, is smooth, uncluttered. There are no tube trains, very few car doors, lots of open countryside, smooth hills, a general feeling of smoothness and well-being and non-hysteria."[76]

The criticism did not stop the album from selling, and the record swiftly passed one million in worldwide sales. No, it didn't blow past the sales of *Tubular Bells*, but what could? No one could tell what Oldfield was doing. A *Sounds* reporter, on site in Oldfield's lair, inspected a record collection of "only a handful" of albums—mostly Bach, Sibelius, Ravel, Delius, and what he'd borrowed from Steve Winwood "to find out what's going on."[77]

Karl Dallas, the *Melody Maker* reporter who had given Oldfield such conniptions, returned to Oldfield's home for a 1975 profile and called his subject—with some hyperbole—"the best-selling twentieth century composer, with gold records up in the loo to prove it."[78]

By then, Oldfield had started living in a pattern. He would ignore Virgin as much as he could and record an epic whenever he was inspired. When Dallas sought him out in 1975, Oldfield was readying a new one-song-two-sides epic called *Ommadawn*. "I just had two tunes which ran together on acoustic guitar, and it sounded nice, and I developed it from there," he said, cryptically. "After *Hergest Ridge*, I couldn't imagine me doing any more. But after this, I can imagine me doing loads and loads more."[79]

Oldfield had found a way out of the muck. "Ommadawn (Part Two)" ended the way the previous two opuses had, and then transformed into a completely different type of song. There, for the first time on record, was Oldfield singing—talking really. "I like beer," said Oldfield, picking an acoustic guitar. "I like cheese. I like the smell of a westerly breeze. But I love, more than all of these, to be on horseback."

The great composer was singing, with no irony, about the joy of riding. "Big brown beastie, big brown face, I'd rather be with you than flying through space," he sang. When Dallas asked about the meaning, Oldfield described the song as a kind of therapy, a way to reverse the negative energy of part two's ripping guitar solo. "When I did that electric guitar, I found it really frightening. I couldn't sleep," he said.[80]

It was around this time that the documentary filmmaker Tony Palmer profiled Oldfield. The composer didn't know what to make of the guy, other than that he drove a Maserati with personalized plates. But Oldfield allowed himself to be filmed in his studio, marking up charts for his songs—a few bagpipes here, some African drums there, a mandolin over there. Cameras followed him as he took introspective walks along the vale. They tracked him as he talked in bland terms about how he composed, then sat for a quiz session about how the rock business worked.

"The pop business?" said a distracted Oldfield, his eyes looking in every direction where the camera wasn't. "It's a bit silly isn't it? I don't really get involved in it."

"What sort of things?" asked Palmer.

"What *sort* of things are silly?" laughed Oldfield. "Well, I can't pretend at all. Unless I'm very drunk, then I don't pretend. I just make an exhibition of myself. I suppose most of it is making an exhibition of yourself, isn't it? I'd just rather do it here."[81]

It was Richard Branson, filmed separately, who got to do most of the talking. Oldfield, he explained, was an artist who had sold millions of albums and never been limited to one style. "He works more or less entirely on his own, in isolation and in peace," said Branson. With a chuckle, he recalled how Oldfield's album had been rejected, how one company had called it "self-indulgent rubbish" and missed out on a sensation. "A composer such as Mike Oldfield is among the best hopes we have for contemporary popular music."[82]

Neither Branson nor Oldfield got to see the results of these interviews until 1977. Palmer's documentary *All You Need Is Love* told the full history of pop music in seventeen segments. Oldfield closed out the series. "Ommadawn (Part One)" was the last song music viewers would hear, all of the elements—African drums, bagpipes, electric guitar, everything he'd looped—blasting over images of Chuck Berry and *Jesus Christ Superstar* and the Beach Boys and Mississippi delta blues.

"I was the last chapter in the story," Oldfield wrote in his memoir. "So, at the time, *Tubular Bells* was thought of as the zenith of the achievements of rock and roll, where it was all supposed to be heading. By then, though, I was not happy with *Tubular Bells* at all. To me it represented nothing but stress and hard work."[83]

7

COMPLEXITY FREAKS

n 1971, the government of Ontario made a decision that would alter the history of progressive rock. The Canadian province dropped its drinking age from twenty-one to eighteen. It was a moment of liberation for high schoolers. It was especially good for Geddy Lee, Alex Lifeson, and John Rutsey, teenagers who had been playing high school dances and had hit a wall. "We played a lot of dances where nobody could dance well, because we weren't a dance band," said Lee, the band's bassist, whose reedy voice handled the vocals on countless cover songs and blues-based originals. "We probably bummed out a lot of people on their high school memories."[1]

Lee, Lifeson, and Rutsey had grown up a thousand miles away from the wellsprings of progressive rock. The bassist was the son of Jewish immigrants; Lifeson, the guitarist, was the son of immigrants from Serbia. He'd met Rutsey when they were teenagers and formed a series of bands. In 1968 they added Lee, and in 1971 they could play the bars. "It was like when the Beatles played for weeks at a time in Germany," said Ian Grandy, the band's first roadie, of the drinking-age breakthrough. "So much time to fill, so songs would come and go, and you're playing them again and again. We were a big band on that circuit and filled the bars, leading you to think you could actually make a living doing this."[2]

Rush delivered what was in demand: hard-riffing, Led Zeppelin–esque rock music. In 1973 the band self-released its first single, a cover of "Not Fade Away," a Buddy Holly song that the Rolling Stones had turned into a shuffling hit. Rush deconstructed it, silencing its famous beat for the entire first verse. There was Lee's controlled squeal, wrapping around the lyrics; there was Lifeson's guitar, chopping out the chords. The drums kicked in, turning a simple song into an invitation to headbanging.

The band's eponymous first album followed that pattern. Lee's vocal mannerisms sounded so much like Robert Plant that American DJs, spinning the record, began to get questions about the new Led Zeppelin album. There were few hints of progressive rock, though the band was absorbing it. "I have a very high voice," Lee conceded to an interviewer from *Circus* years later. "So does Robert Plant, but it's an entirely different voice. Both bands play at a pretty high volume, but the music is different. And when you look inside at what motivates the music, you see it's very different."[3]

The departure of Rutsey came just as the band was earning major label success, as their own Moon Records became a unit of Polygram. Rush, with a two-record deal, found a replacement drummer in Neil Peart. "To be a drummer in 1965, all you had to do was play one beat," said Peart. "Suddenly, through '67, '68, '69, what happened? What it took to be a drummer was so daunting as a teenager at the time. 'That's what I have to do to be a good drummer? I have to play a complicated time signature, exotic percussion instruments, intricate arrangements, inventive drum fills?' All of that was coming at me as a teenager. That became my new benchmark."[4]

Peart was also a lyricist, with an immediate impact on the band's approach. For their second album, he dug into Tolkien for inspiration ("Rivendell"). Blues rock was subsumed by progressive rock. "We were influenced by bands like Yes, Genesis, Van der Graaf Generator, Gentle Giant and ELP," Lee said. "When the progressive movement came along, we were so impressed with the musicality and the complexity, we became complexity freaks. So we wanted to write things that were heavy but complex." It was not calculated. "There was no, 'Let's synthesize these two styles; if we take that element and combine it with this element, we'll have something new,'" said Peart. "It was nothing like that. We were not that self-aware, let alone that calculating."[5]

Rush's new material sent it even further into the unknown, and almost at odds with what had been commercially successful. The band's third album, *Caress of Steel*, offered some proudly Canadian rock in "Bastille Day" and chased it with "The Fountain of Lamneth," a side-long epic to match anything by Yes. "The idea originally came from a time when I was driving from the top of a mountain to the bottom," Peart explained to *Sounds*. "Seeing the lights of the city beneath me, I got to thinking, 'What would life be like if you could only measure your position as a person by the level at which you lived up the side of a mountain?' I got to drawing relations, seeing kinds of comparisons in this metaphor, and eventually put down a rough sketch of the six different parts I thought there would have to be . . . it was all very naïve, I admit that now, it was a ridiculous thing, like writing a thesis on metaphysics or something."[6]

The album was a costly flop, and the material was not finding an audience. As they gigged across Ontario, the band made up passes commemorating the "Down the Tubes Tour," bowing to the judgment of the ticket buyers and the panicky label. "The worst was Northern Ontario," Geddy recalled a few years later, when the gigging had finally paid off. "They don't care what you do. They don't *care* if you do the greatest original material in the world if their ears haven't heard it before. They just want to get drunk and hear their favorite tunes."[7]

Polygram now had the option to drop the group. "There was a lot of pressure from us, from the record company, and, to some degree, from management to go back to our rock roots, make another Rush album," said Lifeson. "And we basically said, 'You know what? That's not what we're about. If that's what everybody wants, then that's what they're not going to get. If we go down we're going to go down in flames.' "[8]

The result was *2112*, the fusion of the rock sound, the progressive influences, and Peart's libertarian-humanist fantasy lyrics. Its entire first side was taken up by the band's most ambitious song, the eponymous seven-part hero's journey of a lone man taking on the priests of the "Temples of Syrinx." There were briefer songs on the second side, but nothing devised as a radio hit, nothing watered down for single status. "Our manager went in and lied to them and basically told them, 'Yeah, the band is working on a great record. It's gonna be a real commercial success and the songs are very straightforward,' " said Alex Lifeson. "And then we delivered it. The fortunate thing is our deal at that time was a production deal. So, really, we had full control over content, including artwork. Once we delivered it to the record company, it was theirs to work with. So we were really lucky."[9]

The album was released on April Fool's Day 1976. Just months after "going down the tubes," Rush had crafted a slow-burning success. In six months, two hundred thousand copies of *2112* were sold. The band was playing larger venues and had a less depressing theme for the tour: "All the World's a Stage." Just five months after the album dropped, that tour was culled for a live album. A band that had struggled to back up Kiss had built a reputation as a touring act, and in 1977 it would go international. "The next album," Lee told *Circus* that year, "will be recorded in England."[10]

PROGRESSIVE MUSIC, INSPIRED by American rock and roll and by the roiling scenes of Europe, took new forms when it returned to those countries. From the beginning, bands from continental Europe shared billings and influences with bands from the UK. In the early 1970s, when the music was dominant, the first wave of progressive bands found themselves the accidental fathers of similar-sounding acts, competing for the same market.

It was England, at first, where the early bands got their breaks. Aphrodite's Child was one of the earliest and luckiest, releasing the 1967 single "Plastics Nevermore" shortly before a coup overthrew the socialist government in their native Greece. The four-piece ensemble of Evangelos Papathanassiou (keyboards), Lucas Sideras (drums), Demis Roussos (bass), and Anargyros Koulouris (guitar) headed north—until Koulouris was conscripted. The band could not get a visa until it proved that it was, indeed, a band.

Once it did, the hits seemed to flow like water. "End of the World" was the first hit, a song with plenty of Procol Harum DNA and a dark lyric. The most striking element was the keyboard, played by Papathanassiou, and clearly the dominant force. He had taken a new name: Vangelis. And conquest, easy as it came, seemed to bore him. "We had one million-selling single after another," he told an interviewer years later. "I hate it when a project I'm involved in, but don't particularly like, becomes successful. I found myself doing things that I couldn't bear at the time, but I don't have any regrets as they were the means to an end."[11]

The "means" included the group's final album, *666*, a two-LP concept about the apocalypse. The "ends" were the makings of Vangelis's studio, where he would compose and produce with no care for whatever trends wound through rock music. A visiting journalist recorded his setup with awe: a Hammond B3, a Fender Rhodes, a "little semi-pro keyboard called a Torendo" to simulate church organs. "Keyboards today are more polyphonic and have many other possibilities and they are also popular because they are new," Vangelis told an interviewer. "Today we are very well equipped, but we don't have the people to play. People buy synthesizers and things like that, and they can't play them. I have the synthesizer because it has been used very badly and for very cheap effects—cosmic things, just to try to impress."[12]

Holland's Focus began in much the same way, as a Jethro Tull soundalike. It broke out in 1972, with a single that deployed a sound that few bands dared use: the yodel. "Hocus Pocus," a lyricless song with an unforgettable riff, anchored the band's hit record *Moving Waves* and established guitarist Jan Akkerman as one of the great players of the genre. "We never listened to English guitar players except maybe the Shadows and Clapton," Akkerman told an interviewer. "I was into jazz and rock and roll. When I heard somebody like Beck or Clapton playing they just dated what I was already doing. I was doing it before them, as simple as that."[13]

Moving Waves ended with Focus's other persona, a side-long suite called "Eruption"—again with no lyrics. "We don't go back to, let's say, Bach and stuff like that," Akkerman said in 1973. "No, we even go back a little further, and I like that. By the way, the whole point of bringing classical pieces into pop music is what I really like. Pop music will be enriched by that."[14] Akkerman talked freely about the influences of the composers. "[Bach's] Fuga for instance, it's very well built, very major," he said. "A composer like Bartók, is the opposite. He tried to create heavenly music, but it became very earthly. In his music I hear waterfalls, I see beautiful trees and butterflies, alternated with weirdness, strange dissonants, and so on."[15]

English bands had not been shy about their influences, but the continental bands were even prouder. Premiata Forneria Marconi, which translated in English to "award-winning Marconi bakery," formed in Milan in 1970 when drummer Franz Di Cioccio, guitarist Franco Mussida, bassist Giorgio Piazza, and keyboard player and vocalist Flavio Premoli of the group I Quelli met multi-instrumentalist Mauro Pagani. They joined forces, and Pagani helped expand their sound with such instruments as flute and violin. In 1971 they released their first single, "Impressioni di settembre," intended to break the usual patterns of pop music. "The most important thing is that the musical phrases sound very strange and its sensation is like being in another world," said Di Cioccio. "We are very proud of this sound."[16]

The band's debut album, *Storia di un Minuto*, came out in the prog salad days of 1972. While other progressive music swaggered between modes, this was all moodiness, channeling "The Court of the Crimson King" and "Lucky Man." A rerecorded version of "Impressioni di settembre" opened the album; it ended with "Grazie davvero," the sort of music that could sound-track a Disney villain's death march.

Premiata Forneria Marconi kept recording and put out *Per un Amico*, their first album with access to sixteen-track recording technology. The opener, "Appena un po," recalled Genesis circa *Foxtrot*; and "Generale!" recalled Emerson, Lake & Palmer.

Soon enough, Greg Lake signed the Italian band to ELP's

own Manticore label. With their name now shortened to PFM as a favor to native speakers of the English language, the group's first album for Manticore was *Photos of Ghosts*, which was basically the *Per un Amico* album released with English lyrics written by King Crimson's Peter Sinfield. It also contained one anglicized song from the debut album *Storia di un Minuto* ("È festa," changed to "Celebration") and a new track, "Old Rain." The album was released widely throughout Europe, the United States, and Japan, and even cracked the U.S. charts. "It was the first and only time that an Italian band was on a Billboard chart," Di Cioccio told the Greek publication *Hit Channel*. "I'm very proud of this."[17]

Bassist Giorgio Piazza left the band and was replaced by Patrick Djivas. The next album, *L'Isola di Niente*, came out in 1974, with an English-language version released by Manticore at the same time: *The World Became the World*. The band's sound began to incorporate hints of fusion, as shown on "Is My Face on Straight."

Americanization did not change the band, but it changed the audience. PFM toured the US to support the album, accompanying such completely unsuitable acts as the Allman Brothers Band, the Beach Boys, Poco, Santana, and ZZ Top. Nineteen seventy-five's *Chocolate Kings* saw the debut of lead singer Bernardo Lanzetti, formerly of another Italian prog group, Acqua Fragile. Because Lanzetti spoke English, the group could record "Chocolate Kings" in a more marketable tongue. The song was successful in the States, despite lyrics about the American soldiers who had stayed in Italy after the war, doling out candy to the children of the conquered.

The Italian band Banco del Mutuo Soccorso—which translates literally as "mutual aid bank"—followed in PFM's trail. The group released its self-titled debut in 1972: three main pieces and three moody instrumental showcases. "R.I.P.

Procol Harum, 1967

The Moody Blues, 1967

Keith Emerson and
the Nice, 1968

Soft Machine, 1967

King Crimson, 1969

Virgin Records founder Richard Branson, 1969

Mike Oldfield, 1970

Genesis, with Peter Gabriel in costume and Phil Collins on drums, 1974

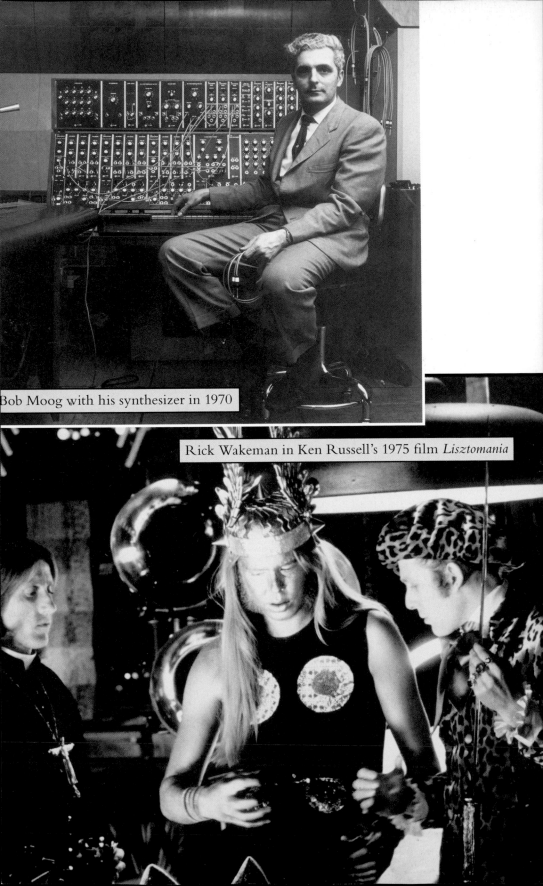

Bob Moog with his synthesizer in 1970

Rick Wakeman in Ken Russell's 1975 film *Lisztomania*

Gong, 1974

Kevin Ayers (bottom left), with (clockwise) Brian Eno, Nico, and John Cale, 1974

Pink Floyd, 1973

Van der Graaf Generator, 1975

Magma, 1974

Rush, 1976

Jethro Tull, 1976

Styx, 1978

Yes, 1978

Kansas, 1978

Asia, 1983

(Requiescant in Pace)" offered a compact, six-minute dose of up-tempo, odd-metered riffing, which was buoyed by the twin keyboards of brothers Gianni and Vittorio Nocenzi and the soaring tenor of Francesco Di Giacomo, which carried much of the album, right through the two extended pieces, "Metamorfosi" and "Il giardino del mago."

Like PFM, Banco chased the debut with a same-year album that got even more attention. *Darwin!* was a concept album about the birth and evolution of man, beginning with the fourteen-minute "L'Evoluzione." The story continued with a furious keyboard and drum workout in "La conquista della posizione eretta," which told the story of early man learning to walk upright. That was nothing compared to the maniacal sixteenth-note keyboard runs in "Cento mani e cento occhi."

The group followed *Darwin!* in 1973 with *Io Sono Nato Libero*, and then began to shed members. Guitarist Marcello Todaro left after gracing Banco's first three albums—a huge loss to the band's sound. However, some famous Englishmen were about to enter the picture with an irresistible offer—again, from Manticore.

"If you delve into their lyrics and direction, you quickly realize that it's very similar to Italian opera in its truest sense, and seeing as opera originated here in Italy, they have almost turned the wheel full circle," Keith Emerson told *NME*. "In the past, Italy was always regarded as being the center of musical culture and now it would seem that it's spreading out again. I honestly feel that, very shortly, America will start listening quite seriously to a lot of new European bands. I don't think it will be restricted to Italy."[18]

Throughout the decade, "progressive" music came to include ever-more-exploratory sounds from Europe. The British press embraced, and unfortunately named, the "Krautrock" movement of German bands that were more experimental and less wedded to old European song structures. Daevid Allen's Gong, built when he was separated from Soft Machine by the English Channel, returned triumphantly to England as a hippie group unfrozen from a cryogenic sleep, with lyrics about flying saucers and "glissando guitar" hypnotics by the English guitarist Steve Hillage.

Even Gong was startled by Magma, the French band led by drummer, singer, and composer Christian Vander. Having once suffered nightmares about the fate of humanity, Vander felt compelled to form the group to exorcize the resulting anxieties through music—abrasive, uneasy and difficult music, which was sung in a wholly fabricated language called "Kobaïan."

"The sounds of the English language weren't necessarily suited to this kind of music," Vander said of the process that led him to inventing his own language. "When I wrote, the sounds came naturally with it—I didn't intellectualize the process by saying 'Ok, now I'm going to write some words in a particular language,' it was really sounds that were coming at the same time as the music. And often they expressed more than if I had translated them."[19]

The band's 1970 self-titled debut told the story that formed the Magma mythos—enough to start a religion on, and more than enough to start a band. In it, earthlings escaped to the planet Kobaïa after their home planet had been rendered uninhabitable by disasters of man's own doing. That album and the follow-up, 1971's *1001° Centigrades*, were jazzy and almost accessible. But 1973's *Mëkanïk Dëstruktïẁ Kömmandöh* introduced a new nightmarish sound. It featured such signature elements as the vocals of the drummer's wife, Stella Vander, and the bass playing of newcomer Jannick Top.

The album began with "Hortz fur dëhn štekëhn ẁešt"— all buildup and none of the expected release. The lead vocal was a chanted, staccato nonsense overlaid with bleating horns and shrieking female screams. Next came "Ïma süri dondaï," an urgent, looping sequence in 7/4 time, which led seamlessly into "Kobaïa is de hündïn." It followed the structure of "Ïma süri dondaï" carried by the piano, breaking after two minutes into a repeating, midtempo, 4/4 chant. It even had a brief rock guitar lead as it faded out. "Da zeuhl wortz mëkanïk" continued the 7/4 motif and led into the moodier and more restrained "Nebëhr gudahtt."

Wurdah Ïtah followed in 1974. None of its twelve songs exceeded five minutes, but it was no pop album. It was carried mostly by piano and avoided the 5/4 and 7/4 time signatures that Vander seemed so enamored of, preferring instead to pound away at the same quarter note for ten minutes before the up-tempo, cruising speed of "Fur dïhhël kobaïa."

Köhntarkösz came in 1974, featuring just four songs, including the two-part title suite. After the 1975 live album *Live/ Hhaï*, Magma released 1976's *Üdü Wüdü*. There was something approaching funk in "Tröller tanz (Troll's Dance)," carried by Jannick Top's throbbing bass, a tritone keyboard figure, and high-pitched shrieking. The second side of the album was taken up by the eighteen-minute "De futura," with room for Vander to play every polyrhythm, texture, and breathtaking sideways fill he could summon.

"There was no outlet for musical creativity at all in France when Gong and Magma were born," Daevid Allen told Richie Unterberger. "We were like the alternative, had no road to follow. And they basically created this incredible network throughout the whole of France, and allowed a whole generation of very interesting bands to come up."[20]

ON APRIL 27, 1973, a King Crimson that was nearing the end of its natural life shared a bill with a new band—Todd Rundgren's Utopia. The Philadelphia-born Rundgren had been writing hits for years, and he had followings in England and the US for a style of music that borrowed as much from garage rock as it did from Carole King.

He was trying something new. *Something/Anything?*, a double album that had produced the biggest hits of his career, was played almost entirely by him alone; only the fourth side used a full band. His follow-up, *A Wizard, a True Star*, relied on different audio tracks to enable him to compose everything. The Utopia project was coming from another direction, an experiment to see what he could achieve with a full band and ambitious music. "It was a disaster," said Rundgren. "We were a highly technical sort of production. King Crimson—they were playing the kind of music that we all sort of admired, but they pretty much based their show on that, on their musicianship. And while we considered ourselves adequate and progressive, we had this layer of theatricality that wasn't necessarily an aspect of progressive rock."[21]

Rundgren's vision of a stage show that simulated a war was part boldness and part goof, inspired by the excesses of progressive rock. "More or less everything went wrong," said Rundgren. "We set ourselves up every night for spectacular success or for spectacular failure. We had these things that were as big as your head, a dozen of them on the stage, and at a certain cue we'd play the Utopia Theme, with the stage supposedly looking like a Martian invader movie. Unfortunately, none of that happened. Half the flashbulbs didn't go off, my guitar never made a sound, and then we were just like chickens with our heads cut off."[22]

Rundgren persisted, and in the mid-1970s he dabbled in progressive rock—the parts of it he liked. He was joined by a plethora of American bands that processed the progressive rock they'd heard and introduced more of a rock sound. In 1974, with Utopia, he tried his hand at a progressive song, "The Ikon," a rambling monster of ideas that was inspired by jazz fusion.

"In some ways you have to slow the process down to something that makes sense or advances the larger musical agenda," said Rundgren of progressive rock. "Yes was a band that really embodied that: 'I'll be the roundabout.' I'll be a traffic circle for you, right? Progressive rock has two almost competing aspects to it. One of them is compositional—how do you, in the traditional way, find something for everyone in the band to play. The other is improvisational. You want to allow the players to get their rocks off but still find a framework to have it that evinces the traditional aspects of songwriting."[23]

Progressive rock was a persona for Rundgren, one of the many he changed into from year to year. In a 1975 interview, he pronounced the death of the pop Rundgren that people knew. "That *is* my official goodbye to those who want the romanticist Todd Rundgren," he said. "He's not coming back. Or, there again, it could literally be goodbye. I might move into another medium or I might not express anything and become contemplative—absorb as opposed to produce."[24]

The product of that thinking was his most ambitious album, *Initiation*, with the longest song that Rundgren ever wrote: "A Treatise on Cosmic Fire." It stretched over thirty-five minutes, longer than anything by Yes, longer than most LP sides had allowed. The theory behind it: "Go crazy and get it all on tape."[25]

Kansas also started off as a progressive band, with a self-titled debut in 1974. "Can I Tell You," its first song, set the mode for plenty of American rock-forward progressive music. The odd-metered song is upbeat and up-tempo, while still operating in an unconventional meter. It led directly into "Bringing It Back," a shuffling rave-up carried by thirty-second-note violin runs. But "Journey from Mariabronn" was the band's first truly progressive statement, an extended and meandering piece with colors from Yes and Deep Purple. The other side showcased

"The Pilgrimage," offering pure southern rock—before a head fake back into ambition with the ten-minute "Aperçu" and the "Death of Mother Nature Suite," alternating between Black Sabbath riffing and quieter, sparse playing.

British critics did not know how to handle this. In a typical pan, *NME*'s Max Bell mistakenly identified the state of Kansas as part of the Confederacy and surmised that its album art portrayed "North and South being held apart by a gargantuan figure, presumably Kansas State." (It was John Brown, the abolitionist.) "All the elements for subtlety are there; good violinist, guitarist, keyboards, busy rhythm section, not to mention the Confederacy theme itself," joked Bell. "Bristling with hard rock commonplace, speed and beat, they rapidly cancel any hints of originality."[26]

But Kansas was less interested in originality than in fusing what worked. The band's cofounder, Kerry Livgren, listed his influences as British bands like "Yardbirds, Kinks, especially Procol Harum, and some of the psychedelic American bands such as H. P. Lovecraft, Touch, Iron Butterfly, Quicksilver Messenger Service, Spirit, the Doors."[27]

It was derivative, and critics noticed, but the band pushed on. The year 1975 brought *Song for America*, featuring only six cuts, dominated by the eight-minute "Lamplight Symphony" and the twelve-minute "Incomudro—Hymn to the Atman." Later that same year, Kansas released *Masque*, and their approach came more sharply into focus. Even the epics, such as "Icarus (Borne on Wings of Steel)," began to flirt with hard-rock territory.

In 1976 the band released *Leftoverture*, and with it, a hit that scaled back on the length but kept the progressiveness: "Carry On Wayward Son." Rife with tempo changes, dynamics changes, and multiple solos, it was nonetheless a pop song, and it broke the band. The album's extended pieces—"Cheyenne

Anthem" and "Magnum Opus"—were tucked away at the end of the album, a reward for fans who successfully completed the laborious task of flipping the record over.

Next was 1977's *Point of Know Return*, distinguished by the presence of "Dust in the Wind." Consisting of nothing but acoustic guitar, vocal, and a violin solo, it brought Kansas to their absolute commercial peak. Its origins were in nothing fancier than a Kerry Livgren finger exercise. "My wife was listening to me play it one day and she said, 'You know, that's really pretty. You should make a song out of that,'" he said. "I didn't think it was a Kansas-type song. She said, 'Give it a try anyway.' Several million records later, I guess she was right. Musically, though, it's not one of my favorite songs. I tend to like the more bombastic things."[28]

Toronto's FM followed the same path. The group was founded by vocalist and multi-instrumentalist Cameron Hawkins, who was joined by drummer Martin Deller and violin and mandolin player Nash the Slash, who performed while wrapped up in bandages like a mummy. This lineup created the group's debut, *Black Noise*. The 1977 album was slick, cobbling from new wave and fusion, and was initially released by CBC Records in a limited run of five hundred copies. It was sold exclusively by mail order and advertised only on the radio. Despite its limited availability, it sold out, and it received a wide release the following year, eventually going gold—Canadian gold, with fifty thousand copies sold.

Nash the Slash left the group for a solo career and was replaced by Ben Mink. This lineup produced 1978's *Direct to Disc*, which consisted of just two extended tracks, "Headroom" and "Border Crossing," each taking up an entire album side. The group was dogged by lineup changes and problems with the newcomers' labels throughout most of its existence, and those problems, combined with the quirky nature of the music, conspired to keep FM permanently obscure below the forty-ninth parallel. Indeed, the most high-profile thing associated with the band was Mink's guest appearance on the song "Losing It," on the 1982 Rush album *Signals*.

THE SUCCESS OF *2112* pushed Rush into international markets, outside of America. For the first time, on June 1, 1977, they played for an English audience. Backed by the progressive rock also-rans of Stray, they took over Sheffield City Hall, then traveled south. The mythos of the journey was not lost on them. "We've always looked up to the English progressive bands and it's gonna be a good opportunity to go over there and try to capture the same sort of atmosphere," Lee told *Circus*. "We're also expanding what we can play. We're getting into more instruments, there will be more texture. We would never forsake our hard rock framework, though! We'll just update it."[29]

The timing was perfect, in a way. Progressive rock was, at that exact moment, being chewed up by a critical backlash. The fans showing up to hear Rush were the wrong kind of fans— the mockable ones, with mockable taste in music. "Rush failed to deliver the killer punch I had half-hoped was coming," Paul Morley wrote in *NME*. "Instead it was heads down for the first of their long Science Fantasy epics and, after that, epic after epic. As far as I could tell, there was little point to them. They were no more than a lot of riffs, mostly derived from Sabbath, Purple and Zeppelin, and loosely thrown together around various concepts. Titles like 'By-Tor And The Snow Dog' and 'The Fountain Of Lamneth' give a fair indication of what to expect—the fairytale castles of Yes meet Sabbath's headbanger."[30]

The rise of punk benefited Rush, and painted a target. The bar for entry was dropped so low that a band with actual prowess, and ambitious songs, looked positively virtuoso. "Punk legitimized us immediately," said Lee. "We were adept and competent musicians. Punk threw us to the top of the pile."[31]

But the authenticity and left-wing politics of punk, embraced almost immediately by critics, made a poor contrast with Rush. The band found this out in a rough landing of an interview that they gave to Barry Miles, a reporter for the *New Musical Express*. Like seemingly everyone on staff, he was cold on the music. Unlike his peers, however, he had read up on Ayn Rand, and was utterly offended that Rush had written a paean to her with *2112*.

When the band met with Miles, Lee and Lifeson sat gobsmacked—"bystanders"—as Peart and Miles went multiple rounds over libertarianism. "The thing for me about Ayn Rand is that her philosophy is the only one applicable to the world today—in every sense," Peart insisted. "If you take her ideas, then take them farther in your own mind, you can find answers to pretty well everything on an individual basis. Putting the individual as the first priority, everything can be made to work in a way that it can never be made to work under any other system."[32]

When the interviewer started to raise his doubts, Peart tore into him. "You're living in the best example," he said. "Look at Britain and what socialism has done to Britain! It's crippling! And what it's done to the youth. What do you think The Sex Pistols and all the rest of 'em are really frustrated about? They're frustrated because they're growing up in a socialist society in which there's no place for them as individuals. They either join the morass or they fight it with the only means left. They have literally no future and I lived and worked here and I know what it feels like and it's not very nice."[33]

Miles was dumbfounded. Was his subject, was this rock star, not being arch? Was he actually explaining to English readers that socialism was breaking their country? Was he putting the Sex Pistols in that context? "Yeah!" said Peart. "Why is there no future in England? What other reason is there? I really think that's the root of it."[34]

If it felt rough at the time, it was scabrous in print. The leading music paper and taste maker branded Rush's music—music partially composed by a Holocaust survivor's son—as "fascistic." The reputation, which the band rejected, was folded into a narrative of Rush as a throwback band for slow-witted listeners. "The reason for Rush's actual popularity becomes clear: It's rooted in the immaturity of both the group and their fans," wrote Paul Morley in *NME*, reviewing a 1978 box set of the first three Rush albums meant to reintroduce them to Britain. "Immaturity of emotions, responses, ideals, character. A striving for something they'll both never have. Rush are musically a superficial splodgy mess of the stun of Led Zeppelin, the excessive structures of Yes and the melody of later Beatles. There's six sides of music here in this package, 24 songs and two suites. None, except for maybe the title track of *Fly By Night*, has any genuine melodic and structural presence."[35]

But Rush was an international act now, with a fan base inherited from progressive rock. Most of the first-wave bands had wound down by 1978. It was the three Canadians who were producing thorny, proudly metaphysical albums and suites. The band's 1978 album, *Hemispheres*, included a Peart composition whose libertarianism was almost mockingly obvious. "The Trees," a sort of inverted Lorax tale, was an *Animal Farm*–styled story about punier trees forming a union to chop oak trees down to size. "La Villa Strangiato" was inspired by Lifeson's dreams. "Sometimes, when we're all supposed to be fast asleep in our hotel rooms, he'll wake up either Geddy or me with a phone call in the middle of the night and start telling us all about these terrible dreams he's been having," said Peart. "When you're barely conscious, some of the stories he comes up with can be quite mind-blowing."[36]

Years later, and without endorsing the snarky critics' critique, Lee appraised *Hemispheres* as the rough end to an old and spent style. "We burned ourselves out on the concept," he said. "The music was becoming slave to the concept, instead of being lifted by it. We were suffocating, becoming formulaic. It was time to break the mold."[37]

THE "NEW" SOUND of Rush was defined by an instrument that had been lurking: the keyboard. Lee, who had taken piano lessons in his youth, began adding textures to the band's music. That was the extent of it; there was no fancy playing, just colors underneath some slightly more accessible rock songs.

Lee's gadget came into full view on *Permanent Waves*, the band's first album of the 1980s. "Freewill" galloped along with 13/4 and 4/4 time signatures, and a smooth synthesizer emphasizing the Peart-provided libertarian lyric. (Decades later, the libertarian-leaning Republican senator Rand Paul would walk out to the song, until Rush asked him to stop.) "The Spirit of Radio" was a bigger hit, cracking the top twenty in the UK—rising after punk's popularity had ebbed away.

The album might have been more ambitious; for a short while, an epic suite about the tale of *Sir Gawain and the Green Knight* was written and revised. But it was scrapped, component parts turned into a shorter environmental song called "Natural Science."

From that point, Rush abandoned the old tropes of progressive rock and developed songs that retained all the allegory but ditched the zigzagging between musical themes. Lee's Oberheim polyphonic was a source for sweeping, futuristic bleeps. A band that could seemingly do anything created a defining electronic sound—the mashed opening chord of "Tom Sawyer," a blunt story about modern alienation that led off the next album: *Moving Pictures*.

The Rush fan base had already been growing, but "Tom Sawyer" became a crossover hit. The storming progressive sounds were blended with something metallic—not new wave, but not far off. "The fact that it is so popular still just confuses the heck out of me," said Lee.[38]

On the strength of *Moving Pictures*, Geddy Lee, the bassist and singer, was named *Keyboard* magazine's newcomer of the year. Later, he would talk down his use of the instrument. "Keyboards are a necessary evil to me," said Lee. "I have an arsenal of sounds, and that's really what keyboards represent to me: Sounds and textures."[39]

Yet as Rush progressed further into the electronic sound, they were in sync with the 1980s. Critics still welcomed new records with spittle; Rush was able to ignore that. *Signals* was even more programmed than what had come before—a function of what Yes had heard from the synthpop of producers like Trevor Horn. "I think we were influenced a lot by those kinds of bands at the time," said Lee. "They seemed to bring keyboards into it in a very cool way."[40]

By the early 1980s, Rush had elbowed into the pantheon. The progressive bands that had preceded it, and inspired it, had gravitated toward the same new sounds. "I remember a lot of musicians saying, 'What am I supposed to do? Forget how to play?'" said Peart. "You know, 'I'm not doing this crap!' And okay, bye. Whereas others . . . think of Peter Gabriel coming out of Genesis and becoming so influential and so vital at the time. Trevor Horn came out of Yes, and look what he spawned, a whole plethora of interesting and vital music of its time. Some people were able to adapt to the modern-ness without losing anything of what they had."[41]

8

FRIPPERIES

In 1974, Robert Fripp made a final tour of Britain's music reporters to explain why King Crimson had to die. In one interview, he recalled the grimness of a show in Rome, where the band had nearly been ripped off and the crowd had nearly rioted. In another interview, with *Melody Maker*, Fripp waxed much more philosophically about the reasons for the split. There was no saving King Crimson, because there was no saving the system that people were then living in. He provided three reasons. "The first is that it represents a change in the world," he said. "Second, where I once considered being part of a band like Crimson to be the best liberal education a young man could receive, I now know that isn't so. And third, the energies involved in the particular lifestyle of the band and in the music are no longer of value to the way I live."[1]

The way he had been living would no longer be available to him—to anyone, really. Fripp shared a sort of apocalyptic vision, based on conversations with "people I respect who have direct perception of these matters." Society was in decline. He'd seen it. "The transition will reach its most marked point in the years

1990 to 1999," he explained. "Within that period, there will be the greatest friction and, unless there are people with a certain education, we could see the complete collapse of civilization as we know it and a period of devastation which could last, maybe, 300 years. It will be comparable, perhaps, to the collapse of the Minoan civilization. But I hope the world will be ready for the transition, in which case there will be a period of 30 or 40 years which will make the Depression of the Thirties look like it was a Sunday outing."[2]

This was not a one-off joke. Fripp told basically the same Cassandra story to *Rolling Stone*, adding that as society collapsed, he would be "blowing a bugle loudly from the sidelines." And there were more explicitly musical reasons for ending the band. Fripp had been talking for a while about the megatouring rock group as a "dinosaur," unfit to survive in an individualist future. The ideal situation for any artist was as a "small, self-sufficient, mobile, intelligent unit." This was what Fripp could have with Brian Eno, with whom he'd never stopped collaborating, making music he found more adventurous.[3]

"It won't reach the mass of people in the way King Crimson did," Fripp admitted. "I hoped, you see, that Crimso would reach everyone. In terms of most bands, of course, it was remarkably successful. But in terms of the higher echelon of bands like Yes and ELP, it didn't make it. My approach, therefore, has now changed and what Eno and I will try to do is influence a small number of people who will, in turn, influence a great number. I've always known that I will not be a rock 'n' roll star, the guitar idol that millions of young guitarists learn their licks from. I'm not prepared to get involved with that star syndrome, if you like. Eno and I will be creating energies different to King Crimson."[4]

The band scattered. Bill Bruford went to play with Hatfield and the North, an experimental offshoot from the Canterbury scene. John Wetton joined Uriah Heep, a long way down from Crimson's headiness. "I always found a certain frustration playing with Crimson," said Wetton. "Basically I had come in through rock and roll. I was never a jazz player. I was never really interested in jazz."[5]

And what interested Fripp? He took a short respite, then reunited with his electronic muse. In April 1975, they met again to marry Eno's looping experiments with Fripp's improvisations. Their first new piece was their most pristine yet. Eno played a small, slight melody on a VCS3 synthesizer. He made some small changes to the timbre but otherwise let the music play, produced by an echo box as it looped. "The phone started ringing, people started knocking at the door, and I was answering the phone and adjusting all this stuff as it ran," Eno would tell *Interview* magazine. "I almost made [the song 'Discreet Music'] without listening to it."[6]

In May, when Fripp and Eno traveled through Europe for six shows of experimental music, this tape loop would be a "landscape"—Eno's word—for whatever the guitarist wanted to build. A half-hour segment, sans Fripp, would become the eponymous first side of Eno's November 1975 album *Discreet Music*. A smaller, isolated section, titled "Wind on Wind," would appear on the duo's December 1975 album, *Evening Star*. "It's one of a very select handful of pieces which I constantly return to and which I never seem to exhaust," Eno later told *NME*. "They have this capability of being appreciated on any level. They don't dictate their terms. They're always fresh because they're always modified by their context."[7]

The tour ended, but the small, mobile Fripp-and-Eno unit continued its experiments. In late summer, Fripp joined Eno in the studio as he laid down the songs for a third solo "pop" album. *Another Green World* would feature three Fripp guitar solos, none of which sounded alike, and none of which sounded much like Crimson. All were pop songs. On "Golden Hours," a languid and gently self-pitying song about passing time, Fripp played a series of burbling sixteenth notes. The bashful love song "I'll Come Running" found Fripp playing a lightly distorted, loping solo over the second refrain.

"St. Elmo's Fire" was a deceptively eerie pop song built on a hammering piano figure and a synthesizer that twinned Eno's vocals. Eno talk-sang about "splitting ions in the ether"—Fripp's cue for a thrilling guitar solo that changed speeds and timbres, jumping in and out of sync with the vocal melody. "I had this idea and said to Fripp, 'Do you know what a Wimshurst machine is?'" Eno told Lester Bangs in an interview for *Musician*. "It's a device for generating very high voltages which then leap between the two poles, and it has a certain erratic contour, and I said, 'You have to imagine a guitar line that has that, very fast and unpredictable.' And he played that part, which to me was very Wimshurst indeed."[8]

Both albums fell into shops at the end of 1975. It was time for Robert Fripp to disappear. Other members of King Crimson had done it; David Cross, Fripp reminded one interviewer, had left the band and gone to traipse around Ireland with his violin. Fripp became intrigued with a higher pursuit: the theories and guidance of George Gurdjieff, an Armenian spiritual teacher who died in 1949. When Fripp gave a particularly loping interview, there were echoes of Gurdjieff, of his advice.

> Remember that here work is not for work's sake but is
>   only a means.
> Man is given a definite number of experiences—
>   economizing them, he prolongs his life.
> The highest that a man can attain is to be able to do.[9]

Long before he died, Gurdjieff told an English adherent named J. G. Bennett that he needed to found a school where this way of living and thinking could be shared. Bennett did so in 1971 and then died three years later. Robert Fripp was among the people who came upon Gurdjieff's work. "The top of my head blew off," Fripp said. "I needed someone who knew a lot more than me, and not only knew, but knew how to do something about it."[10]

Gurdjieff's work made the rounds with progressive musicians, none of whom seemed as thrown as Fripp. "What I really liked about him was, he was a total charlatan," said Kevin Ayers. "He didn't make any bones about it. His thing was that you cannot present the truth to people in simple form. You have to elaborate. Otherwise they're not interested. Did you ever read his book? It's just bullshit, absolute bullshit."[11]

In the fall of 1975, Robert Fripp arrived at J. G. Bennett's International Academy for Continuous Education at Sherborne House in Gloucestershire, England, intending to complete the first ten-month course not led by Gurdjieff's pupil. The man who'd played in Hyde Park and Central Park shared a room with four other men. "The place had a chill about it," Fripp told an interviewer years later. "The place was also haunted, and any kind of school which works like that obviously attracts the other side, if you like. The opposition poke around."[12]

Days at Sherborne began around 6 a.m., when students woke up. They would continue with psychological exercises, then on to breakfast, and then to practical training, like the metal workshop where Fripp became a pupil. "[On] the outside . . . if you're feeling a bit pissed off you can go to the pictures or watch television or get drunk or do whatever," Fripp explained. "But in Sherborne you had to sit there and find a way of dealing with it—the expression would be *working* with it. Not easy. The woman I was living with left me while I was there, which was awful for me. I was pretty suicidal. It was not easy. But, on the other hand, that was certainly the beginning of my life."[13]

WHILE ROBERT FRIPP was scattering King Crimson, the five members of Genesis were busy at work at Island's studio in Wales. They'd really broken out in 1974, a year that started with an American tour that one *Rolling Stone* reporter captured in dazzled quotes from the audience.

> I haven't cried at a show since I saw Nureyev dance,
>   until now.
> This reminds me of the response Jethro Tull was getting
>   when it was starting out.

The Genesis live show had become hypnotic—had been hypnotic for a while, actually—but Peter Gabriel was aware of how the "Brit puts on silly outfit" pull could look to people. "The gimmickry is remarkably good at getting pictures in the paper," said Gabriel during the tour. "I'm only too happy to play that game, because I enjoy playing it. It does make a difference. It's a means to an end."[14]

They were cutting back on costumes, but not on scale. In October 1974, as *The Lamb Lies Down on Broadway* was being mixed, Gabriel told *Melody Maker* that the band had made a double album "split up into self-contained song units," but "based on one story, happily more direct than in the past, although still involved with fantasy. . . . This will break all bounds and records previously set for pretentiousness," he deadpanned. "No—nobody's said it yet—we're waiting, in anticipation."[15]

The band had held a vote, and Gabriel's concept had won out.

The new album would tell the story of Rael, a name chosen because it had "no traceable ethnic origins" apart from being the name of the rock opera hero on *The Who Sell Out*. "I don't know if my memory has been playing subversive tricks on me but I was annoyed," said Gabriel of the coincidence.[16]

Rael, to be played on stage by Gabriel, was "a greasy Puerto Rican kid" (Mike Rutherford's view) who found himself on a spiritual and sexual journey through New York. "I was trying to give it a street slant, and that was before punk happened," Gabriel told one biographer. "I felt an energy in that direction, and it seemed that prancing around in fairyland was rapidly becoming obsolete."[17] This was the condensed version. The album was not meant to be digested easily. Record buyers unfolded the package to find not just lyrics, but a narrative that darted between verse and prose.

The new references, untethered from fantasy, were meant to drive Genesis into the heat of the 1970s. When audiences showed up for the 1975 tour, they could buy an official booklet that began with a lengthy essay placing Genesis in the history of progressive music and explaining how they'd broken loose. "Back in the late 60's progressive music seemed all but dead," read the booklet, "barely kept alive by the faint spark of a lingering mellotron. Rock audiences had overdosed on loud psychedelic riffs and gentle acoustic flower-power tunes, wondering all the time if there was anything more to progressive music than strobe lights, incense and the odd synthesizer. Just when adventurous rock seemed forever moving backwards, Genesis began flirting with multi-media concepts."

The booklet promised that Genesis, "not a terribly wealthy band," was plowing its earnings back into a one-of-a-kind stage show. "To convey the complex story line of the new album, visual aids will be used on three backdrop screens, hinting at three dimensional illusions, slowed down slides will also add to an animated feel. As always, these new technical improvements will serve as painted landscapes adding to the fantasy and clarifying the story line."

This description might have undersold the drama of the show. Gabriel appeared on stage in jeans and a leather jacket, as Rael. "We'd like to play the whole thing for you tonight," he would say. "It tells of how a large black cloud descends into Times Square and straddles out across 42nd street, turns into a wall, and sucks in Manhattan island. Our hero, named Rael, crawls out of the subways of New York and is sucked into the wall to regain consciousness underground."[18] Gabriel stayed in costume for most of the set, until reaching "The Lamia," when he descended into a rotating cone called "the tourbillion," Rael's portal to a new world. When Gabriel emerged again, he was clad in a yellow body sock decorated with bulbous objects somewhere between genitalia and gourds.

In February, with most of the tour left to go and positive reviews from every city, Gabriel decided to tell Genesis that he would leave the band. He was unshakable; they were distraught. "Their position was that we had worked eight years to get this far," said Gabriel, "and now, finally, we were about to make it, and I was pulling the carpet out from underneath it all."[19]

Yet nobody broke faith with the press. Genesis did no interviews for the rest of the tour. In July 1975, *NME* reported on the rumors of a Genesis split. Phil Collins remembered picking up a better-sourced *Melody Maker* story—a cover story—and readying for the press to completely write off the band. In August, Gabriel asked the papers to publish, in entirety, an essay about his departure. They complied. "I believe the use of sound and visual images can be developed to do much more than we have done," wrote Gabriel. "But on a large scale, it needs one clear and coherent direction, which our pseudo-democratic committee system could not provide." This, even though he had won the most recent committee vote. "My future within music, if it exists, will be in as many situations as possible."[20]

Gabriel slowly—very slowly—retreated from the music scene. On the way toward his hiatus, he gave a few interviews about the new sounds he'd been hearing and the directions Genesis could not have gone. "I'm optimistic about the future," he said at the end of 1975. "There's plenty of people going to get their bits out—your Patti Smiths and your Bruce Springsteens."[21]

Todd Rundgren approached. "He was a very quiet, shy guy, and it seemed like he was in this transitional space and not super confident about where he was going with everything. I think he was looking for me to give him something 'certain' to hang onto, but I didn't know what exactly it was he should do at that point."[22]

The rest of the band was accepting demo tapes from aspiring singers. "He's got to be able to be a stage performer who can jump in at the deep end," Tony Banks told *Melody Maker*. "Either he's got to have had some experience or he's got to be a natural." This was not easy to find. In one promotional photo, the band hoisted a portrait of Frank Sinatra—problem solved! The actual submissions from vocalists, more than four hundred of them, were landing with wet thuds. "We had a guy called George Gabriel, would you believe?" Steve Hackett told *Melody Maker*. "That was really his name. Doing 'Norwegian Wood.' Then we had a transvestite." Mike Rutherford confirmed this. "Yeah, a guy who called himself the Red Hooker," he said. "He sang a song called 'I Got the Sex Blues, Baby,' and sent us a picture of him wearing what we assume was a red dress, singing the sex blues."[23]

"We're looking in a leisurely manner," said Phil Collins.[24]

How leisurely? Fans figured that out at year's end, when Genesis pushed Collins to the front of the stage as the new, full-time singer. "People are going to be looking for a great gap but they won't find it," Collins told *Sounds*. "It's not as if we've lost an Ian Anderson leader and here we are, a band without a leader."[25]

Genesis was actually thriving without its star. They released *A Trick of the Tail* in February 1976, backing it with a full tour, and musically the album grabbed the baton from *Lamb*. "Dance on a Volcano" began with Hackett playing eighth notes that zoomed from speaker to speaker, leading into a burst of synthesized chords from Banks and beats from Collins and Rutherford.

Then came Collins's voice, approximating Gabriel's in a few ways—the quick leap up to high notes, for example—but telling simpler, more optimistic, romantic stories. The title track bounced along with a nursery rhyme flair—something that had been traded away in the *Lamb* days. "Ripples," which was adapted into one of the band's earliest videos, was a nearly straightforward song about love. "I think people who had found Peter a bit difficult maybe preferred the album because it was a little bit less dense," said Banks.[26]

The new Genesis made its debut one month later, at the London Arena in London, Ontario. Collins was replaced on the drums by Bill Bruford. He hadn't settled into a new progressive band after Crimson went defunct; Genesis would pay him £500 a week to fill out the tour. Bruford considered Collins a "soul mate," but found Genesis a bit too rote. "My nature is to play a piece differently every night," he explained, "even though there are only so many ways you can play 'Supper's Ready' on a drum kit without the song unraveling. . . . In the first break between songs, I saw Phil go up front with a piece of paper in his hand, his hand shaking, so nervous," Rutherford recalled. "But it worked great."[27]

GAUGING SUCCESS, or predicting a breakout, was an inexact science. Peter Hammill reconstituted Van der Graaf Generator in 1975, promising a revision of the sound. "Previously we were very much an overdubbing band, which at the time wasn't something that people did all that much," Hammill told *Melody Maker*. "The great problem with the whole psychedelia era was that the wall of sound was being produced but totally without control. There wasn't, in fact, the degree of musicianship behind it which would make it valid."[28]

The new band had the full support of Charisma, which released a series of comeback albums and paid for ambitious tours. In 1976 the band put out two melodic albums: *Still Life* and the ironically titled *World Record*. An American tour, outfitted with a full road crew and light show, simply could not make back its cost. The crowds diminished as the band returned for shows in England. At the final gig of the tour, in Germany, no one missed the joke of a bill that allied VdGG with the band Farewell. The result was that "Farewell Van Der Graaf Generator" appeared on all of the badges. "It was demoralizing for all of us," said bass player Pete Donovan. "I left halfway through."[29]

A similar drama afflicted Daevid Allen's Gong, but the ageless pixie of the progressives went along with it. In 1975 he parted with the radically transformed group. Steve Hillage, a proudly unevolved hippie who fascinated the music press, became the creative force in the group. "There had been a punk revolution in the ranks of Gong," Allen said. "After I left Gong in '75, I grew quickly tired of the clean hair, white clothes, and glistening instruments of the prog rock coterie and fell into bed with the UK punk revolution, which was extremely raw, dangerously violent, and as wild as a cyclonic updraft. Maybe I was lifted up into the land of transcendental punkadelics."[30]

Once again, Allen found himself outside of a group he'd created, happily building from the spare parts. He teamed up with the musicians of Here & Now, old associates of Gong, for a project that would be released as *Floating Anarchy 1977* by Planet Gong. Punkadelica was born; extraterrestrial bleeping and Allen poetry were brought into the zeitgeist by reliable, thudding riffs. A single, "Opium for the People," fit more naturally in the moment than most of what Allen's peers had done.

"Curiously, the UK press kept publicizing Gong as the most likely band to be assassinated by the kill-the-hippy extremists while I was running with the assassins and misbehaving in their ranks," said Allen. "Seven or eight of us would rampage through London in a battered Bedford van and conduct lightning graffiti raids on everything we could get away with. We toured the UK for free in an outrageously antique bus with a coal stove at its rear. It had a top speed of about 50 mph and would black out the motorway behind us with great clouds of smoke from the stove. Barely a day would pass when we were not stopped by local police."[31]

Allen proved that there was a way out of the progressive fog. Promptly thereafter, he "got pneumonia and staggered back to Spain."[32]

Allen's old bandmate Kevin Ayers was dislocated too—but even less sure of how to respond. In 1978 he released *Rainbow Takeaway*, a collection of fractured pop songs that sold less than ever. It took work not to notice how bored he had become by performance. "I kind of numbed out on that," Ayers admitted to an interviewer in 2007. "I kept working, but obviously *it* wasn't working. I mean, another generation had just clocked in, you know?" Ayers continued, "The best of punk rock is great. I was just rather out of context."[33]

ROBERT FRIPP'S NEAR-YEAR at Sherborne removed him from the music industry, but not from music. "Some people had brought guitars and I played," he confessed to one interviewer. "There was a concert about once a month. I played at three of those concerts."[34] Peter Gabriel and his family dropped in for a few visits.

Before entering the house, Fripp had gotten to know a Philadelphia musician named Daryl Hall, who had started spending more time in England. The two of them kept in touch; Hall was convinced that Fripp was communicating with no one else in the outside world. This was during a period that Fripp would admit was "both physically painful and spiritually terrifying." In a 1978 interview, he would count three fellow students who had left the school for the bosom of mental asylums, and he estimated that it took a full year to relocate to a place in society. Sherborne filled its residents with "the kind of cold that freezes the soul," said Fripp.[35]

Fripp escaped. Gabriel talked him into playing on his first post-Genesis solo album. The guitarist arrived in Toronto in July 1976, suddenly working under Alice Cooper's producer Bob Ezrin, who had assembled a crew of people he knew and people recommended by Gabriel. Larry Fast, a synthesizer designer who had helped Rick Wakeman build his Moog and had imported Genesis albums into American markets, arrived on Gabriel's recommendation. Steve Hunter, an axman on Cooper's albums and Lou Reed's harder-edged work, arrived to fill out the guitar sound. "Bob hedged his bets," said Fast. "He had Steve Hunter sitting next to Fripp, and Steve was given 'Solsbury Hill.' He knew Tony Levin as a bass player, so I think he knew very well what to expect there."[36]

Levin had been playing with experimental bands for a long time. Years earlier, he'd missed a shot at joining John McLaughlin's fusionist Mahavishnu Orchestra when he was out and his in-laws took the call. "I was given the message that I'd been called about a job with Murray Vishnu and his Orchestra," Levin remembered. "I didn't take the job."[37]

Ezrin brought Levin into the studio. His new bassist produced a new instrument, which he'd been sold on by the inventor himself—Emmett Chapman's "Chapman Stick." Levin, theoretically, could use the girthy ten-string to play a family of notes that other instruments had to collaborate to imitate. "Bob took one look and insisted I put it away immediately," said Levin.[38]

Fripp went on the road with Gabriel. "Robert is my favourite guitarist," Gabriel told an interviewer, "but there's only a few places where he puts his own style in as opposed to just decorating as a session player. He was more against going on the road as Robert Fripp than actually going on the road." The solution: He did not go out on the road as "Robert Fripp." In billings, Gabriel's guitarist was "Dusty Roads." On stage, he was often concealed from view, paid tribute only when Gabriel was announcing his band at the end of the set. But one night, a roadie sidled up to Gabriel with a new instruction. He could go ahead; he could introduce his guitarist as Robert Fripp. "It's whether the white star or the black hole is more attractive," explained Gabriel to an interviewer.[39]

The tour went on without Dusty, and Fripp stayed in New York. "It was magic," Fripp told *New Hi-Fi Sound*.[40] "I had a flat on the Bowery; I'd walk out and Richard Lloyd of Television would generally be staggering by, whatever time it was. There was this incredible openness."[41]

Fripp was at home in July when the phone rang. Brian Eno was calling. "He said, 'Hang on, I'm here with David Bowie.

I'll pass you over,'" Fripp would recall, in a story told many times. "David Bowie says to me, 'Do you think you can play some hairy rock-and-roll guitar?' I said, 'Well, I haven't played guitar for a while. I'm not sure, but if you're prepared to take the risk, so am I.' Shortly afterwards, a first-class ticket arrived, on Lufthansa, to Germany."[42]

He landed and headed to the studio for three short days of recording, possessed of a mission, wholly unsure of what to play. "When I did that album I was completely out of my brain," said Fripp. "I went in to listen to what they'd been doing and they said, 'Well you might as well plug in.' 'I suppose I might,' I said. And the very first thing they did was put up 'Beauty And The Beast.' And I played straight over it."[43]

The note that came out of Fripp's guitar was unclassifiable, bent and distorted, not unlike the noise from a vocoder but with no voice. Eno and Bowie's chugging, piano-driven song was suddenly dressed up with metallic bends and whinnies. As the intro faded, Fripp played something that sounded like water falling through tin. Fripp had achieved a similar effect on "The Heavenly Music Corporation," but in this case it was hooked to a melody. "This is the way I did the rest of the album," Fripp told *Melody Maker* in 1979. "They'd put up a track and I'd play. I wouldn't bother rehearsing it. I'd just play."[44]

That collaboration worked best on the album's title track, a ballad about lovers by the Berlin Wall that Bowie sang as producer Tony Visconti moved the microphone further and further away. Fripp played three completely divergent takes. One took him up the fretboard, staying there, letting a note sustain. Another was sheer, shredded feedback.

"Fripp had a technique in those days where he measured the distance between the guitar and the speaker where each note would feed back," Visconti explained. "For instance, an

'A' would feed back maybe at about four feet from the speaker, whereas a 'G' would feed back maybe three and a half feet from it. He had a strip that they would place on the floor, and when he was playing the note 'F' sharp he would stand on the strip's 'F' sharp point and 'F' sharp would feed back better. He really worked this out to a fine science, and we were playing this at a terrific level in the studio, too. It was very, very loud, and all the while he was playing these notes—that beautiful overhead line—Eno was turning the dials and creating a new envelope and just playing with the filter bank."[45]

None of the experimentation was cut. "I casually played the three guitar takes together and it had a jaw-dropping effect on all of us," said Visconti.[46]

Not long after, Fripp was on his first-class plane back to New York. Just days later, he was in the studio again, writing and producing music with Daryl Hall, who he'd known since before the end of King Crimson. "I would stay at his house, and he used to stay at my house, and all that," said Hall. "We were really good friends."[47]

Hall's career had taken off since the Crimson days, with music that sounded nothing like Fripp's. In 1976, his band Hall & Oates had gone to the top ten with "Sara Smile." One year later, and just months before collaborating with Fripp, they'd scored another hit with "Rich Girl." Both were uncomplicated, melodic slices of white Philly soul.

The music that Hall would record with Fripp started like that, then careened on the power of Fripp's sustained notes. The lyrics they came up with were more searching, and rich with irony. "Something in 4/4 Time," the second track on Hall's *Sacred Songs*, was a joke at the very idea of pop song structure, a lecture to an unwilling musician that "ya gotta have something that always rhymes," if there was any hope of making a career. At the second chorus, Fripp's guitar buzzed in with a sequence of floating notes.

On other tracks, Fripp and Hall bent the ambient guitar sound into something new, something warm, living outside the structure of a pop song. "The Farther Away I Am" contained just three sounds: Hall's voice, an electric piano, and Fripp's guitars. "Is it just a cloud passing under?" sang Hall, as one clean note from the guitar drifted into another sustained note—this one defined by feedback.

Hall knew that he and Fripp had discovered something new about their music. "Hall is the first singer I've met who can sing anything at all the way I ask him," Fripp told one interviewer. Hall repaid the compliment, without the edge. "When he plays," Hall told one interviewer of Fripp, "it sounds like the universe crying."[48]

It did not sound like Hall & Oates, certainly, and that was not what RCA expected from a signed artist. Hearing no singles, the label shelved the album. Hall said nothing about it. In 1978, the two men collaborated on more songs for an album of Fripp's own. RCA had Hall's vocals stripped from those songs—a breakneck rocker called "You Burn Me Up I'm a Cigarette" and another ambient soul ballad, "North Star."

Still, Hall said nothing. Fripp was not so reserved. "Daryl is a remarkable singer and his solo album is fantastic," Fripp told Jean-Gilles Blum in an interview. "It is too bad RCA is limiting the scope of his career. As for Hall and Oates, they are a very professional group. They limit their format and possibilities on purpose, as part of a commercial compromise they accept."[49]

"Robert was being a girl," Hall said decades later. "He got very burned by this all. We had a very close relationship, and my manager at the time, Tommy Mottola, came into it, and Robert got really hurt by it. I mean, when you get into a relationship or a collaboration with a musician, it's almost like a romantic relationship. And that's the best way I could put it. You get into somebody's heart. And Robert I think had visions that he was going to steal me away from John."[50]

While *Sacred Songs* gathered dust, Fripp was being heard again, and recording new music on two continents. Bowie's "Heroes," the song, did not chart, but it made it onto FM rotation. "The title track is easily the best thing Bowie has put on plastic in three years," wrote a critic for *Crawdaddy!*, crediting its pull to "Eno's spine-tingling synthi-guitar." (Close enough.)[51]

In November 1977, Fripp was back in the studio, in Amsterdam, taking over for Bob Ezrin as the producer of Peter Gabriel's second album. Most of the pivotal musicians had stayed on: Tony Levin was back on bass, and Larry Fast had returned to the keyboards. But where Ezrin had built vast worlds of sound, Fripp demanded that the band draw in. First takes, with their tiny flaws, were kept. "Robert was very keen to get everything fresh," Gabriel explained. "Robert did not take on the role of a military commander taking his troops into musical battle, as Bob [Ezrin] did. But he was steely, in a quiet firm way, in defending his approach from any challenges from the musicians and even from the artist."[52]

EMERSON, LAKE & PALMER had finished their *Brain Salad Surgery* "Someone Get Me a Ladder" tour on October 24, 1974, with a benefit in Central Park. That month, they released the entirety of a show from Anaheim, California, as a triple LP, with the breath-exhausting title *Welcome Back, My Friends, to the Show That Never Ends—Ladies and Gentlemen*. The three musicians retreated to their homes in England. And for the next two and a half years, they released almost no music at all.

This was not the original plan. In November 1974, *Circus*'s Jim O'Connor reported that ELP had commenced work on solo albums. "Right now Keith and Carl are both about fifty percent finished with theirs," Manticore's Mario Medious told O'Connor. "Greg's written his whole album, but so far he's only recorded one track."[53]

The process took much longer than all that. It was not enough anymore to write a mere album. Emerson wanted to compose a "once-and-for-all statement to shut up the critics," a history of piano music in one suite. "I wrote a series of piano variations inspired by Brahms's 'Waltz No. 6 in C,' wanting to create the huge tenth interval leaps after the great man's fashion," Emerson would recall. "I then wanted to create a gigue. I wanted rhapsodic, fugal development sonata form, if there was such a thing. I wanted Schonberg's 12-tone scale! The more I wanted, the more the notes poured out of the piano."[54]

Emerson put that on paper. "Allegro Giojoso," the first movement, began with a chaotic chord, and with strings playing sixteenth notes that seemed to run aimlessly up a scale. The theme was there, exposed just moments later. A battle raged for nine minutes, between Emerson's pastoral, Aaron Copland–flavored melodies, and the banging glissandos and ostinatos that grew out of rock. The second movement, "Andante Molto Cantabile," was pure melody, and pure peace.

In April 1975, with the concerto not quite done, Emerson and his family went on vacation. When they returned, "loaded down with bottles" of French champagne, the pianist got a call from a neighbor. His home, Stone Hill, was engulfed by flames. "What is it you're looking for, exactly?" asked a fireman as Emerson approached. "Tapes in the dressing room on the first floor," said Emerson. "That doesn't exist anymore," said the fireman.[55]

The Emerson family had no choice but to find another home.

Once ensconced, Emerson wrote the third and final movement
of his concerto. "The final movement became, ah . . . more—
fuck you. Aggressive," Emerson would tell an interviewer. There
was nothing pastoral about "Toccata con Fuoco"—literally,
"with fire." Emerson attacked the low notes of the piano, punc-
tuating it with orchestral stings, like flames licking the stage.[56]

Toward the end of 1975, Emerson went into the studio to
record the concerto. But there was no sign of a solo album.
Palmer and Lake were just as wrapped up in experimentation. It
was with Lake that Emerson started using cocaine. "I suddenly
went from being a loner, lost in creative dreams, to some manic
expressive that finally got his point across verbally, vertically
and unhorizontally while others seemed to listen upright for the
first time," Emerson recalled in his memoirs. "If cocaine did
anything at all, at that time, it was to drag me out of my shell."[57]

There was no shell for Lake to crawl out of. He entered the
recording sessions with a surplus of swagger. For him, the pause
after the exhausting worldwide tour reinforced his need to assert
his place in the musical cosmos. "Keith can relate to Carl musically but neither of them can relate to me musically," Lake had
told journalists Rick Sanders and John Wells. "My art is as far
away from what they do as a painter is. . . . I think if you can
have any gift in music, the greatest gift is to be a singer."[58]

Yet Lake was making this art with a collaborator, Peter
Sinfield—and the collaborator was less impressed than the singer.
"Greg always wanted to be as great as Keith Emerson," argued
Sinfield. "Unfortunately, his guitar playing was pretty basic and
folky. From a technical point of view, he was never going to be
as great a star as Keith Emerson. He resented that, thinking his
singing would make up for it."[59]

The Sinfield-Lake collaboration, uneasy as it was, produced
a real hit: "I Believe in Father Christmas," an atheist hymn for

guitar, which Emerson adorned with a section from "Troika," the third movement of Sergei Prokofiev's *Lieutenant Kijé* suite. It was a number two hit, a near-winner of the British Christmas chart race, which progressive groups did not tend to win.

It was the only piece of ELP music released in 1975. In February 1976 the band relocated to Montreux, Switzerland. Emerson was bored, with no entertainment apart from his Kawasaki 1100 motorcycle and his Jet Ski around a private lake. "My contacts had grams of coke shipped in from Zurich inside the covers of album sleeves," said Emerson. "But with no one to share, it was wasted along with myself. . . . The best one was nestling in a box set of *The Complete Organ Works of JS Bach*, but it was never enough."[60]

It was worse for Sinfield, who had been assigned the task of matching lyrics to a musical suite. The band, initially, asked for a song cycle about mercenaries; Sinfield talked them down to one about pirates. Even then, he found himself delivering material to Lake and being waylaid by random taste. "I was in Montreux, and I was saved by the roadies," recalled Sinfield. "I went up in Greg's chalet, way up the mountain, and delivered the lyrics. Greg went, 'I don't know, maybe a six, not good enough.' Five days later, I head back up the mountain. Now, Greg says, 'That bit you wrote about the rose and the pistol, that was good.' Well, I happened to be looking over the edge of his chalet. And I thought, Perhaps that will do. Perhaps I will jump now."[61]

Lake also wanted the use of an orchestra. Emerson asked how much it would cost. "Don't worry about that, sunshine," said Lake. "You just go and write the fuckin' music while I have a chat with Stewart."[62]

Carl Palmer's music was less cumbersome—and easier to push aside. He and the composer Joseph Horovitz produced their own "percussion concerto," put on tape in collaboration with the London Philharmonic Orchestra. It would stay in the box for twenty-five years. Palmer put forward an adaptation of Prokofiev's *Scythian Suite*, "The Enemy God Dances with the Black Spirits," and *that* was given the orchestral treatment. "We were going to record 'The Enemy God' with the group originally," he said, "but found that it sounded better with an orchestra, so I immediately recorded it that way."[63]

The budget for the recording sessions ballooned accordingly. "When we were recording 'Pirates,'" recalled Sinfield, "Greg said, 'I'm not coming to the studio today. Keith didn't come yesterday; he said he had a cold, so I'm not coming in 'til Friday.' To teach him a lesson. This is ridiculous! The studio's sitting empty at £500 a day. But that's how stupid and childlike big rock stars can get. Small people with big ideas."[64]

Material piled up, but there was no outward sign of dread. ELP were using space, time, and money to take progressive music to its natural, higher plane. When Ahmet Ertegun, president of Atlantic Records, arrived in Switzerland to listen to the tapes, the band played him a cover of Aaron Copland's *Fanfare for the Common Man* that stretched to nearly ten minutes, each member of the band playing over the hard-fought orchestra. "That's a hit, man!" he said.[65]

There was no question that it would sell. It just wouldn't sell in the form of solo albums. The new music—Emerson's concerto, Lake's popular songs, Palmer's jazz experiments—would be sides of a new ELP album. The fourth side would consist of "Pirates" and "Fanfare." Instead of atomizing, the band would unite behind a statement. "Say Keith would have released a solo album," Palmer argued to *Sounds* reporter Barbara Charone. "Later, perhaps I'd release an album. But what happens is you blow each other out, steal each other's sales. You lose group unity. See, the public like *unity*. If they see 3, 4, 5 guys playing together for X amount of years, they see unity. It's like a family, right?"[66] The album was to be packaged in a barely adorned sleeve, and a simple title. "I'd suggested *The Works of Emerson, Lake and Palmer*," Emerson later admitted, "from all the coke sent to me in box sets of *The Complete Organ Works of Bach*."[67]

As the album was being compiled, Emerson relocated to Nassau, in the Bahamas. It was there, powered by "three grams of coke, accompanied by three bottles of Cognac," that he looked across the water and decided to swim to England. "We realized that it was quite a long way," Emerson would say, "but we had a compass." The effort failed. Keith Emerson was pulled wheezing from the water. January 14, 1977, was the last day that he would use cocaine.[68]

Just two months later, *Works* landed in record shops. There was not, at first, any dog pile by the critics. *Rolling Stone* judged the album's orchestrations to be "flaccid" but suggested that "the final side triumphantly demonstrates that as an ensemble ELP has lost none of its expertise."[69]

In May, Atlantic released the single of "Fanfare," and gave ELP its biggest hit—the third-best-selling instrumental rock song of all time. Aaron Copland had graciously cleared it, and given it something close to an endorsement. "I allowed it to go by because when they first play it, they play it fairly straight and when they end the piece, they play it very straight," he told the BBC. "What they do in the middle, I'm not sure exactly how they connect that with my music but they do it someway, I suppose."[70]

The number one song in Britain was Rod Stewart's cover of "I Don't Want to Talk about It." In America, the *Billboard* chart had been conquered by the Eagles' "Hotel California." ELP's music, thrown into that mix, was as radical as ever. And the band played up that impression, as it began to promote its unheard-of new touring strategy. It would stalk North America with a full seventy-piece orchestra. Three buses would carry them from gig to gig.

The band's own sound system, as *Sounds* noted, blasted out 72,000 watts and weighed 25 tons.[71] After welcoming ELP back, the music press was being bludgeoned into awe. Emerson, who'd blanched at Robert Moog's departure from the company he had founded, had taken on a GX synthesizer that was moved and reassembled by "eight roadies."[72]

"The wave of the future is not in smash-bang, nor is it in electronics," Lake told *Rolling Stone*. "It is in musical expression. And just as we once opened doors for other groups electronically, we're now going to do it musically. Where we once had six hands, we now have 140." "Some of the percussionists are so good I'd like to cut off their arms," said Palmer.[73]

On July 2, the three artists appeared on the cover of *Sounds*, standing on an anonymous rooftop. Emerson and Palmer, clad in leather jackets, were pictured in conversation. Lake had his eyes trained on the camera. The cover line was a dare: "Would you pay two million dollars to see these men?" Above their heads, above the magazine's title, the reader was promised a story about the Sex Pistols. But the tone of the piece was triumphant. Given a preview of the new ELP tour, the music paper found its snark arsenal running dry. "Visually the stage looks incredible, with the orchestra circling above the band in Stanley Kubrick type silver enclosures," wrote Barbara Charone. "They all wear t-shirts that say ELP in bold silver lettering. Conductor Godfrey Salmon towers above them, moving his baton and occasionally shaking ass."[74]

The orchestra appeared to be a masterstroke. "We didn't want to come zipping back with the same old show," Palmer told *Sounds*. "An orchestra seemed like a natural progression. It was the only way we could reappear after 2 and 1/2 years. But it's not a permanent musical direction. It *all* works but ELP would work without the orchestra. The orchestra just puts the cream on top of the cake. Actually, just the cherry right in the middle."[75]

The band gave *Rolling Stone* extended access to the tour, and reporter Charles M. Young came away skeptical but moved. "The orchestra, ELP's biggest excess ever, has had the effect of smoothing over their other excesses," he wrote, after seeing a "short-of-sellout crowd" be entertained in Cincinnati. The band made no attempt to explain away the scale, and the risk, of what it was doing. It was blowing a fortune to send an orchestra around North America. "We're risking everything we ever made and everything we're ever likely to make on this tour," Lake told *Rolling Stone*. "I'm talking about our families, our possessions, everything we believe in. We'll have to sell our houses in England if it flops." "If we lose money, so what?" asked Emerson. "There's no way we can make money."[76]

And the band did lose money. The shows were transcendent, and Emerson held off illness with a nightly "vitamin cocktail" that he credited for grand, newfound energy. After a while, he wondered if the front rows could see the marks on his arms. "I could almost read their minds—'no wonder he plays so fucking fast,'" Emerson remembered. "Sometimes the doctor could find a vein, sometimes he couldn't. When he couldn't find one in my arm, he'd find one in the back of my hand."[77]

Fripp saw ELP at one of the Madison Square Garden gigs. "As I'm walking past this barrier I see Robert, and I was shocked," Lake would tell Sid Smith. "So I asked him what he was doing there and said to the roadie, 'Get him out of the crowd and get him back into the dressing room and look after him.'"[78]

After the show, Lake recalled, "we went off in the limo, and we're going down the road. I said to him, 'You know, Robert, one day we ought to get our guitars out and play together again. It's been so long since we did that.' " "I don't think so," said Fripp. Lake told his driver to pull over. He opened the door for his former bandmate. "Out you go," he said. "I thought, why was he like that?" Lake recalled later. "It must have been jealousy. There was ELP, selling out three nights at Madison Square Garden, and you couldn't get arrested in King Crimson at the time."[79]

The guitarist remembered it differently. He went to every show at the Garden; Lake invited him to a dinner for the band, held after the triumphant final performance. "Greg was vibrating with various suits," said Fripp, "and at the end of the evening, sat me down to talk with him. Greg presented, in strong terms, the idea of a KC69 reformation." Lake gave Fripp a ride to his New York home, and only at the end did he ask about the reunion. Fripp said he'd call.

"That's it? You want me to call you?" asked Lake.

"You already know my answer," said Fripp.

"You mean, 'no'?"

"That's right."

"I was really hoping to see him again last summer, but, apparently, he didn't feel like it," Fripp told an interviewer in 1978. He and Lake had drifted apart. That was that. And ELP? "They are part of rock industry's dinosaur structure."[80]

ON FEBRUARY 5, 1978, a line formed outside of a Soho, New York, art space called the Kitchen. Robert Fripp was playing, for the first time since the collapse of King Crimson. No music had been published under his name since Gerald Ford's presidency. His music with David Bowie and Peter Gabriel had been overpowered by their gigantic personalities; his collaboration with Daryl Hall was locked in a vault.

At the Kitchen, at the appointed hour, Robert Fripp walked out with an electric guitar and a tape machine. "He said that the performance was conceived as a 'salon piece'—improvisations intimately and informally presented—and reserved the right to be boring and unintelligent," wrote John Piccarella in the *Village Voice*. Fripp sat down and began to play music that might have been called ambient. Fripp had a better name, simultaneously more branded and more silly. This was "Frippertronics."[81]

"The music is organized around drones, and Fripp's performance let us in on the process by which these backgrounds are created," wrote Piccarella. "A guitar note is picked with the volume off, and then swells into the foreground as the sound level is turned up. There it is augmented by another note, until a layer of tories and trills is built into a repeating loop of tape. The guitar is then switched out of the tape loop and Fripp solos, accompanied by the receding wash of recorded sound."[82]

It was as unclassifiably new as ELP was stodgy, circusy. "Fripp has found a structure of improving consciousness that allows for the repetitive rigor of a composed minimalism like that of Reich or Glass," summed up the *Village Voice*. At intermission there was an abstract theater performance called "Mooncowisms," designed by an artist named Joanna Walton, who used Brian Eno's "Oblique Strategies" cards to shape an abstract performance around the quotes of great thinkers.

Walton, at that time, was also collaborating with Fripp on some lyrics for new music. Over the course of 1978, he widened his network and put together, song by song, a solo album. Ideally, it would have been the trilogy in a series that began with Peter Gabriel's second record and Daryl Hall's *Sacred Songs*. Yet Hall's label was unmovable. Two songs cowritten by Hall and Fripp—"Chicago" and "Mary"—were stripped of his vocals.

The key part on "Mary," a song that combined the waving ambience of Frippertronics with a gnostic lyric, went to a new

Fripp acquaintance named Terre Roche. Terre, with her sisters
Maggie and Suzzy, formed the Roches, a band that might have
been mistaken for a folk group until the listener moved in closer.
Their music was unpretentious and whimsical, with interlocking guitar parts and harmonies that were never saccharine. Fripp
came into their life after the band played at Kenny's Castaways in
New York. "A woman named Charlene whom I'd worked with
as a clerk typist at a music business management office called me
up and said she'd brought a friend of hers named Robert Fripp
to the show," recalled Terre Roche. "I'd never heard of him,
but she said he'd been in a group called King Crimson, and the
big red album cover with the wide open mouth came to mind.
Oh, yes, aren't they a really loud rock band that appeal mainly
to men?"[83]

The sisters were surprised at the man who turned up. "He
was a very proper, buttoned-up-to-the-collar type," recalled
Suzzy Roche. "At the same time, when you got to know him,
he was goofy in a childlike way. He loved sweets and pastries. He
was eccentric. And he wanted to record us the way we actually
sounded."[84]

Fripp embedded with the band. He did not want to alter their
sound on record, but he played with them to develop their natural sound. Everything he learned, they were welcome to. "He
taught us these exercises for the guitar, which both Terre and I
did for years," said Suzzy Roche. "They were much like med-
itations. They were extremely useful in a couple of ways; they
involved going back and forth between two strings with a pick,
going up the neck fret by fret, and then scales. We were surren-
dering to this very simple-seeming but deep repetitive action,
regardless of how you're feeling about it, without any expecta-
tion of what might come of it."[85]

The King Crimson sound, the pomp of progressive music, was
far behind Fripp now. On his own songs, Joanna Walton's lyrics

and George Gurdjieff's teachings gave the music even greater distance from rock's norms. "Mary" was the rare song named for a woman that—thanks to Walton—had nothing to do with puppy love. "She was, among other things, a Reichian therapist and wrote the song about one of her patients," explained Terre Roche.

With the Roches, Fripp brought in Larry Fast to add synthesizer textures, and Tony Levin to play bass. Fripp's own guitar, and influence, were almost wholly removed. The sound was as labeled on the finished album: "audio verité." One of the few exceptions came when the band was playing back "Hammond Song," a mysterious, romantic song based on strummed C and F chords. At the second chorus, the three sisters sang in harmony, and Fripp played an impromptu guitar solo, perfectly in tune. "He was sort of just fooling around," said Suzzy Roche. "He just played that solo, and we said, 'Oh, wow, that's great!' He said 'Oh, I couldn't possibly put that over your song.' But that was a beautiful solo he played. I believe it was the first take. And it made it on the album."[86]

The Roches would be released in April 1979; on the cover, the record buyer was informed that it had been "produced in audio verité by Robert Fripp." Two months later, Fripp released the long-fiddled-over solo album *Exposure*. The title track had appeared on Peter Gabriel's second album, as an instrumental, with Tony Levin's bass carrying a melody and Fripp's guitar in full waterfall burble. The "completed" version of the song featured lyrics, of a sort. Terre Roche howled the title, and a male voice spelled it out in monotone.

That set the tone for the album, which was not supposed to sound like anything Fripp had done before—or any prior music recorded by anyone. Fripp and Hall had composed songs that fit the 7-inch pop format, but bent in upsetting, disorienting directions. Van der Graaf's Peter Hammill had stepped in to record some of Daryl Hall's parts, which only added to the jaggedness of the sound. "I May Not Have Had Enough of Me but I've Had Enough of You" was a tangle of chords matched with lyrics that circled in an endless loop.

By the time *Exposure* hit shops, Fripp seemed to do more than transcend the old progressive rock. He had outlasted it. Emerson, Lake & Palmer went on hiatus, the wreckage of the orchestra tour never fully cleared. Yes, seemingly revivified at the height of punk, had lost Jon Anderson and Rick Wakeman. The need for King Crimson music was seemingly sated by U.K., a collaboration between John Wetton and Bill Bruford alongside the Roxy Music and Curved Air virtuoso Eddie Jobson and the progressive jazz guitarist Allan Holdsworth.

Fripp, meanwhile, was announcing his album as the start of a personal revolution: "a Drive to 1981." The meaning was gnostic. "This Drive to 1981 commits me, for two and a half years, to be working substantially in the marketplace, in positions of public access and accessibility," Fripp told the interview series *Boffomundo*. "The details will be filled in as the drive continues." It had been years since the exit from Gurdjieff, but the self-denial and ritualism he'd learned there still defined him. "There's a little story of a Sufi master who says: 'Choice, choice? Freedom? I have no choice. I can only do the will of God,'" said Fripp. "This is freedom. Now, from one point of view, I would view this Drive to 1981 as being a personal discipline."[87]

9

DEATH KNELL

his is getting to be a bit of a habit with us," said Mike Rutherford. "Isn't it?" Genesis's bassist was at his Notting Hill home, suffering through an interview with a *Melody Maker* reporter who wanted to know how the band could keep playing. It was October 1977, and Steve Hackett had followed Peter Gabriel out the door, into a solo career that followed more of the patterns of progressive music.

"His decision to go freed up the band," Tony Stratton-Smith would say, "especially once Mike had decided to handle the guitars, because a three-man unit is a much easier relationship to make work. It opened the door to a new way of writing in which Phil could participate more."[1]

That left Rutherford with more playing duties, and he was too honest to pretend he was as adroit as Hackett. Genesis was a three-piece now. "The new album's definitely going to be a lot different," Rutherford told *Sounds* reporter Hugh Fielder. "Whereas in the past a song could have been seven minutes long we now said we can say it in five minutes just as well, and you end up with more variety."[2]

Rutherford's musings appeared next to ads for new singles from Ian Dury and the Damned. Genesis would end up topping some of the reader polls at year's end, but 1977 had been the year of punk, of DIY, and of a rock press coming with pitchforks at ELP. Phil Collins was spending downtime playing with the jazz fusion band Brand X, and using whatever time was left trying to rescue his marriage.

"We had dropped down to a three-piece, which might have been a drawback," Tony Banks admitted. "Punk music was coming in and was supposed to be doing away with groups like us. But at exactly that moment we had our first hit single, and so the first of our albums that sold in any quantity."[3] The song was "Follow You Follow Me," a trifle that came together when Rutherford found a simple ascending riff, Banks added chords, and Collins decided on a soft beat. Rutherford estimated that it took him five minutes to come up with the lyrics.

Rutherford's piece was placed at the end of . . . *And Then There Were Three . . .* , the trio's first album, with a title that began as a joke to the music press. No member of Genesis thought it was their best. Yet the single reached into the American top ten. Banks was quite honest about the track. "If Genesis had never released 'Follow You Follow Me,'" he said, "if we'd split up before it came out, most people would never have heard of the group."[4]

Critics welcomed the new sound, and the new appeal, with a raspberry. *Rolling Stone* accused the band of losing itself "in a pea-soup fog of electronics" and gimmickry. "The melodies have never been less substantial, while the songs revel in pettiness and two-bit theatricality. In short, this contemptible opus is but the palest shadow of the group's earlier accomplishments."[5]

Was it fair? Genesis's songwriting had been simplified. There were eleven songs on the new record, and none of them were particularly fantastical. The longest composition, "Burning Rope," was extended by a meandering guitar solo and some optimistic block chords from Tony Banks. Block chords were everywhere, as were inspirational or glancingly introspective lyrics; "Undertow," the most driving ballad on the record, was basically a sheet of inspirational advice for anyone feeling defeated. "Stand up to the blow that fate has struck upon you."

Genesis was becoming a pop group, as it had been in the Charterhouse days. The difference was in a decade-plus of adult gravitas, and heartbreak. "Until then eighty percent of our audience had consisted of earnest spotty young men," said Stratton-Smith. "Suddenly we had this hit single and girls started turning up."[6]

THE DOWNFALL OF PROGRESSIVE ROCK happened quickly, with an entire critical establishment seemingly rooting for its demise. In just a year, bands like Yes and Jethro Tull—winners of reader polls for the whole of the 1970s—became soft punch lines for music writers. Band after band moved away from the complicated songwriting that had defined them. More important, the labels were dumping progressive music as fast as they could. "Bands were getting six-figure advances and years to make records," producer Tom Newman later told the author Paul Stump. "The accountants moved in. They make things work, but at the same time they spell the death knell for up-and-coming creative and progressive stuff."[7]

The number crunchers saw no other choice. According to the Record Industry Association of America, record sales doubled from 1973 to 1978, then tumbled, not to reach a new peak until 1984. The doom year was 1979; the music historian Simon Frith tracked the decline of sales as twenty percent in Britain and eleven percent in the United States.[8] That accelerated the decline of bands that were being waylaid by trends.

In 1980, as he toured Jethro Tull's formless album *A*, Ian Anderson explained to an interviewer that the flight of investment was killing creative music. "Ten years ago, there was a great deal more flexibility and freedom both in radio programming and in terms of the record company policy, as to what they would take a chance on," he said. "The profit margins were higher—simple as that. There wasn't quite the same desperate competition that existed between artists, between record companies, for a limited number of dollars. . . . what gets most programming, in terms of radio play, is that sort of top forty-ish kind of format, or MOR sort of format. You don't get the same absurd extremes occurring, which were very beneficial to music as a whole."[9]

When Anderson said that, Tull's era of experimentation had already ended. Other bands were smoothing out their sounds. In 1978, Gentle Giant completed its move away from renaissance influences and into pop tones with *Giant for a Day!*—ten driving rock songs, none longer than five minutes, designed for a hit. "We certainly weren't driven to be a commercial pop band," said singer Derek Shulman. "We tried things. It was an experiment. Some things kicked off well, and some sounded terrible. It wasn't three-chord silly songs that sounded like anyone else. Yeah, they were a little less intricate. They were a bit more pop—which is a horrible word. But they were good songs. Apparently our fans were not that thrilled by it."[10]

Gentle Giant would produce one more album, *Civilian*, and then call it quits. From hiatus, Greg Lake was finding new collaborators, and stewing over the biases and distortions that had displaced his sort of music. "The punks were standing in the King's Road in London, dressed in kilts, with their hair greased into spikes," remembered Lake. "They had nothing going for them, they had no motivation. They were rebelling against nothing. Look, if you want to talk about punk bands, let's talk about the Who. That's a real punk band. There's nothing new about the Sex Pistols. What's new about them? Nothing. Absolutely nothing. There was nothing new about punk, except it was crap. It should have been called crap really, because that would have been more honest."[11]

"None of those genres had any musical or cultural or intellectual foundation," continued Lake. "They were all propositions of the media or record-company-stroke-media conspiracies. They were invented by music magazines and record companies talking together—you know, how can we whip up a storm? It was good for both of those entities. It was good for the record company, and it was good for the newspapers, the music press."[12]

THE LAST YES TOUR of the 1970s had ended in disaster. The *Tormato* tour had not. The venues still sold out. Pranks aside, the Yes-in-the-Round setup came off as intended. The critics, though fully committed to punk's rise, had saved their brickbats. Still, when the tour ended, the band found the old energies spent. They started recording new songs in Paris, getting nowhere. After Alan White injured his ankle roller-skating, Jon Anderson and Rick Wakeman found themselves bonding over their shared desire to flee. "After *Tormato* everything started to go horribly wrong because punk was hitting big time and Yes was out of fashion," Wakeman recalled. "Jon and I got paralytic on Calvados in the bar and left. . . . We began crying on each others' shoulders. Jon was saying, 'This isn't the band I loved.'"[13]

Wakeman was bored. Anderson was simply exhausted. Atlantic had laid on hands to change the band's sound, assigning producer Roy Thomas Baker to the Paris sessions. Baker had twirled the knobs for Queen's first four albums; more relevant, he had produced a massive new-wave hit in the eponymous debut album

from the Cars. In his hands, Yes's new music continued the sty-
listic slide from *Tormato*. "Dancing through the Light," one of
a handful of tracks from the sessions, sounded almost nothing
like the band—all processed vocals with Wakeman limited to
a light, plinking melody. "Groups like The Cars and Foreigner
were having big records with sales of eight million," Wakeman
said. "The record company said, 'This is what you've got to do.'
They put us with Roy Thomas Baker as the producer and that
was a complete disaster."[14]

Chris Squire understood why the sound was changing. "Punk
rock had come in while we were doing our mega tours of America," he told author Chris Welch. "It was a good thing for the
evolution of music as a whole but it wasn't the best thing that
could have happened to us at that point."[15]

Yet there was no saving Yes. In March 1980, the split was
official. Jon Anderson and Rick Wakeman were no longer part
of Yes, but there would be no talk of hiatus. Chris Squire had
discovered replacement musicians in the studio next door. The
Buggles were a young new-wave band, consisting of Trevor
Horn on vocals and strings and Geoff Downes on everything
else. Just months earlier, they'd had a transcontinental hit with
the nostalgic, metallic single "Video Killed the Radio Star."

No one would have associated the band with Yes, until Yes up
and did so. "It just so happened that Geoff Downes and Trevor
Horn had come to Brian Lane and asked him to represent them
for management, so they were in our office," Chris Squire told
Welch. "We said, 'Why not get together with us, then?' Trevor
Horn kept saying to me, 'I can't possibly fill Jon Anderson's
shoes.' I used to keep telling him, 'Yes you can, yes you can!' I'd
tell him to go away and sleep on it, and then he'd come back to
me and say, 'You know, you're wrong. I can't do this!' "[16]

Before joining Yes, Horn had taken pains to explain why the

Buggles were not just another new-wave group. "Our records have an intelligence layer in them—they're not just pop pulp," he told *Smash Hits* that winter. "You can take them on a superficial level but there's another layer too. That's something that's been the hallmark of most successful bands, right from the Beatles. And though we have got this synthetic, arranged sound, it still doesn't really come out as total synthesiser music."[17]

Horn had also been a fan of Yes, ever since he'd combined an opportune LSD trip with a listen to a local cover band. He heard "I've Seen All Good People" and was spellbound. "I said to the girl I was with, 'That's fantastic. What a brilliant song.' The girl said, 'That's by a group called Yes. You'd like them. They've got a good bass player.' On Monday I went out and bought *The Yes Album* and more or less played it non-stop for months. It just blew me away. . . . I had started out in dance bands, but I'd never heard a group that was as musical as Yes."[18]

Years later, Horn would play *Tales from Topographic Oceans* to get a feel for the sound in a studio. And like the rest of Yes, he had been left cold by *Tormato*. "Don't Kill the Whale—dig it, dig it? No, I didn't get that. Times were changing, and at that point in time I thought, 'well, that's the end of them.'"[19]

The "Buggle-ized" Yes, as the *Los Angeles Times* called it, was announced in May 1980, and it was strange enough to pique new interest in the band. It was stranger for Downes and Horn. They collaborated instantly with the rest of the band, churning out songs that advanced the style of Yes. Downes was not a virtuoso, like Wakeman, but he had a crisp command of melody. His Fairlight keyboard never noodled; it only provided hooks or countermelodies. Horn's voice, which lacked some of Anderson's high end, was a close-enough simulacrum to avoid any real disruption to the sound. It was the lyrics that changed the most. "White Car," a short almost-instrumental that was sandwiched between two of the band's anthems, had nothing in common with Anderson's old tales of enlightenment. It was about the synthpop star Gary Numan driving a white Stingray. "Trevor saw him driving along one day and he wrote the song about it."[20]

The Buggles-Yes hybrid finished its album, *Drama*, in the spring, at a sprint. Horn, who'd committed himself fully to the project, got married, then drove back to the studio to keep recording. Atlantic gave the album a Roger Dean cover and a worldwide release date of August 18. Eleven days later, the new-old band was headlining in Toronto—to a sold-out stadium crowd. Everything seemed to be in its right place.

"Brian Lane, in his wise way, said, 'Don't tell anyone we've changed the singer and the keyboard player!'" Squire remembered years later, and with no small amount of wryness. "So we just showed up and there were like two different people in the band, and the audiences were saying, 'What's going on?'"[21]

The fan who showed up to hear this iteration of Yes usually heard the entirety of *Drama*, alongside a mélange of hits. Horn and Downes did not change their style at all; instead of Jon Anderson floating around the stage in a kaftan, there was the man from the Buggles, complete with goggle glasses and suit, scaling to play the right notes. During keyboard intermissions, Downes would sprinkle in the hooks from "Video Killed the Radio Star."

On the tour's first leg, the whole thing seemed to jell. Even the snark from critics was tinged with respect. "One tends to think of rock institutions like Yes as unchanging monoliths, and to a considerable extent such groups are trapped by the expectations of their audiences, who come to concerts expecting to relive special moments spent with the band's music," wrote a critic for the *New York Times*. "But since Mr. Downes and Mr. Horn joined Yes, the group's corporately composed music has shown signs of getting more simple structurally and more direct rhythmically."[22]

The band cooperated with the narrative. "I'd say we're more concise and clear now," Steve Howe told one reporter, who naturally was trying to understand the survival of a dinosaur in the era of punk. "The top-line guitar and keyboard concept has changed quite radically, been modernized. Instead of padding and thickening agents, we've gone back to lines much, much more. We're using the orchestral side of Yes much more selectively, limiting the gloss, you might say. Whatever's been leveled at us in the past, we want to be re-judged. We're saying to everybody, 'Yes might have been this, and might have been that, and you might have loved us or hated us, but now we're re-presenting ourselves to you.'"[23]

Rolling Stone was harsher. "Visions of Jon Anderson in his silken sugarplum-fairy robes surely danced in the heads of the 20,000-plus faithful gathered here when Horn—looking pitifully alone on a raised platform in the center of the circular, revolving stage—hit several horribly flat notes during the old Yes song 'Yours Is No Disgrace,'" wrote David Fricke. "In Wakeman, rock's answer to Liberace, Downes had an even tougher act to follow. But he didn't try very hard, playing familiar lines from such Yes hits as 'And You And I' and 'Roundabout' as if he were reading them from an exercise book. His only acknowledgement of the Buggles' success was a snippet of their hit 'Video Killed the Radio Star' in his otherwise inconsequential solo keyboard spot."[24]

Years later, without renouncing the music, Howe would admit the problems with Buggle-ization. They became starker when the American dates ended and the band toured the UK. "The two failings in that version of Yes were that when we came on stage people were quite disappointed that the Jon Anderson larynx wasn't there and that old twiddly fingers Wakeman wasn't there," he said. "We walked in everywhere and seemed to slay them. We did three days at Madison Square Garden in New York with this hodge-podge version of Yes . . . meanwhile, the audiences in England were shouting out 'Jon Anderson—we want Jon!' And then they shouted 'We want Rick!' usually at the most crucial moment. They really did it to us on that tour."[25]

The band knew how this was weighing on Horn. Before one of the band's three-night Newcastle shows, Howe told the singer, "Just imagine this is your dream come true—you are playing and singing in Yes. Just go on and enjoy yourself." Horn was not moved. "Don't you think I've tried everything to make it work for those people?" he asked Howe.[26]

No one was more aware of the limitations—of the unanswerable expectations—than Horn. Chris Squire kept trying to convince him that he sounded exactly like Jon Anderson, but Horn wasn't buying it. "He's got a much higher voice than me, at least three tones higher than mine," said Horn. "The idea of sticking somebody who was a second rate singer, who was really a producer, up front in a band like Yes and sending them out on a 44-date tour of America playing every song in the original key was ludicrous. . . . The opening note in the set was a B, and the highest note I can sing is a B."[27]

England was where the structure finally fell apart. The hecklers were only one problem; they had bought tickets, after all. It was with the newly booked concerts, the ones where Horn and Downes were promised as part of the band, that the sales dropped off. "We got away with it in places where the dates were sold out," said Brian Lane. "Such was the strength of the Yes cult. . . . But when we got to places where they knew about the changes, whereas before we were used to playing to 20,000 people, only 3,000 people showed up."[28]

At the end of 1980, when the tour sputtered out, the five members of Yes huddled and came to a conclusion. They brought Brian Lane forward to break the news. "We've all had a meeting," said Squire. "We've decided that enough is enough, and we've decided to fire you as the manager of Yes."[29]

In Squire's memory, Lane was bristling, unapologetic, and final. "Fine, if that's the way it is," he said. "Yes have peaked so it's a good time to get off the boat. But let me give you some advice. If you are going to continue as Yes, can I suggest that you get down on your hands and knees, kiss Jon Anderson's feet, and beg him to return to the band." Horn interjected. "What am I supposed to do?" "Why don't you become a fucking record producer?" snapped Lane. "Making dumb remarks like that is one of the reasons we're firing you," said Squire.[30]

Lane was out. Yes was effectively finished. But the erstwhile producer would remember how right he was. "Steve Howe and Geoff Downes must have agreed with my thoughts, because a few weeks later they were back in the office with John Wetton and we formed the embryo of Asia," he said. "Carl Palmer joined the band and suddenly I had the first corporate rock band of the Eighties."[31]

AFTER ROBERT FRIPP terminated King Crimson, John Wetton and Bill Bruford walked into the welcoming arms of several other groups. Bruford joined Genesis on tour, freeing up the limbs of Phil Collins as the new singer roamed the stage. Wetton played with Roxy Music; in 1976, when the band went on hiatus, he backed up Bryan Ferry. "People were just coming out of the woodwork," remembered Wetton, "and journalists and people were asking: 'What happened to King Crimson?'"[32]

Wetton and Bruford were not cold to the idea. Near the end of 1976, the two of them collaborated with Rick Wakeman—

then just about to re-join Yes—on new, progressive music. The project never jelled, and Wakeman walked. "We spent six weeks of our lives doing it, and even had photographs done on the set of a James Bond movie," Wetton recalled.[33] "Mercifully," said Bruford, "A&M Records was unwilling to let its 'star,' Wakeman, walk off with a used, slightly soiled King Crimson rhythm section, and the idea folded."[34]

Wetton, undeterred, suggested that the band bring on a fellow late-stage veteran of Roxy Music. Eddie Jobson, who was still just twenty-two years old, had been playing with Frank Zappa after the Roxy hiatus. Bruford dropped another name: Allan Holdsworth. Bruford had collaborated with the progressive jazz guitarist in 1977, when recording his first solo album, and after Holdsworth had recorded with the umpteenth iteration of Gong. "I didn't speak French and they were always arguing in French, so I never knew what the hell they were arguing about," Holdsworth said. "I think the band had a lot of potential; it was just never reached."[35]

Everyone in the Bruford band—which included bassist Jeff Berlin and Canterbury veteran Dave Stewart—spoke English. "The sounds in his [Stewart's] head were hard to realize pre-synthesis, but when the Sequential Circuits Prophet 5 appeared toward the end of the 70s, it was the answer to his prayers," said Bruford—who himself was saving money on drums by using a new pair of RotoToms.[36]

"Allan brought forward this heavy armament, more commonly found in classical composition, as source material for improvisation in rock and jazz groups," Bruford said. "Many was the night you could find Allan, soldering iron in hand, five minutes before the audience was let into the hall, wiring together three complaining amplifiers, their guts spilling out onto the stage."[37]

Wetton greeted the new guitarist with awe. "When he gets

onstage in front of 3,000 people he'll destroy the place."[38] The band set to work on material that could fill arenas, without repeating any previous work. "Collaboration" was not quite the word to describe it. Bruford portrayed the band's writing style as "like four writers all trying to write the same novel simultaneously, with only the barest common understanding of the plot." The recording strategy was "lock the rehearsal room door and . . . fight for what you believe in."[39]

Holdsworth and Bruford were inclined to write experimental, jazz-influenced music. Wetton was not. "From my perspective, it was more of a puzzle than a fight," said Jobson. "We had maybe forty or fifty musical ideas, like jigsaw pieces, and the trick was to piece them all together to make one sonic picture and a cohesive album. John was on the mainstream right, and Allan was on the dissonant left, so they perhaps had to work harder to get their compositional identities voiced. I was lucky in that my compositional style met with the most consensus, most easily."[40]

The music that survived the process was a hybrid—strong melodic hooks, sharing space with long periods of improvisation. *U.K.*, the self-titled debut, began with a three-song suite, titled "In the Dead of Night," that had two recurring themes. In 7/4 time, Wetton laid down a steady bass line. Jobson joined him with fast block chords from the synthesizer. When Holdsworth joined in, gaining power as the song lurched toward his solos, Bruford found places to add percussion flourishes. "The little hole in the bass line was crying out for a rachet," Bruford said.[41]

U.K.'s music thrived on that tension. It was no sequel to King Crimson; it was, as Wetton would reflect, like two bands of equal power fighting for control. And it could not last. After limited touring, and after Wetton considered splitting the band in two, Bruford and the introverted Holdsworth simply left. Wetton recruited new musicians, touring U.K. as a pop-oriented group, but by 1980 it had faded. "Not a nice experience," Holds-worth recalled years later. "Nice chaps and everything. But a very miserable experience."[42]

Wetton followed the U.K. breakup with a solo album, *Caught in the Crossfire*. He was consciously finding a new sound for the 1980s; doing that meant moving even further from the tropes of progressive rock. "In the 1970s the tradition was to take 4 minutes from something I had brought in for King Crimson or UK, take those 3 or 4 minutes and turn them into a complete song," he would say. "Starless is a perfect example: I brought in the first three minutes of the song, and they extended it into 12 minutes. A very similar thing was happening with UK. What I did with 'Caught in the Crossfire'—I cut down 8 minutes of the additional stuff, and just gave you 4 minutes of the song."[43]

The album did not sell, and in early 1981, Wetton met with his manager, John Kalodner, about setting up a new band and began a round of speed dating with musicians who might complement his style. A South African guitarist named Trevor Rabin, whose own solo career was sputtering, didn't click with Wetton. Geoff Downes, now free from the ersatz Yes, was another story. "I saw a great deal of potential in his approach to the keyboard, which was less of a virtuoso," said Wetton, "but more into the textures and quite modern sounds with computers."[44]

Wetton had also been talking with Brian Lane, spitballing with him about the next project. What Lane had in mind was a "supergroup," like U.K.—a designation coined by the press, then irksomely unshakable. His initial vision was for a five-man combo. Atlantic and David Geffen wanted the same thing. "Brian Lane wasn't quite sure that I could cut it, and he was always used to a band having someone who sang and didn't do anything else," claimed Wetton. "His new Yes."[45]

Wetton worked his way into command, but the band came

together in pieces. Guitarists would audition, then Geoff and John would leave in their separate roadsters. They'd pull up alongside each other at traffic lights and give the thumbs down on whoever had auditioned—until Steve Howe came in. Yes's erstwhile guitarist signed up, and then came Carl Palmer, two years free of ELP and looking for something else to do.

The name was decided by committee, after Brian Lane pitched a series of powerful words. "Asia" just clicked. "It looked right," said Wetton. "Four letters, four people; a very symmetrical looking word."[46] Lane fretted over the choice only when he discovered the existence of a small American band that had obviously used the name first.

Lane, according to Wetton, was confident that he was about to launch "the biggest band in the world," and to protect that, he arranged a photo of the four members and a full-page ad in *Melody Maker*. There, among the stories about the new, young, DIY stars of British music, appeared a shot of four progressive rock warhorses, all approaching forty. "This is Asia," read the text. That was it. "It gave us a bit of security, but that's when the 'supergroup' tag started happening," Wetton recalled. "I felt uncomfortable with it. It made me cringe."[47]

The musical direction of the group came from Wetton and Downes, who steered everything toward hooks and melody. The technique of Howe and Palmer, two of the greatest players of their era, was spotlighted without allowing the music to slow down. Of the songs written for the debut album, only a few stretched for more than six minutes. Each was a self-contained pop symphony, in and out, with some time for solos but no structural inventions. "David Geffen was keen on having great musicians playing some commercial music and some prog rock pieces, but obviously a lot shorter," Palmer said. "Asia had exactly that."[48]

Downes was crafting simple, powerful hooks out of his Fair-light. Wetton was conspicuously writing his most personal lyrics ever. "Heat of the Moment," which would become the album's lead single, began in 7/4 time and moved to 4/4 at the chorus. Both Downes and Howe claimed bars as chances to play solos. The lyrics, though, were all nostalgia and romance. Instead of writing for the tropes of progressive rock, Wetton was writing like a folksinger. "Before then, I hadn't been really touched by Joni Mitchell," he would explain. "Everything she does is first person. Up until then, I'd been groping about with abstract stuff. Suddenly, Joni Mitchell hit me right between the eyes and said, 'No, come on. This is your pain. You write about it.' By the time Asia came out, I was writing all first-person lyrics. My transfor-mation was complete. I was the butterfly."[49]

Even with the packaging they took no chances. Roger Dean was commissioned for the cover, and produced a painting of a dragon reeling out of an angry sea, contemplating a magic sphere. "Bless them, John and Geoff really did take the bull by the horns and started writing endless songs," Howe said. "But we could have done it with a few less of them and a few more songs that didn't rest on the keyboard direction."[50]

Critics had already bludgeoned progressive rock with a rusted shovel, and buried it deep under the dirt. In 1982, when Asia's album dropped, the same critics blasted it with all available ammo. "The sound of Asia is as homogeneous and inoffensive as Cream of Wheat," wrote Boo Browning in the *Washington Post*. "Asia is nothing less than a turning-in upon itself of late-'70s commercial cynicism, spawned by the very 'progressive' musi-cians that initiated rock's backslide. It is the autotelic summation of binge/purge radio rock—a winking man's Toto."[51]

The album was critic-proof. "Heat of the Moment" went to number one—the first song to do that in any of the band members' careers. Its video, which interspersed quick shots of the band with on-the-nose illustrations of the lyrics, went into heavy rotation on the nascent MTV. The video revolution was not supposed to elevate the survivors of the 1970s, and yet that's what it was doing. When Asia went on tour, the bricks kept flying.

"In Yes, early King Crimson and Emerson, Lake and Palmer, Asia's members played music full of technical hurdles and symphonic pomp," wrote Jon Pareles in the *New York Times*. "Soon groups like Kansas and Styx picked up on the pomp, minus any experiments. Asia imitates the imitators, inflating conventional pop songs with pseudosymphonic grandeur. While Geoff Downes plays churchy keyboard chords and John Wetton sings in a heavily echoed, humorless tenor, Steve Howe adds the upper-register guitar runs that he brought to Yes. Occasionally, they insert a fast unison passage to remind listeners that they're virtuosos."[52]

"Everyone assumes it's easy to get a hit single," said Wetton, "and, my God, it's possibly one of the most difficult things to do."[53]

IT WAS *NOT* EASY—not necessarily, as Steve Hackett was learning. He had recorded one solo album, *Voyage of the Acolyte*, before leaving Genesis. When he walked out, Charisma kept him on, and went on releasing his work for the better part of a decade. *Please Don't Touch* came in May 1978, with a cover by Hackett's future wife, the artist Kim Poor. It showed toys coming off a shelf to attack an understandably surprised couple.

Vocal duties went to Steve Walsh from Kansas, whose voice one expected to hear with this sort of music. But there was also Richie Havens, as well as Randy Crawford, a soul singer from Georgia who turned an already-soulful song, "Hoping Love Will Last," into a pure love ballad. That sat next to a title track

that liner notes warned, cheekily, was "not to be played to people with heart conditions or those in severely hallucinogenic
states of mind."

"*Voyage* was a bit elitist," Hackett told *Sounds*. "I've really gone
anti-concept. I keep thinking that concept albums require an
explanation sheet with them. You should ideally be able to just
enjoy a piece of music when you're doing the washing-up or
buying a shirt somewhere or in a restaurant or whatever."[54]

The album did not make much of a commercial impact. "Nar-
nia," an obvious single, ran afoul of Kansas's label, which didn't
want Walsh playing out of school. (The cover art fared better,
and according to Poor, it inspired a scene in Ridley Scott's 1982
film *Blade Runner*, in which android toys spring into violent
action.) Charisma kept backing Hackett, but he knew he wasn't
writing commercial music. "Record companies were getting
away from album sensibility and moving more towards singles,"
he said later.[55]

The three-man version of Genesis was having no problems
with that. "Follow You Follow Me" had broken the band in
the US, finally, and put new pressure on the trio to record and
tour. The songs that would make up *Duke*, their first album of
the 1980s, swerved even further into pop. Ambitious music was
still there, and Banks took the lead on a suite of "duke"-themed
compositions that opened and closed the album. Collins, however, wrote another hit, "Misunderstanding," and an even more
searching song of heartbreak titled "Please Don't Ask."

That music had its origins in the collapse of Collins's family
life. "My first wife just didn't understand what I needed to do to
be happy, which is work," he would explain.[56] During the late
'70s, that meant he was away from England for months, which
tested a marriage that had started to fray. While Genesis toured,
Collin's wife Andrea had an affair with a man doing renovations

on their home. "I had an awful lot of songs that were not really Genesis-ey, and songs that if I brought into Genesis would not end up sounding like I wanted them to," Collins told *Melody Maker.* "I played them 'In the Air Tonight' and 'If Leaving Me Is Easy' but it was kind of too simple for the band."[57]

Collins appeared on *Top of the Pops* to promote "In the Air Tonight," sitting behind his keyboard, nearly alone on stage. That framing made an odd stage decoration stick out even more: a splattered paint can, with a brush sticking out. The TV audience got no explanation. Andrea knew what she was seeing: the father of her children shaming her for the affair. "That hurt me more than anything, caused me a lot of pain," Andrea told Collins's biographer, Ray Coleman. "I spoke to him many times about those kinds of comments and he just basically said: 'I'm allowed to do whatever I want. It's artistic license.'"[58] (It was thirty-five years before Andrea finally came out and said that she had not had an affair with the decorator and that the marriage had broken up for other reasons, most of which had to do with Collins himself.[59] And in his own 2016 memoir, Collins denied that the paint can had been placed to convey a message.)

Collins meant nothing by it. In his memoir, three decades later, he bemoaned how a random staging decision had come to haunt him. But it haunted, and hurt, because of what he was quickly becoming. Phil Collins was a pop star.

"Our most difficult moment could have been when *Face Value* [Collins's first solo album] was such a massive success," Tony Banks told *Mojo.* "We were all writing *Abacab* at the time. *Face Value* goes in at 29 and Mike and I think, 'Pretty good.' The next week it's Number Two and you think, 'Oh shit!' No matter how strong your friendship, there is rivalry too. You feel he's transcended the band and you wonder what effect it's going to have. But I think we could take it because we were 30-ish by then. Anyway we carried on joking about how short he is, and that defused it completely."[60]

Hackett became more of a cult figure. The full extent of Hackett's new persona was evident on TV in early 1983, when he appeared on a music show hosted by Rick Wakeman, another virtuoso whose old band was reaching new commercial heights without him. After a jam session, the two of them sat to talk about how they were doing just fine, really. "You went 'round areas in Europe, in eastern Europe, and you broke areas whereas before nobody had ever broken," Wakeman said, helpfully. "I'm always pleased that I can go into a territory where it hasn't been done by Genesis," said Hackett, "and I can walk in there and people say, 'Oh, yes, that's it, yeah. We know this guy; he plays, he sings, you know. It's like, we're not sort of totally concerned with his past.' "[61]

Wakeman knew the feeling. "Do you feel sometimes annoyed that people in this country don't realize that in fact you are bigger in certain eastern European areas than in fact most other bands . . . are at the moment?" he asked. "Um, I dunno," said Hackett. "I've always got the feeling that however a record does, you know, you kinda go out and play in front of people and that's the affirmation of it."[62]

"I did have a hit single at that time, with 'Cell 151,' and there are some things that I'm proud of on that album," remembered Hackett. "But it marked a transition. This was at the time when we started to do things to a click track. At the same time, I wasn't able to work with big budgets. There was a lot of paranoia in the music business at that time. People were so keen on getting a hit single but didn't have a clear idea of what a hit single was. I kept telling people that it's not actually the hit single; it's what goes on around it—how it's being sold by the record company. I think it's possible for record companies, if they want to, to pull out the stops and sell refrigerators to eskimos."[63]

IN AUGUST 1979, shortly before a Frippertronics performance at a Winnipeg art gallery, Robert Fripp sat for an interview about where his music might be heading. There would be a record of his new experimental music—actually several records. "*Frippertronics Volume One: Music for Sports*," Fripp told his interviewers. "Probably be a double album. There is also *Music for Palaces & Kitchens*, which may well be incorporated into that particular double album. But I anticipate it will be a whole series of albums."[64]

The "Drive to 1981" was on, as Fripp toured with his ever-transmogrifying music. At a July 30, 1979, concert, a fan-cum-heckler had yelled for the "Star-Spangled Banner." Fripp responded with a variation on "God Save the Queen," one that left almost no trace of the melody. Over the year, Fripp amassed tapes of these performances; at year's end, he cut them into a surprise album of Frippertronics and other experiments.

God Saves the Queen/Under Heavy Manners was bisected as the title suggested—ambient sounds on the first side, and "discotronics" on the second. The liner notes explained what Fripp was doing more succinctly, and less obliquely, than the many interviews. The tours, he wrote, were a protest against "the general acceptance of rock music as spectator sport, to humour each other's mutual pretensions, egocentricities and conceits."[65]

The music followed from there, without explanation. Discotronics sounded unlike anything Fripp had done before, with "Under Heavy Manners" itself bringing in a new vocalist, David Byrne. The Talking Heads singer winced and emoted through a list of terms, each seemingly unconnected to any other. It was likely the first song to use the terms "cataphatacism" and "apophatacism"—and it used them as a couplet. "The Zero of the Signified" twinned the fluttering Frippertronic sound with a danceable 4/4 beat.

What did it mean? The music press handled the question gingerly. No one was making music like Fripp—not even Eno—but the direction was hard to figure. "Discotronics is defined as that musical experience resulting at the interstice of Frippertronics and disco," explained Fripp in the sleeve. "True, you can dance to it," wrote Michael Davis in *Creem*. "Big deal, you can dance to a lot of things, from eggbeaters to washing machines."[66]

Where to run with that? Fripp had been talking about the idea of a "mobile unit" for music—what less contemplative types might call a "band"—during much of his return. In March 1980, he announced the first such unit as the League of Gentlemen. Barry Andrews, who had just left the postpunk group XTC, came on as a keyboard player who owed nothing to progressive rock. No one in the band did. "It is very difficult to play Frippertronics to drunk people at rock 'n' roll clubs," Fripp told one interviewer. "The League of Gentlemen works from outside the music inward, while [Frippertronics] works from the inside outwards."[67]

Fripp biographer Eric Tamm described just how much the guitarist was able to innovate when the songs were boiled down. "Cognitive Dissonance," a song that began with a standard pop beat, was his example. "The organ presents a harmonic entity based on the augmented triad Gb-Bb-D, over drums and bass," wrote Tamm. "Fripp's guitar enters playing a broken Gb dominant seventh chord with added flatted third—Fripp's beloved major/minor ambiguity. The harmony shifts systematically to $Bb7$ and then to $D7$, as it were developing the implications in the original augmented chord."[68]

Still, this was Fripp's first touring band in six long years, longer than King Crimson itself had existed. And this, by intention, was nearly a parody of a band. When it got to New York, Fripp introduced the band with patter as far away from rock standards as possible. "Welcome to the League of Gentlemen," he said. "This is another improbable event, full of hazard. We suggest that you listen and dance simultaneously."[69]

The crowd had been warmed up already by a largely unknown act—one with a pedigree. GaGa was led by guitarist and singer Adrian Belew, who'd just come off a tour with David Bowie, and who before that had been part of Frank Zappa's band. The rangy Tennessean had a clear, Lennon-esque voice, and a technique that thrived on experimentation.

"One of the best things I took away musically was to take a piece of music and treat it so many different ways, from arranging and rearranging," Belew said. "In the three months time that we did very intense rehearsals—five days a week, eight hours a day—of Frank's music, he would often take something that we'd already learned and say, okay, now, we're going to do it this way. Completely different arrangement. Different instrumentation. Different style. I watched him do that over and over again. That was very important to me."[70]

David Byrne was in the audience for one of these shows. Belew soon found himself playing the role that Fripp had played so briefly: the experimental lead guitarist for Talking Heads. A world was opening up for Belew, and Chris Blackwell of Island offered him a record deal of his own. But Fripp had been watching Belew for years. He had seen him with Bowie, playing the parts from "Heroes" that Fripp had written in Berlin. They'd talked for the first time when the three of them—Belew and Bowie together, Fripp separately—took an off day to see Steve Reich at the Bottom Line.

The League of Gentlemen fell apart at the end of 1980—

accidentally, yet almost on schedule with Fripp's Drive to 1981.
There was energy, and purpose, and he recognized it. "I decided
to have a go at a first division band," he would tell *Creem*, introducing another concept into the lexicon. "King Crimson had
never died, in the sense that the interest in the band is still
out there, probably greater than when we were first playing,
and also, this is hard to get across, it looks a bit silly in print, I
think. . . . I became aware of the iconic aspect of King Crimson,
that there was a potential energy there, that was kind of hovering behind the band and that was available to us if we wanted to
plug into it."[71]

Fripp did not set out to reunite King Crimson, but the first
recruitment he made was Bill Bruford. He was lucky, taking
accidental advantage of Bruford's faltering tour with National
Health. The drummer, who had parted with Fripp on such
seemingly capricious terms, was on board when Talking Heads
reached England and Belew was summoned for a conversation.
They cut a deal—Belew could make solo records while in the
band—and the new unit was a trio.

That started the search for a bassist—one who would have to
pass an unusual test. Before the band had come together, Fripp,
Bruford, and Bruford's bassist Jeff Berlin had knocked together
a complicated piece of music. "Jeff and I had written this lovely
ostinato in 17/16," recalled Bruford, "and Robert was sitting on
the sofa, and said: 'I've got something that could go with that.'"[72]
That became "Discipline," an intricate song that incorporated
looping techniques through traditional instruments. The next
bassist had to play that. "Robert and I set up in a rehearsal room
and a line rapidly formed around the block," recalled Bruford.
"We auditioned them with 'Discipline' on the grounds that, if
they could play that, they'd probably be all right. After about an
hour of this, Robert announced he was leaving."[73]

Another day of rehearsals came, and ended, with no optimism.

On the third day came Tony Levin. "The afternoon with Tony was one of the best musical experiences of my life," Fripp told biographer Sid Smith. "Bill was showing TL a rather difficult 9/8, grouped 5 and 4. Tony had it before Bill completed the sentence. Adrian was trying to remember some queer accents BB had shown as rhythm shots on top of the 9/8, which we had worked on the day before. TL played them as well as his own part, to make them clearer for Adrian! And TL, who had never heard 'Larks Tongues in Aspic II' in his life, played it in spirit perfectly."[74]

This was when "Discipline" fell away as the name of the new project. "In the first week of rehearsal," Fripp told *Creem*, "I knew the band I was hearing. There was no doubt that the band playing was King Crimson."[75]

JON ANDERSON WAS COPING with the separation from Yes. In short order he sought out Vangelis, whom he warmly remembered trying to court for the band when Wakeman originally quit. "I saw photographs of him playing four or five keyboards at the same time, and laser beams behind him," Anderson would recall. "It was unbelievable. I had to meet this guy." When he did, Vangelis greeted the singer in "a kaftan way down to the floor and a big bow and arrow around his shoulders and arrows coming out of a quiver," displaying archery before he got down to the music. But he was game for an audition—and promptly blew it. Anderson remembered Vangelis making rounds with the group and deciding this was the perfect time to razz Steve Howe. "You know, Steve, electric guitar?" Anderson recalled Vangelis saying. "Not a real instrument."[76]

So, Anderson turned to Patrick Moraz, but he never stopped working with Vangelis. In his postprog life, the Greek had become a purely instrumental composer, pulling electronic sounds out of electronic instruments, rather than approximating anything classical. The post-Yes sessions at the Greek genius's Nome studios consisted, according to both men, of improvisation.

"With Jon, we never talk," Vangelis would say. "We work in a very spontaneous way. This is something I like. Also, we don't plan anything, so it makes it better."[77]

Anderson and Vangelis recorded at a steady clip; the emergent music was shimmering and harmless. The new-age ethos of Anderson seemingly found its match, and the singles did what Yes had stopped doing: they cracked the top 10. That success helped Vangelis reconnect with David Puttnam, a film producer who wanted the artist to record a soundtrack for his film. *Chariots of Fire*, a somber drama about two British athletes who make it to the 1924 Olympics, had been scored to more generic electronic music. Vangelis replaced that with colors from his synthesizer, trying to evoke athleticism through sweeping chords. "What I see creates an emotion which comes out immediately," he told a biographer. "It may be the right one—the first one. The second and third are much more intellectual in approach, which is second best."[78] The 1981 *Chariots of Fire* score won Vangelis an Oscar, which he did not fly to Hollywood to accept.

Daevid Allen, as usual, took the opposite path. Like Fripp, he had decamped to New York and relocated there to find whatever Gong had been lacking. "My old ally Giorgio Gomelsky had set up a Mani-festival whereby he sought to combine European progressive rockers with the No Wave movement and take Manhattan by storm," said Allen. "In the UK and Europe I had been vaguely aware that New York was experiencing its own punk and then postpunk movement, but my first visit to the Mud Club in 1979 gave the impression that the real gutsy dangerous UK punk movement was being emulated as a pale fashion statement more than a genuine dance with destruction."[79]

One result of Allen's latest meandering was "New York Gong," a collaboration with the bassist Bill Laswell. For the first time, the forty-two-year-old singer was spitting lyrics about aging and feeling out of touch. The psychedelia had been tacked back completely; the new music sped along the rails of 4/4 time and looping bass lines. It departed from the rest of the "No Wave" movement only because Allen said it did. "Yes Wave was a pataphysical reaction to the No Wave club," said Allen. "I never liked joining men's clubs."[80]

GENESIS WAS NOT WINNING awards. It was not repeating any themes from the progressive years. It was still being savaged by critics. "We were supposed to have been killed off by punk," recalled Tony Banks, "and yet we were bigger than ever. And at that point our press just became terrible."[81]

Gabriel had avoided that trap. "Peter was on a journey," recalled Larry Fast, who had played and programmed synthesizers since the start of Gabriel's solo career. "One of the things that became apparent was that his solo career would not be a new version of Genesis. We studiously avoided doing things like bring mellotrons on the road with Peter, because he wanted to establish that break." Fast saw the distinction when Gabriel covered "A Whiter Shade of Pale," Procol Harum's song from the start of the progressive era. In Gabriel's hands, the gossamer fell away, revealing a pure rock song, something modeled after the music he'd heard in New York. "Peter was really just ripping his vocals to shreds," Fast said. "My wrists got really tired playing all those sixteenth notes. Part of what he was doing was mocking the song; part of it was trying to understand it."[82]

In the studio, alongside Fripp and then alongside producer Hugh Padgham, Gabriel was producing more experimental music that was less complicated than anything produced by Genesis. His third album, self-titled like the first two, began with the song "Intruder." A drum loop announced the beginning of the song—drums, and no cymbals. There was no showing off, no use of explosives. Gabriel's former bandmates heard it, and were compelled. "We had already been talking about how much we liked the John Bonham drum sound on Led Zeppelin's 'Kashmir,' and this was even more John Bonham than John Bonham," said Tony Banks.[83] "I wasn't surprised when he started getting into African rhythms," said Mike Rutherford. "Peter has always been a frustrated drummer and he was very rhythmically aware."[84]

Hugh Padgham was tapped for Genesis's next album, *Abacab*, which would veer between pure pop and jokes at the expense of other musical trends. "Who Dunnit?" was an unsubtle joke at the punk trend. When the band debuted it at a Dutch concert, it was blown back by hecklers. "They genuinely disliked the new approach," said Collins.[85] "The band wore silly hats," recalled Banks. "I'd put on a little snorkel and play a Prophet Five keyboard specially tuned just for that one song."[86]

Gabriel, who had dialed down the stage act, was being given more credit for the music. In 1980 he founded the World of Music, Arts and Dance (WOMAD) festival, booking the Royal Bath & West Showground in Shepton Mallet, England, for the debut. It had been the site of the 1970 Bath Festival of Blues and Progressive Music; in 1982, the venue would showcase international acts, curated by Gabriel.

That was not yet enough to foot the bills. With obvious reluctance, Gabriel agreed to an autumn reunion gig with Genesis in the town of Milton Keynes. "The motivation is to pay off the WOMAD debts," he explained. "For me, um . . . I think I will enjoy it but having tried for seven years to get away from the image of being ex-Genesis there's obviously a certain amount of stepping back." Sixty-five thousand people showed up to hear the band. "It was odd," said Tony Banks, "and not as good musically as we had been used to."[87]

In the next years, Gabriel did not cast a glance back at the old group. He went to work on a fourth solo album, working again with Larry Fast, and using the only Fairlight synthesizer in the country. "His music sounds like he's serving penance for the impurity and decay of the entire western world," grumbled Gavin Martin in *NME*. "What are we going to do with these arthouse bores?"[88]

Martin's commentary was cruel but not wrong. Gabriel was winning new respect in the art house. The release of that album was celebrated by the *South Bank Show*, a TV program that filmed months of recording sessions and gave Gabriel time to explain what he was inventing. The artist, according to a narrator, was out to "revitalize what he and many others see as the limited range of rock, by looking outside Europe and America."[89]

The show began as the album began, with the shuffling beat of "The Rhythm of the Heat." Gabriel stared into the camera, face framed by headphones, dressed in a gray blazer, eyes hard and fixated on the interloper. He spat out the first wordless scream of the song, face contorting and then collapsing back into a smile. This song had originally been titled "Jung in Africa," after Gabriel read Carl Jung's *Memories, Dreams, Reflections*. "I love the idea of this guy who shaped a lot of the way we think in the West, who lives in his head and in his dreams, suddenly getting sucked into this thing that he can't avoid," said Gabriel, "where he has to let go of control completely and feels that he has become possessed in a way, not by a devil but by this thing which is bigger than him."[90]

10

NEO-PROG

T he progressive rock revival had come to Glasgow, and didn't it seem like it was time? Phil Bell, a reporter for *Sounds*, found himself at the Dial Inn to review a band whose name was two-thirds of a J. R. R. Tolkien reference: Marillion. "This neo-progressive upsurgence thingy ain't hype, y'know, but something that's being generated by public interest," wrote Bell. "The age of exaggerated musical agility is back."[1]

Marillion, a five-man combo playing small venues, had resurrected the spectacle of progressive rock, at scale and with no visible signs of irony. It was 1982, yet here was Fish—just Fish. He was a towering Scotsman—six foot five—with echoes of Peter Gabriel when he rose from a shout to a yelp. He was acting out songs that stretched to about ten minutes. "Forgotten Sons" was a standout, starting fast and then slowing as it gained mass, a guitar and a keyboard trading melodies.

Bell captured some of this, then apologized to readers, for words could not quite capture the feeling of "Forgotten Sons" being acted out. He could only try.

I'll only say that it thickens and heightens in vigour until everything blacks out and enigmatic frontman Fish, all alone, says in a deathly macabre atmosphere: "Halt! Who goes there? Death (echoed whisper). Approach . . . friend." Then everything explodes brite-white-lites-on-crowd etc., into giant ending, blah-blah—got it? Classic stuff. It's in "Forgotten" too that the highly visual aspect of the gig climaxes. Startlingly face-painted Fish dons fatigue jacket and helmet and, transforming his mike-stand into a machine-gun, proceeds to "mow down" his audience (firing tuned in to Mick Pointer's rat-a-tatting drumming). Ending the performance, he mimes the soldier blowing his own brains out.[2]

It had been years since a band needed to be explained in this way. "This drama excepted," wrote Bell in a caveat, "Fish is less prop/costume dependent than Peter Gabriel."[3] He was a head over six feet tall, covering himself in face paint, the design changing from show to show.

Where—where had this come from? It had come from Buckinghamshire. There, in 1977, a kid named Mick Pointer had become the drummer for a group called Electric Gypsy, whose music drew "upon such bands as Camel and Genesis." As Martin Jenner recalled, "The Genesis influence came with things like song construction and, most notably, offbeat timings."[4]

Electric Gypsy worked but did not last. Around 1978, after a string of disappointing gigs, they splintered. Pointer and bassist Doug Irvine formed the nucleus of a new group, courting new members to keep it going. Their first get was Steve Rothery, an acolyte of David Gilmour and Steve Hackett.[5] "It was obvious I was in a similar area of music to them," he said. "Pink Floyd, Genesis, Camel—but not Rush."[6]

By the end of 1980, the band had started to build a reputation. Progressive covers were in the set; so were fresh, ambitious
songs, unlike the rest of what made it onto radio. But Irvine was
out, having pledged to succeed by age twenty-five or hightail
it away. In December, an ad went into the magazine *Musicians
Only*: "Competent bassist/vocalist required for established progressive rock group with own material."

That ad made it to a Scottish bassist, William Minnitt, nick-
named "Diz"—as in "come here diz minnit." He sent Marillion
a tape of his friend Derek William Dick, who slathered on face
paint and went by the stage name Fish. Marillion invited the pair
down, but upon arrival, the two scoffed at the idea of audition-
ing. "Bugger the audition," Minnitt recalled thinking. "We're
here and that's that."[7]

In no time at all, Marillion absorbed the 1,000-watt personality of Fish. One plus was that he tightened rehearsals and had
a knack for conceptual lyrics that bent readily into the music.
Another plus was the stage show. "I recall a gig at the White
Hart in Bletchley where there was a handful of disinterested
drunks in the audience offering low level grumbling abuse,"
recalled Minnitt. "Fish dealt with it by using the opportunity to
accentuate the inclusive nature of his stage performance and per-
cussively beat time on one of their heads with the tambourine.
Needless to say the verbal abuse stopped."[8]

The bet was that Marillion could overcome any resistance
from the industry by melting the audience from the stage. The
bet was right. "We started in March 1981, that was when we
started gigging, and by October we had rejection slips from
every single record company in Britain, including EMI," Fish
told the *New Musical Express*. "Everyone told us, this style of
music is dead, ten minute songs are out the window. We went,
fuck you."[9]

This was the sort of language that John Lydon (a.k.a. Johnny Rotten) used to dismiss the progressive rock movement. In its crudeness, the phrasing marked something necessary and new. Marillion represented a "neo-progressive" movement that the industry didn't seem ready for. Neo-prog arose as the first-wave bands moved further into pop. Genesis, without Peter Gabriel, was becoming one of the world's most successful bands; Peter Gabriel, without Genesis, was becoming an icon for listeners who would never tuck *Foxtrot* under their arms.

In November 1981, after more than seventy gigs, Marillion added Mark Kelly on keyboards. "Fish would spend all day on the phone, ringing up different clubs," said Kelly. "Eventually we were doing three or four gigs a week, which was pretty good for a band that nobody wanted to book."[10]

It was jarring to everyone who witnessed it; progressive rock, obviously, was supposed to be defunct. "Everyone said then that the music Yes did in the Seventies was dead," said Rick Wakeman. "What came along? The gap was filled by Marillion." When Fish himself got a chance to meet Wakeman, he pronounced the disappearance of progressive rock and Yes's rebirth as a pop act to be "crazy." "Yes are our idols," said Fish. "If they're not gonna do that anymore, well, we're gonna carry on doing it."[11]

WHAT MADE MARILLION's appearance so unexpected, so perplexing to taste makers, was Wakeman's observation. The first wave of progressive acts had either vanished or changed their sound completely. It was easy to portray Fish as a successor to Peter Gabriel, because Gabriel had so definitively buried the costumed era of his career. A new Yes had an obvious hole to fill; the old Yes was supplanted by the Trevors, Rabin and Horn. That created a small opening for bands tagged as prog revivalists. "Many journalists' attitude was, we buried all that Genesis stuff in the '70s," said Peter Gee of the band Pendragon. "The last thing we want is for it to come back."[12]

The bands that had transformed into arena fillers weren't winning the critics either. It hardly mattered. Genesis had become a group of hit makers, fame rising in tandem with Phil Collins's. They had not abandoned the experiments; their 1983 self-titled album began with "Mama," its menacing drum track (run through an echo machine) and cackling hook (based, said Collins, on Grandmaster Flash's laugh on his song "The Message") made it sound like the darker side of Collins's "In the Air Tonight." But the hit was "That's All," an "almost Beatle-ish" pop song, according to Tony Banks.[13]

"When Phil started writing lyrics they were coming straight from the center of his heart," said Hugh Padgham, the coproducer of Genesis's early-1980s work. "Your old-school Genesis fan will say that the era I came in on—and I hope they will not necessarily blame me—destroyed Genesis, because when I started working with the band their songs became shorter, more understandable, and subsequently more commercial, and a lot of people thought that the commerciality was selling out. But certainly up until I started working with them, they were still on the bones of their arse financially speaking."[14]

Collins was swiftly becoming one of the biggest stars on Earth, continuing on the lush pop songwriting path that had fit uneasily with the old Genesis. "In America, on the late-night radio, you'd often end up chatting and smoking dope with the DJs," Mike Rutherford recalled. "With the birth of MTV, promo became a bigger and bigger part of our lives until eventually we seemed to spend more time in TV studios than we did onstage."[15]

By the mid-1980s, Genesis was one of the world's major

touring bands. There were no costume changes or DIY light tricks; the new audiences included fans who had never seen that iteration of the band, or didn't care to. The shows, said Banks, "became less distinctive because you are playing endless arenas and stadiums. The very early shows when we were playing to three people in Beaconsfield always stick more strongly."[16]

But when the band seemed to be left behind Collins, there were sore feelings. In 1985, on a hiatus between albums, Rutherford was working in AIR Studios with a series of singers, for what would become the first Mike + the Mechanics album— pure pop, with hit potential. Collins, who had drummed on Band Aid's "Do They Know It's Christmas?" was invited to fill an expanded, historic role at the charity group's Live Aid concert. The concert spread to two venues, in London and Philadelphia. Collins would play in London, race to a Concorde jet, and hustle to Philadelphia's stage. Genesis had not been invited at all. "It was one of those events that became Phil's thing and not ours," said Banks. "I didn't even see it on TV. I felt all the time that we should be there. I just didn't want to watch it."[17]

That was a speed bump, as the improbable superstardom journey that had begun with "Follow You Follow Me" continued. Mike + the Mechanics were produced to a keen pop sheen, with guest vocalists like Paul Young handling Rutherford's 4/4 swingers. "All I Need Is a Miracle" contained no vestiges of progressive rock but cracked the top ten. And in the studio again, the band was producing such hooky material that Collins worried about repetition. "Well, we won some Grammies," said Padgham. "It can't be wrong." It was a tossed-off line, but it stuck with Collins. "Doubt is a good thing," he said. "It makes you try harder, while complacency is the worst thing you want."[18]

There was experimentation in Genesis's next album, *Invisible Touch*: a metallic instrumental called "The Brazilian," and

Banks's multipart meditation on war, "Domino." There were also tremendous hit singles. "*Invisible Touch* was the first album where we suddenly felt that we were going to have a hit whatever we did," said Banks. "That may be a bad thing to think, but that's what we thought."[19]

Asia, less a family than a factory-assembled machine, struggled to remain on top. "In the 1970s, everybody was happy to develop an artist and you were allowed to have a first album that did OK, and a second that did a little bit better and, by the fourth or fifth album, you were starting to make money," said John Wetton. "In the 1980s, you weren't allowed to do that."[20]

The rapid success of the band's eponymous first album had sped up the treadmill. "We fell into the category of about six bands that MTV decided they were going to push that year—that included Duran Duran, the Police, and Def Leppard," said Wetton. "People would recognize me walking down the street. It was quite good fun because it happened in America. It didn't happen in England. In England, we were regarded as another prog rock band, plus there was no such thing as MTV in Britain at the time."[21]

Again, the critics rose up in protest. This time they got more of a hearing: the album's sales were slower, with no breakout single. "We could have toured for another year on that first album," said Wetton. But everyone was very keen to do the same thing again; to get another payday. Everything went smoothly until the cycle of the first album was done."[22]

The problems had been visible in the recording studio. The band moved on to Quebec, Canada, which had a studio (and more forgiving tax laws) waiting for them. "We lost that feeling of a band that we had at first," said Geoff Downes, "that 'we're going to succeed at this and we're going to stick together.' "[23]

The band finished recording with "Don't Cry," a slice of

schlock that immediately went top ten. But as they toured the material, they stared out at empty seats. "We'd been booked into all these huge halls and outdoor shows because we were too big to play the little theaters anymore," said Wetton. "And we went to Toledo and only sold about 2,500 tickets in a 15,000-seat arena. America goes in primary, secondary, and tertiary markets. When you get beyond tertiary, you're playing Amish villages. . . . The longer you're around, the easier it is to sell out the big cities than it is to sell out the smaller cities. It takes longer to filter through. And Toledo was a big reminder that we hadn't filtered through at all."[24]

"The guys in Asia were older than other acts who were breaking on MTV, and that showed in their videos," said John Kalodner, who had helped get the project going. "They had the biggest-selling record of 1983, but they quickly became unhip."[25]

There was no obvious solution, but Brian Lane came up with one anyway. MTV was producing *Asia in Asia*, a concert film about the band's hopefully triumphant arena show in Japan—and one-quarter of the band had walked. Wetton, who was showing signs of strain already, would be replaced.

Greg Lake, who had recorded a solo album that was all bright choruses and soft corners, got a phone call from Carl Palmer, asking for a favor. Lake's first thought was that Palmer needed to borrow a guitar.

"I wonder if you could play with Asia for a couple of weeks in Japan because we've just fallen out with John Wetton," said Palmer. "We don't have a singer and the shows are booked."

"Oh dear, oh dear. When are the shows?" asked Lake.

"It's in three weeks time," said Palmer.

"You can't be serious, man. I couldn't do it in three weeks," said Lake.

"We have to do it," said Palmer.[26]

Lake, like a growing portion of the universe, considered Asia "corporate rock" and uninteresting to play. But he suited up and went to Japan, with MTV's editors explaining away the switch in a quick voice-over and a shot of Lake exiting a plane. "I should have been suspicious at this point because they filmed me walking down the corridor to the plane," Wetton said. "There was no one else in the frame at all; just me walking down the corridor to the departure gate. And they showed me gazing wistfully through the glass at the Detroit airport. They convinced me that the rest of my part was going to be done later. What I would do was walk down the corridor and say 'see you later,' and suddenly appear in Japan somewhere."[27]

"I was expelled from the group in a Machiavellian conspiracy," Wetton claimed, years later. "Management and the record company combined to oust me 'for personal reasons.' They said I drank too much. True. That I was arrogant. True. That I wasn't a team player. True. But did I deserve to be expelled from the group that I started? No. Would the public accept this blatant travesty? No."[28]

But Lane had his way. "I did it as a favor to Carl," Lake recalled to the journalist Anil Prasad. "They had apparently booked this 747 jet to take contest winners of an MTV competition to the shows and none of it could be cancelled, so the thing had to go on."[29]

Unlike the hiccups with Asia, Brian Lane's other project was humming, even after being reconfigured in the same manner as Asia. The deconstructed Yes did not quite come apart. Chris Squire and Alan White continued to work on material, and for Christmas 1981 they released a single, "Run with the Fox," which went nowhere.

They were still working in 1982 when the South African guitarist Trevor Rabin sent a demo to Atlantic Records. Phil Carson, the label manager, informed Rabin that he could collaborate with a duo of Jack Bruce and Keith Emerson, the rump of Yes. "From a selfish point of view," said Rabin, "I thought, 'What I really need is a great rhythm section.'"[30]

Squire was skeptical. The first he'd heard of Rabin was the soothsaying of Brian Lane, who as early as 1979 had been trying to sell him on a talented young South African by giving him another demo tape. "The guy played and sang everything on it and it sounded just like the last Foreigner album prior to that time, whatever it was," said Squire.[31]

To the mutual surprise of the musicians, something was clicking. Rabin had several strong melodies, and the one that carried was "Owner of a Lonely Heart," with a nagging, rising five-note bass line. Rabin had written it during a trip to the bathroom, but it worked. The ensemble brought in Tony Kaye, so unceremoniously replaced by the old Yes a decade earlier. This was a different time; bouncing block chords no longer sounded so bad. "We wanted it to be more modern-sounding," said Kaye. "We wanted to appeal to an audience that the Police and the new Genesis would appeal to. It couldn't just be old Yes and the same old dirge, yet at the same time we knew that it mustn't sound like Styx or Journey."[32]

Trevor Horn went into the producer's booth, mixing the songs for the new band: Cinema. "Owner of a Lonely Heart" took on more heft and more humor after Horn programmed a series of James Brown screams into a Fairlight keyboard and banged the keys.

After a few months, the band nearly fell apart again. Kaye left the group over the technical aspects of the songs. "Tony is a great Hammond player," said Rabin, "but we were getting involved with Fairlight computers, the Synclavia, and there was a whole area of technology that Tony didn't know enough about."[33]

Carson, who was putting out any fire that sprang up, suggested a radical remedy. The new material was strong and hit the marks they'd set when they decided to crack the Genesis/Police formula. But a fractious Cinema would not be the best delivery system for the music. The band needed Jon Anderson; it needed to become a new Yes. "To be frank, if it was going to sell, it had to be a Yes album," said Phil Carson. "Trevor Rabin wasn't used to being a front man for a serious rock band. He couldn't cut it and they needed somebody good. So Jon came back in again, while Rabin did harmonies and some lead vocals."[34]

Squire had not spoken to Anderson since he'd quit the band, at the end of the previous decade. He was dispatched to share the new music and make the pitch. Ostracized by Anderson's wife, Squire drove to the singer's house anyway, and coaxed Anderson into the car to play him the songs. Anderson was back, and on board with the mission. "It was imperative, coming back after such a load of shit, that Yes have a single," Horn said.[35]

"Owner of a Lonely Heart" did everything that Atlantic asked for. It shot to number one on the *Billboard* pop chart, the first and only time Yes would land there, almost fifteen years into its existence. The label shot an evocative video that barely featured the band at all; one version actually began with a goof, as the new-new Yes plunked through the song, looking as out of time as Asia had. The video suddenly froze, and Anderson, in a voice-over, announced that the band would "try something different."

The single led off *90125*, the anonymous title—based on the expected Atlantic catalogue number—that replaced "The New Yes Album." "I wanted to make something more of an experi-ence in music," said Anderson. "I wasn't really creating that with Trevor and the guys."[36]

After his cameo with Asia, Greg Lake lacked that kind of direction. So did Keith Emerson, to his frustration. He had com-posed scores for a run of action films, but by 1984 the work had dried up. It had been six years since ELP's three-way divorce;

Emerson informed Polygram that he was ready and raring for a solo project, carrying on the sort of work he'd loved. "I've been speaking with Greg," said Jim Lewis, a vice president at the label. "Why don't you do these with him?"[37]

It was not the chemistry of 1970, but it was a deal. Emerson and Lake were back together, each adding to the other's music, but with no intent of reuniting ELP. But Polygram liked what it heard. In just six years, the technology of Emerson's music had altered dramatically. The Moog, for all of its theatricality, had been replaced by a Yamaha GX-1, a Hammond C-3, and a Kurzweil K250—a smaller setup with vastly more options.

Polygram wanted a new band. With Palmer on contract, the Lake-Emerson duo recruited Cozy Powell, a journeyman British drummer. The jokes told themselves—here was ELP, with an all-new "P"—and Emerson couldn't stand it. "We do not refer to ourselves as ELP," he told a journalist. "We are Emerson, Lake, and Powell."[38]

Indeed, they didn't; the Emerson, Lake & Powell album was released under that name, the old and iconic logo left behind at some Manticore rummage sale. "The Score" was the album's epic track, and "Touch and Go" was its single. Both shone a different hue from anything that had appeared under the ELP name. "In the 'old days,' Emerson would have launched into a gonzo synth solo over the underlying chord progression of the verse," wrote ELP scholar Edward Macan in an analysis of "The Score." Instead, Emerson was playing sustained chords.[39]

Critics, who were skeptical of the idea that this was not a cash-in, found it easy to punch around the album. "These guys are literally the only ones left in 1986 who still have the balls to serve up vintage crap like this," wrote *Rolling Stone*. "Pomp fans shouldn't worry; the short ones have just as much hot air as the long ones."[40]

The ELPowell tour did not go well. In San Antonio, they got three thousand at a venue where ZZ Top had gotten fifteen thousand. Emerson took that as an affront. "It's bordering on impudence that a simple band like that can draw so much more people than we can," he said.[41]

The corporate birth of Emerson, Lake & Powell gave way to a very corporate breakup. "By the time it came to making a second album, there wasn't any money left," said Emerson. "And Greg said, 'Well, if there isn't any money left, and Polygram isn't interested in putting any more money up, I'm not interested.' And, of course, Cozy was being offered jobs and he got fed up with the indecisions and said, 'I'm leaving.'"[42]

The three of them returned to side projects, picking up largely where they'd been before the quasi reunion. It was important to Emerson, and difficult, that he move faster than the pace of musical change. "I really need to get my own identifiable sounds again now that I've lost the GX-1," said Emerson. "It's like Eric Clapton's guitar; nobody sounds like that."[43]

KEVIN AYERS HAD less to do, and less of a stated interest in doing it. "Between the ages of 17 and 40 I had a great time, no grounds for complaint whatsoever," Ayers said in 1992. "My problem is just that I don't know what to do with the rest of my life."[44]

The 1980s found Ayers back in Spain, where he would stay, occasionally recording a new album through a lazy haze of alcohol. In 1983 he released a new collection of songs titled *Diamond Jack and the Queen of Pain*. The closing track, "Champagne and Valium," imagined a series of distracted scenes, including a visit to a worried doctor. "Can't taste no wine if you don't drink," Ayers sang. Years later, he would admit that he could not remember recording the album.

In 1987, Ayers reconnected with Mike Oldfield for what would be Ayers's last stab at the charts for the rest of the century. "He liked to enjoy life, take it easy and not take things too seriously," said Oldfield in 2013. "Unfortunately, his attitude was not suited to being tremendously successful in the music business, in which you do need a lot of drive, savvy and street smarts. If you don't have those things, there are so many people who either take advantage of you or don't listen to what you have to say because you didn't sell enough albums the last time out."[45]

The product of the Ayers-Oldfield reunion was "Flying Start," an evocative pop song with lyrics that referred forlornly to Ayers's career. "You lost your dream in a bottle of wine," Ayers sang. The chorus included a cheeky reference to the early times: "Made the Whole World sing, they had no choice."

The album cracked the top forty, as did the single. In 1988, a revised version of "Flying Start" appeared on Ayers's *Falling Up*, a clearheaded comeback album. But that was all he did, for years. "In the 1960's he was lovable, passionate, a brilliant compulsive songwriter and driven to succeed," said Daevid Allen. "In the 1970's after the Soft Machine tours in the US, he had become damaged, domineering, and self-centered. After that he was nervy, extremely abrupt, impatient, and highly sensitive to the quirks of Murphy's law, which in the performance space appear at every turn. Sadly for me, who loved him deeply, he had become almost impossible to work with."[46]

ON AUGUST 25, 1982, Marillion signed with EMI. There would be no change in style and no obvious search for a single. The proof that none was necessary came whenever the band played live. At that summer's Reading Festival, Marillion was low on the bill, sandwiched between comfortable, identifiable heavy metal groups. "We were showing our influences maybe a little too clearly," shrugged Rothery. "It was clumsily done, but it was sincere. It wasn't done to be pompous."[47]

The Reading set sounded like no one else. There were moments when Rothery's guitar supplied only colors. "He Knows You Know" asked an audience of metalheads to meditate on a dark story of addiction, the only solace coming from a swinging keyboard hook.

Marillion's lineup, now set, was confident in its talent and its approach to music. Under the trappings of old progressive rock, there was rawness, postmodern honesty. "Script for a Jester's Tear" was inspired by a Fish breakup. "When I was doing the vocal I actually cried in the studio, it hit me that bad," he told an interviewer.[48]

"There were plenty of similar bands around," said Mark Kelly. "The difference was that the lyrics and musical content were always more important to us than how much we could show off. We weren't in the same instrumental caliber as Yes or ELP. But we knew how to construct a song, whereas I don't think ELP have ever written a song in their lives."[49]

Still, Marillion trusted its sound to one of the elite group of producers who could connect them to the first stirrings of progressive rock. David Hitchcock, who had produced their favorite Genesis records, said he was ready to go, and ready to shake up his approach for the 1980s. David "said he would do anything to avoid getting a sound like Genesis or Camel," Fish said.[50]

"Script for a Jester's Tear," the opening and title track from the album, leaned into everything that had been judged and found uncool. It began with a soft Fish vocal and arpeggiated piano, which led into a waltz-time section starting about a minute in, with vocals over keyboard and bass. When the full band rushed in, playing in 7/4 time, the echoes of Genesis were unmissable.

The song shifted into straight 4/4 time then, in a hard-rocking section at the 2:30 mark (complete with wailing guitar solos), which was interrupted by a quiet, waltz-time section with bass, acoustic guitar, and synthesizer. Something new was being built; it harked back to what the band members had grown up on, but it showed off the edge of pop metal.

"He Knows You Know" was the single, at number thirty-five. "Marillion think the Peter Gabriel incarnation of Genesis was shit hot, so much so that they feel compelled to hobble into a recording studio to transfer their necromantic urges to record," declared Edwin Pouncey in *Sounds*.[51]

The disbelief at something like this—something wrenched out of time and thrust into the 1980s—was a ready source of amusement. Fish delighted in poking the interviewers who probed him. "I stay in the bath for too long," Fish would tell an interviewer for *NME*. "Nothing cosmic. Look, I'm too aggressive to be a hippy. I go straight for the throat. I do not take shit."[52]

"Judging by the band's dreadfully corny costumes, Marillion's budget doesn't stretch very far," quipped the reporter Bell.[53] "The effect *Script for a Jester's Tear* will have on one section of the public ought not to be understated," Bell wrote in another review for *Sounds*. "At least, it's the coming of age of an exciting new British talent. At best, it could instigate a new musical awareness among the whole post-punk generation."[54]

"Complete with boils in his ears and harlequin pants, he [Fish] acted the part of the court jester, getting off to a healthy start with sexist jokes about herpes," wrote Lucy O'Brien in a review of a Bournemouth show. "Unfunny jokes directed at poufters, queers and 'pathetic girls in Chelsea bedsits with Marks and Spencer duvets and a letter from the bloke they first slept with' raised a few guffaws, though most of the crowd (90 percent men) remained, in Fish's words, '*unnaturally* quiet.'"[55]

The band leaned into the image. Whenever he was asked about his influences, Fish not only rattled off progressive groups, but spotted dishonesty in the bands that would not admit their fan base. "You've got your Yes, Genesis, Soft Machine," Fish told an interviewer. "A lot of Floyd stuff. King Crimson. Gentle Giant. That's what I was brought up with. The punk thing made it embarrassing for anyone to stand up and actually say that 'I like Genesis or Floyd. . . .' But we stood up right at the beginning, and said our influences are '70s bands. I was too young for the Beatles. The Beatles and the Stones were somebody's big brother's music, you know? By the time I was switching on the radio, it was the new album by Tangerine Dream or *Topographic Oceans*."[56]

In command of his own band, Fish was a taskmaster. After Mick Pointer blew his part on "Charting the Single," Fish demanded that he be fired, and Pointer went. "I was playing Hammersmith Odeon one night and two weeks later I was standing in the dole queue," Pointer said. "I had my dream taken away from me."[57] Many years later, Pointer would say, "They are part of my past, and I'm happy about it, but I've moved on."[58]

Andy Ward, whose work with Camel gave Marillion a link to progressive history, lost favor over his drinking. "They had a ridiculous opinion of themselves," Ward assessed, years later.[59] (Ward declined to be interviewed for this book.)

"The audience hated us," said Mark Kelly. "I remember one guy standing on a seat in the front row with his trousers down."[60]

The group was welcomed more warmly by the bands that had clearly been its inspiration. Peter Hammill lent Fish an album that inspired the song "Assassing." It was more of a problem for aspiring "third wave" progressive acts. The music press's aperture was small; so, went the belief, was that of the potential market. Pallas, another revivalist group, enjoyed the full support of EMI for its first album, only to see the label's enthusiasm vanish with the second. "We were supposed to be the flagship for the relaunch of Harvest," Pallas's Mike Stobbie told the author Paul Stump. "Whether they thought it was too much competition for Marillion and the market wouldn't support two bands, I don't know."[61]

In November 1984, as the breakout band of the new scene, Marillion went back into the studio. "We were so useless at coming up with starts and finishes to songs," admitted Kelly.[62] The noodling led to some successful, wide-open songs. It also began to lay the seeds of a band split. "Fish grabs me and holds me up against the wall, screaming that I'm holding back the best songs for my solo album . . . and here's a six foot six Scot hurling abuse at me!" said Kelly. "Any friendship that was left in me for Fish went away at that moment. It was like a switch flicked off."[63]

To the rest of the world, outside of the band, Marillion was finally breaking through. The painful studio sessions produced the album *Misplaced Childhood*, which gave up none of the band's pretensions but carried two melodic, radio singles. "Kayleigh" became a hit; the album itself broke past the critical consensus and went to number one.

Marillion's crossover fan base was like nothing else in the 1980s. The singles brought pop fans. The prog anoraks had always been there. But there were metal fans too. During the band's 1986 tour, Fish's voice started to go. "Something had to give," said Fish. "I ended up paying for my sins by losing the use of my voice for a month."[64]

The band truly started to fray after the long tours ended and EMI was owed a follow-up. *Clutching at Straws* would be a concept album, the story of a character named Torch who was remarkable for being sadly unremarkable. "Warm Wet Cir-

cles" and "That Time of the Night," interlocking songs that
stretched over ten minutes, were about nothing larger than "getting trapped in the 9–5 syndrome."[65]

Of Fish, Mark Kelly said, "He used to stay long enough
to tell us the music we were working on was 'shite' and then
leave. To be fair, we were as complimentary about the lyrics he
showed us."[66]

When the tour was over, Fish acted on years of impulse and
packed it in. He would remain with the label; the band would
have to move on without him. "The musical directions of the
band have diversified to such an extent I realized the time had
come to embark upon a solo career," Fish wrote in a message to
fans. "We weren't as devastated as people might have thought,"
said Kelly. For Rothery, it felt like a weight had been hefted off
his shoulders.[67]

ROBERT FRIPP'S LATEST "small, mobile unit" avoided the pop
dynamics of the 1980s. It had been several years since anything
was recorded under the name "King Crimson." The guitar had
not changed in that time, though Adrian Belew, like Fripp, had
been an experimenter. The bass had changed, with Tony Levin
bringing the Chapman Stick, a fretless instrument with greater
diversity of sound, into the studio. And Bill Bruford had begun
adding electronic drums to the repertoire.

With his typical combination of aplomb and mystery, Fripp
announced the new band to the media as a happy accident, a
reformation that he had not intended. "King Crimson has a life
of its own, despite what its members say and do," he said. "Any
thought-form which attracts interest becomes partly iconic and
since the group 'ceased to exist' in 1974 interest has continued.
At the beginning of rehearsals during the first week of April, I

recognized this potential hovering behind the band, an available energy if we chose to plug in."[68]

Bruford was the only member familiar with how Fripp really worked. Levin, wrote Fripp in his diary, seemed to have no stress at all about the group's improvisational approach. Bruford knew what he was in for. "It starts out as a stream of negatives first off, which cracks many a lesser man," said Bruford. " 'Don't do this, don't do that, and I suggest you don't do this. By the way, I also recommend you don't do that.' You're in a prison and you've got to find your way out of things. I quite like that. I must be a masochist or something, but I don't feel right unless I'm imprisoned and told to find a way around it."[69]

Belew became the closest collaborator in songwriting—a process that involved intimate time in the studio, trading ideas, and being ready when one was trashed. "The difficult part being me and Robert sitting down hours and hours and hours every day trying to figure out how to do something and how to make a two-man guitar team something," said Belew. "Then me going away with anything that's supposed to turn into a song and figuring out how to do that—ha, ha, ha! How to write a melody over some of these crazy figures we were coming up with and odd time signatures."[70]

In his diaries, Fripp expressed a joy about what the band was writing—the vindication of the "Drive to 1981." He and Belew would throw notes to each other. One might lay down the tricky melody of a piece; the other would strike out with a solo. "Elephant Talk," which became the first song on the new band's album, began with the low flutter of Levin's bass, which picked up speed and then slowed, like a dropped coin spinning around a sink. The guitars slowly joined in, over a Bruford drum pattern that crashed at the end of every bar. Belew, the new vocalist, introduced himself with *Sprechstimme*. "Talk, it's only talk," he sang. "Arguments! Agreements! Advice! Answers! Articulate announcements! It's only talk." Ninety-nine seconds into the song came the revelation of the name. As Fripp clipped out notes, Belew strangled his guitar and coaxed a sound that really did approximate the moan of an elephant.

"Discipline" synthesized everything Fripp had done in his postprog years, with some of the ambient experimentation replaced by Belew's pop. "Thela Hun Ginjeet" was the band's first dance song, albeit one with Belew describing a mugging attempt where one might have expected to hear vocals. "Matte Kudasai" was an elliptical love song, with its lover saying the title phrase (Japanese for "please wait a second") to a boisterous American. "The interest from foreign press is remarkable, while the English press contributes permanent cynicism," Fripp wrote in his diary, portions of which were published by *Musician* magazine.[71]

Like the new Yes, the new King Crimson threatened to split before anyone could see it. Levin worried about the opportunities he was pushing off in order to tour as a full band member—a new experience for him. Belew, with his more melodic, Beatles-esque tendencies, deeply felt material, sometimes went around the unwritten rules of the unit. "AB has written lots of 'simple, commercial songs' which seem out of place with the 'serious, influential' people he works with," said Fripp. "He needs to record them and get them out of his system."[72]

The deal, quickly reached, would allow Belew to record his own solo albums in between his Crimson duties. With no other problems to sort out, the band was able to release *Discipline* in September 1981, seven years since the end of the band's previous lineup, and four since the Drive to 1981.

Critics, who could be so harsh to the old progressive groups and the revivalists, knew that Fripp was building out something else. There were holdouts; *Melody Maker* turned its lasers on "The Sheltering Sky," an instrumental track in which Belew pulled notes that sounded like a Muslim call to prayer, labeling it "a drippy, overlong piece of doodling that should have Genesis fans closing their eyes and muttering phrases like 'distinguished musicianship' while the rest of us fall asleep."[73]

The problem inside King Crimson, at that moment, was not that anyone agreed with the critics. It was a creative tension that usually aided the band, and occasionally caused it to split. After one disagreement during the recording of *Beat*, the second album, Fripp bolted the studio and had to be begged back by Bruford. "Heartbeat," a Belew composition more easygoing and melodic than almost anything else in the catalogue, held no interest for Fripp, who considered his solo "limp." "I had nothing to do with the mixing of 'Beat,' nor did I feel able to promote it," said Fripp.[74]

The band did splinter, re-forming again for a tour—and one last album, as the label had contracted. *Three of a Perfect Pair* showcased even more of the creative schisms in the group—all in ways that worked for the music. The title track hypnotized listeners with a looping Belew guitar figure, then smashed the calmness with a scale-breaking Fripp solo that jumped from note to note with no obvious design. "Sleepless" was the first and only King Crimson song to be remixed as a club single.

There was a tour—then another end to another experiment. As Bruford recalled, on Sunday, July 12, 1984, Fripp had breakfast with the group and announced its termination. Belew remembered it differently: reading Fripp's pronouncement in *Musician* magazine, which had celebrated and published him throughout the years of experimentation. "That's how I learned I was no longer in the band," said Belew. "After that I went a year or two where I didn't want to write songs anymore. I was kind of finished with all that. I realized as I said earlier that I didn't really care that much about being a star and I cared more about being a musician."[75]

The liberated musicians picked up the careers they'd had before Fripp's *Discipline* head-hunting. Levin, who had taken a pay cut to join the group, returned to session work. Bruford returned to jazz. Fripp himself teamed up with Andy Summers, more than two decades after they'd first met. With the end of the Police, Summers was game for experimental and instrumental music; the fame he'd earned in the Police gave the first Fripp-Summers collaborative album, *I Advance Masked*, a serious label push.

Belew, at first, recorded some effects-heavy music that he thought could sell. "I wasn't sure that King Crimson would ever happen again, and what I thought was, 'What I want to do now is be a creative artist,'" he said. "I'm fed up with the idea of trying to make it in the music business on a pop level. So I created *Desire Caught by the Tail*, and it nearly bankrupted me."[76]

Belew's next move was to join another group—actually, to take it over. The Raisins, an Ohio band that he'd seen before and liked, had a local following but no national reach. "I thought maybe I should give it one more big try, to have a band that could really be exciting, to write a lot of three-minute hit songs, and just see if that could happen again," said Belew. "I was kind of inspired by the Police, because they came out of nowhere, and within a year they were huge."[77]

Belew's friendly takeover of the band came with a name change: the "Bears." Just three years after cowriting "Larks' Tongues in Aspic (Part III)," Belew was the front man of a pop group, revising some of their old material and collaborating on new ones. "Fear Is Never Boring," one of their pre-

Below singles, was rebuilt with him sharing vocals and soloing after the hook.

None of Crimson's players were allowing themselves to backslide.

"By the time John Wetton's Asia had sold millions of copies of its bland radio-friendly pop in the 80s, the post-hippie extension of the counter-culture that was progressive rock, based on the idealistic impulses of the 60s, had finally run its course," Bruford wrote. "The dream, or illusion, of individual and global enlightenment was over. Progressive rock, like the period that gave rise to it, was essentially optimistic."[78]

"The whole underlying goal—to draw together rock, classical, and folk music into a surreal metastyle—was inherently an optimistic ideal," said Bruford. "At its best, the genre engaged the listeners in a quest for spiritual authenticity. We took ourselves too seriously, of course, and its po-faced earnestness could lapse into a moronic naivete, but it never gave way to bitterness, cynicism, or self-pity."[79]

FISH WAS GONE, but there was no talk of ending Marillion. There was no talk, really, of continuing along the path of *Clutching at Straws*. No one within the band was a natural singer, so a call went out for someone new. Steve Hogarth, who sounded nothing like Fish, was one of the try-outs. "I expected them to say, 'we're this big progressive rock band and we sell this many copies. It's a good living, and do you think you can sing like this?'" Hogarth told author Jon Collins. "They said, 'we've heard you singing, we've heard some songs you've written and we really like what you do.'"[80]

Hogarth was flattered, but not sold. "To be honest, I wasn't terribly interested in doing it," Hogarth said. "I had no income and was completely skint."[81] With that motivation, and with some respect for what the band had done, Hogarth tried out and joined an all-day jam session. He tackled unfinished Marillion tracks, or attempted to. "I thought I was out of tune and horrible," he recalled.[82] But the band warmed quickly to Hogarth's approach. Fish had swung wildly and emotionally; Hogarth exuded a sort of sincerity. "Everything just clicked," said Rothery. "The minute Steve started singing it was like our whole creativity became supercharged again."[83]

Hogarth hesitated before signing on. Had he remained solo, he was set to tour with Matt Johnson, the artist who recorded and toured as the The. "Matt was about the hippest artist in England and Marillion were about the least hip artists," said Hogarth.[84] But soon enough, Hogarth was in, hauling along a red bucket of tapes containing song ideas that had never made it. When the band hit an impasse, a hand went into the bucket. "Easter," a deeply literal song about the Irish rebellion, had been kicking around on a magnetic loop. Tolkien was out; lyrics about "a tattered necklace of hedge and tree" and "where Mary Dunoon's boy fell" were Marillion's now.

The new Marillion introduced itself in 1989, with a set of songs called *Seasons End*. Mark Wilkinson, the painter who had produced the first four studio albums' iconic scenes, had stayed with Fish. Marillion blew that off. "Graphic artists are so much quicker than proper artists," said bassist Pete Trewavas.[85] Instead, there would be a photo illustration, with four frames depicting both the literal seasons of the year and the ways in which Marillion had broken free from its past.

Wilkinson's revenge came when Fish released his debut, *Vigil in a Wilderness of Mirrors*. The painter had hidden insults in the artwork. Mark Kelly and John Arnison became derelicts, heating themselves by a fire. Steve Rothery's white Porsche sat on a scrap heap. "It was mischievous," Wilkinson admitted. "So was having my illustrated clown from 'Fugazi' drowning in a muddy pool."[86] The band understood exactly what Wilkinson was up to. "I told EMI I wanted all the albums destroyed," said Mark Kelly.[87] As a compromise, later versions of the album would ship with altered art; Kelly would no longer be mocked as a hobo.

But there was no truce when Marillion toured and promoted the new music with Steve Hogarth. When journalists asked, the other band members were contrite: they had replaced a fallen-off singer with a dynamic artist. "He didn't seem to be inspired anymore by the music we were writing," Rothery said of Fish, with Hogarth at his side. "On the other hand, we didn't like his lyric direction either."[88]

"Everybody keeps asking me if it was difficult, expecting me to say how difficult it was," said Hogarth. "As soon as we made music, we just made bags of music."[89]

Seasons End did not sell the way that Fish's Marillion albums had sold. The band shed the fans who had come in through the progressive revival, and through heavy metal. The new Marillion, with Hogarth amplifying tendencies that had bubbled under, was more raw and political. When it came time to record a follow-up, the band and label agreed on Chris Neil, whose progressive cred topped out with Mike + the Mechanics. "They'd seen how Mike Rutherford brought Genesis into the mainstream, and so they came to me," said Neil.[90]

The new Marillion was not a pop group, but it abandoned what had been so mockable about progressive rock. Hogarth had his own flamboyant stage presence, with costume changes and little set pieces; being hauled off stage by mysterious thugs was the most striking. But in his own words, Hogarth "smashed the progressive approach apart."[91] Fish, keeping up the progressive approach, hoped to surpass the old group's success.

"In musical terms it didn't happen that way, or in business terms because we make more money than him," said Hogarth, years later. "But it did pan out like that in media terms. If the *Daily Mail* ever talks about Marillion they still print a picture of Fish, even now. That's a ghost we haven't been able to lay to rest. But on all other fronts, it's Marillion 1 and Fish 0."[92]

11

THE NOSTALGIA FACTORY

A s the 1980s wheezed to a finish, a seventy-seven-minute cassette tape from an unsigned and unknown band began to arrive in the offices of underground music zines. The title and the act looked equally nonsensical; Porcupine Tree proudly presented something called *Tarquin's Seaweed Farm*. The folded sleeve credited musicians like Sir Tarquin Underspoon (organ, electric piano) and Sebastian Tweetle-Blampton III (delay circuits) and Master Timothy Masters (oboe).

It was a parody, sure—but a parody of what? The first sounds on the tape came from a keyboard, which started low and grew in volume until interrupted by a flute. A few strings were plucked in a vaguely Eastern style. Was this ambient music? No; the entrance of a drum machine, clanging as if a robot had taken control of Janet Jackson's studio, put the lie to that.

The tape spun on, and genres tumbled into genres as a theme slowly emerged. This was progressive music, albeit two decades after the music's era had ended. It had the trappings of a garage band and the ambitions of Yes, or Pink Floyd.

The fake "band members," the "tripping musicians extraordinaire," found their purpose in "The Cross/Hole/Yellow Hedge-row Dreamscape," the final song on the tape. It began as a cover of Prince's defiantly Christian anthem; it morphed into arena rock, with a dubbed "audience" cheering as a singer (Under-spoon) invited them to turn on. "I'd like to take you on a jour-ney with me!" he said, drenched with reverb. "Relax! Open your hearts to the universe. Let the light shine into your hearts. Be at one with the universe. Open your mind. Come with me."

This fantasy had sprung from the mind and hands of Steven Wilson, who was born on the outskirts of London in 1967, and grew up after the progressive moment had passed. Before he turned ten, he was listening to ambitious music through the filter of his parents. "I was discovering the Electric Light Orchestra and Pink Floyd through my father," said Wilson. "He also had *Tubular Bells*. He had the big mainstream cross-over art rock albums of the era. But my best friend had a brother who was five or six years older than us, and he'd been buying records in the seventies. He'd say, 'Oh, you're listen-ing to Pink Floyd? Here's what you really need to hear.' And he had records by Camel, by Hawkwind."[1]

Wilson was transfixed, not least because the music had been willfully tossed aside by the culture. When he was eleven, he trekked to the Berkhamsted Civic Centre for a punk show—the Chiltern Volcanoes—but was early enough to catch some band called Marillion. "I recall that in one song Mick Pointer came to the front of the stage and played some flute," he'd remember. "Although it made a pretty big impression on me, I don't think I really expected to hear the name again."[2]

"We were hearing things like Genesis and these other bands we wouldn't have come across either, because no one was listen-ing to those bands," he said. "We're talking about 1980, 1981; no one's listening to that music. All my friends at school are listening to the Jam, the Smiths. No one was listening to what was comparatively recent. It might as well have been a century ago."[3]

In his teens, Wilson started experimenting with a four-track recording system. By 1987, when the Porcupine Tree project started, he was recording reel to reel, but highly aware of his limitations. His "band" would owe more to Pink Floyd than to Robert Fripp because David Gilmour had drafted the simpler blueprints. "I was never a good musician, and I was never interested in being a good musician," said Wilson. "So I gravitated toward the stuff that was easy to play. That allowed me to continue on my musical journey without having to be very good."[4]

The resulting songs, half whimsy and half ambition, went out to a few hundred people with hopefully overlapping tastes. Nick Saloman, who recorded as the Bevis Frond, suggested that Wilson send a cassette to Richard Allen, a journalist just a few years older, his tastes similarly unstuck in time. Other people navigated through the 1980s with electronic music and New Romanticism. Allen covered the new psychedelia, underground music that survived without much label support. And Porcupine Tree's tape struck Allen as promising—memorable, but not perfect. In the short-lived, low-budget magazine *Freakbeat*, he praised the experimentation of the music, then panned the "long, calculated prog jams."[5]

Still, Allen was interested in where Wilson could take this. He was amusingly committed to the joke of Porcupine Tree as a band of fractured geniuses, rediscovered and newly put on wax. "It was very tongue in cheek," Wilson explained. "It was suggested that the 'band' met in the early 1970s, at a rock festival. They'd been in and out of prison and they'd been busted on various occasions."[6]

Wilson's second tape, 1990's *The Love, Death & Mussolini E. P.*, was just as cracked, down to a snatch of dialogue from the justly forgotten film *The Amazing Transplant* that ended one of the more serious songs with the phrase "I want you to put Felix's penis on me." Only ten copies of the tape were made, and Porcupine Tree remained a Wilson-only affair.

Allen would help to change that. In 1991, he struck out and announced the formation of Delerium Records and courted Wilson for the label's debut compilation. Porcupine Tree provided "Linton Samuel Dawson," a short pop song with sped-up vocals. "I did all the press for the label, particularly for Porcupine Tree," Allen would tell the blog *Psychedelic Baby*. "No other label was interested in this kind of music so it was a real uphill battle particularly for Porcupine Tree a band that to start with was completely unknown, had no fan base, couldn't perform live easily and played lengthy psychedelic guitar based progressive rock at a time when ambient trance and electronic, dance music were hip."[7]

Allen bet again on Wilson, and signed Porcupine to his indie label. The first result of that alliance would be *On the Sunday of Life*, a mélange of everything Wilson had been doing. "It seemed on the surface to be the worst possible time to be trying to make that kind of music," Wilson would admit, with some pride, to an interviewer. "Everyone was listening to Nirvana and Soundgarden and all of the sort of new grunge. Even the idea of a guitar solo seemed like it was completely outlawed. You couldn't do things like that [let] alone 15-minute long tracks and extended improvised guitar stuff. It seemed like the worst possible time but . . . what I found was actually there was a lot of other people like me that kind of missed that creativity and missed that ambition in music."[8]

Delerium printed just a thousand copies of the new record. Interest, if there was any, would have to build from that low base. "It took 10 years before we got any serious interest," Allen remembered. "It was essentially a war of attrition. If you know the music is of a good quality and keep going long enough someone will eventually take notice."[9]

But it did sell. The first thousand copies found homes. In time, twenty thousand units of Wilson's shamelessly progressive record had moved. "This was pre-Internet, and there were no magazines writing about that music, and there were no radio stations playing that music," Wilson said, years later. "You certainly couldn't get that music on TV. So that process of building an audience and finding those people became a word-of-mouth one and a very organic one."[10]

As Wilson found a fan base, he built a band and began touring his material. Porcupine Tree's mid-1990s music continued the scale of progressive rock, as produced by anoraks with keyboards. In early summer of 1993, Porcupine Tree released *Up the Downstair*, and with it, the first collaboration between Wilson and David Sylvian's old bandmate Richard Barbieri. Barbieri's electronic signature was all over the title track, ten minutes of music that welded together the dreamy pop ambience that was becoming popular with Wilson's guitar work, which wasn't.

"It's a strange and wonderful brew, taking in Orb ambience, FSoL dub, Metallica steel and all points in between," wrote Dave Simpson in *Melody Maker*. "I'm remembering Floyd and King Crimson and wondering whether they're aware that their pioneering spirit has been re-incarnated in the Nineties. Mostly (and curiously) I'm reminded of the great 801, a ground-breaking ambient rock 'super group' formed by Brian Eno and Phil Manzanera, who slayed the Reading Festival in 1976 and imploded soon after, leaving a myriad of musical possibilities unresolved. Here's where the gauntlet is finally picked up."[11]

In just a few years, Wilson was being celebrated as the revivalist and torch carrier of progressive music. A press that had

FSOL = Future Sound of London

chased away his predecessors was intrigued; a fan base, which had shrunken but grown more intensely devoted, was buying the records. So Wilson traveled even further into space. "The Sky Moves Sideways," split into two parts, was longer than almost any piece from the progressive era. Over thirty-five dreamy minutes, it advanced through ambient noise, to guitar solos, to native-style drumming, to Wilson's thin but commanding voice reciting wide-eyed poetry.

Wilson was not a show-offy guitarist. Like David Gilmour or Robert Fripp, he looked for spaces between the notes, and for feel. "When I was very young and first heard those King Crimson records," said Wilson, "I would think 'That's just wrong. You're playing the guitar wrong, mate!' But the more you start to listen to Fripp's playing, the more you appreciate his choices of notes."[12]

WHILE WILSON WAS RECORDING to his four-track, a group of American musicians was taking a far more traditional route to the mainstream. In 1985, three kids from Long Island moved into the dorms at the Berklee College of Music in Boston. John Petrucci and John Myung bunked in room 817; Mike Portnoy was two floors below, in room 608. Petrucci and Myung spotted Portnoy on the second or third week of school, playing drums in a practice room. "We looked through the glass window," Petrucci remembered. He "had a Rush shirt or something on . . . and we were like, 'we've gotta hook up with that guy.'"[13]

They bonded immediately—castaways with ears for ambitious British rock, one of them waking every day to sign up for a practice room, six hours a night, every weekday. Myung played bass, Petrucci played guitar, and all three men shared Long Island roots and an education in metal. "We were the only band playing really loud, heavy stuff," said Petrucci. "We were really into, like I said before, Rush, Iron Maiden, and stuff like that. At the same time, we were listening to fusion and jazz and stuff like that, so when we got together at Berklee, even before the stuff that John and I would write, it always had a hard rock edge to it, but it was influenced by all this more progressive music. We were also big Yes fans."[14]

Portnoy on drums, Petrucci on guitar, and Myung on bass became a band whose name took inspiration from a Boston appearance by Rush during the *Power Windows* tour. The friends camped out overnight for tickets, and when day broke, they played Rush through their boom box—"Bastille Day," the sort of song Rush had drifted away from writing. "We were like, oh, they're so majestic," Petrucci said. "Their music is so majestic. Somebody said, 'That's it!' 'Majesty'—that would be a great name."[15]

The trio recruited two Long Island friends to fill the band out: Kevin Moore on keyboards and Chris Collins on vocals. Majesty's sound was well formed by the time it recorded a 1986 demo tape. This was heavy metal music, but with keyboards more resonant in the mix than in anything comparable. Much was owed to Rush, but Petrucci's shredding was sometimes twice as fast as the work of Alex Lifeson.

Lyrically, the band stayed within the lines drawn by progressive rock and metal, even if the results could be hard to parse. "A Vision," an eleven-minute epic that showcased everyone's talents, linked together idea poems like "time to set emotions straight" and "this space is wasting a dream." There was mood, if not yet meaning.

And soon there was no Berklee. Petrucci, Myung, and Portnoy left school to focus full-time on Majesty, swapping out singers, tightening what they had. Their efforts paid off in 1988, when the demo made it to Mechanic, a division of MCA Records where the idea of a progressive revival clicked. "I have always been a big fan of the likes of ELP, Genesis, Yes, King Crimson, and Pink Floyd," said Mechanic's Jim Pitulski to an interviewer. "I was really blown away that there was this young, new band that was playing this kind of music again."[16]

Majesty went into the studio, with Terry Date—a metal producer who agreed to work at roughly one-third the normal cost, for just $30,000—behind the glass. As they finished, and after the paint had dried on cover art of a terrified man being branded with the band's logo, the band learned of a Las Vegas act that had trademarked the name. Portnoy and his bandmates cast around for a new name, hitting dry well after dry well. They almost went with "Glasser," after their attorney, until Collins triumphantly announced that name to a New York crowd. "There was just this dead silence in the room, with absolutely no applause," said Portnoy.[17]

It was Portnoy's father, Howard, who bailed out the group. In November 1988 he caught a movie at a California cinema called the Dream Theater. That was the name that the first album, *When Dream and Day Unite*, was released under, its cover art showing a man getting an especially untimely Majesty tattoo.

The album did not sell, despite flattering reviews. Here was a band, wrote Derek Oliver in *Kerrang!*, "who appear to be anxious to re-experience the years 1972 to 1978, the golden age of progressive rock music." Oliver described playing the tape again and again, searching for brilliant players to compare the new band with. "Here is musical dexterity I have not heard since the glory jazz rock days or Dixie Dreggs or, as a more accurate description early Kansas."[18]

Still, the flop meant that the band had to wriggle out of a contract. It parted ways with singer Charlie Dominici and found

James LaBrie, a Canadian metal singer with a high range. Dream Theater would try again, whether or not people understood what the band was doing.

PROGRESSIVE ROCK, which had not seemed to survive the 1980s, had a curious half-life. Steve Wilson and Dream Theater came from the generations that weren't supposed to like this music. Home recording, with all of the tricks that had taken progressive musicians years to develop, became steadily cheaper. Metal groups harked back to the heaviest of progressive music for inspiration.

Most of the progressive acts, the ones that had lasted, adjusted awkwardly to changing tastes. Genesis released one album and went on one tour with *We Can't Dance*, a slab of pure pop. Jethro Tull never broke up, and in 1987 the band earned a real comeback with the pop-smoothed *Crest of a Knave* album. To the band's surprise, the album was nominated for a heavy metal Grammy. To the world's surprise, Tull won—a shock that shamed the National Academy of Recording Arts and Sciences into changing its standards for the prize. In 1992, when Metallica finally won the prize that the press believed it had been denied, the band's drummer and leader opened his speech with a Tull dig. "We gotta thank Jethro Tull for not putting out an album this year, right?" said Lars Ulrich.[19]

The new Yes fractured after just five years; Jon Anderson had been bored by its second album, *Big Generator*, and moved on. In 1989, Yes reassembled without the band name—largely because Chris Squire was not involved. Anderson, Bruford, Wakeman, and Howe formed a unit of that name, and tapped Tony Levin as a bass player. "In my world, everyone would have worked on ABWH and come up with fresh material," said Bruford. "How-

ever, Yes, as ever, is guided financially. Most of its musical movements now are motivated by sheer lack of money."[20]

Through the machinations of agents and the compliance of
band members, the components of Yes were smashed together
into one unwieldy unit. The Trevor Rabin–era band was back,
augmented by Bruford, Wakeman, and Howe. The album and
tour, with minimal inspiration, were called *Union.* In a witticism
he never tired of, Wakeman said, "I call it the Onion album,
because every time I hear it, it brings tears to my eyes."[21] When
Peter Banks showed up for a show, he couldn't even talk his way
into the dressing room. "The strange thing is that the Union
tour was quite fun once it started," said Rabin. "It was just the
album. In fact, I have never listened to it all the way through. I
couldn't bring myself to do it. Who was in overall charge of it?
Accountants, mostly."[22]

Successors to Yes were hard to spot. Quebec's Voivod began
life as a speed metal band. That changed on its third album,
1987's *Killing Technology.* The music was still dominated mainly
by fast tempos, but Voivod at a fast tempo was an entirely different animal from other high-velocity thrash metal of the period.
The band favored a swinging, jazzy meter. Guitarist Denis
"Piggy" D'Amour's minor and diminished guitar chords also set
him apart. He used the entire instrument, handing off the low,
chugging rhythm duties to bassist Jean-Yves "Blacky" Thériault.
Like Yes, one of the band's inspirations, Voivod pumped the bass
high in the mix and let it carry melodies as strongly as the guitar.

Voivod's 1988 track "Experiment" continued the evolution. It
began as metal; at four minutes, it shifted into a viciously swinging, waltz-time riff over a repeating diminished figure. From
there the songs all flowed one into the next and stayed in dark,
minor-key territory, jumping erratically from one odd-time riff
to the next, the pleasure coming from the erratic flow.

By 1989's *Nothingface*, Voivod was recording with a major label. The title track jumped from a swaying, midtempo riff to up-tempo funk and back before a 7/4 section that jerked back abruptly, and impossibly, into a staccato shuffle time section. If the influences were lost on anyone, the band covered Pink Floyd's "Astronomy Domine." The result: the first Voivod album to crack the *Billboard* charts. They didn't get there again. Part of the problem was also that the band's next, more melodic album was released in 1991, just as Nirvana's *Nevermind* was breaking.

Nirvana, actually, had plenty of time for King Crimson; Kurt Cobain claimed that *Red* was one of his favorite albums. But for a while, "progressive" meant revivalism, with no innovation.

Spock's Beard was founded by brothers Neal and Alan Morse, with a name hailing from the legendary mirror universe episode of *Star Trek*. "Spock's Beard was sort of a phrase that we'd say to each other—my brother and I—when something weird would happen. We'd say, 'Wow, that's like "Spock's Beard,"' meaning, 'that only happens in a parallel universe, right?'" said Neal Morse. "I put Spock's Beard on the list sort of as a joke. Everybody seemed to like it the best, and so we picked that one, and here we are 20-however-many-years later."[23]

Spock's Beard self-financed and released their debut, *The Light*, in 1995. Composed of four tracks, three of them epic-length, it opens with the title track, which remained in the set list for as long as they played.

Sweden's Änglagård was just as faithful. Formed in 1991, wedded to the bygone era's flute and mellotron sounds, as well as the virtuoso drumming of Mattias Olsson, the band was together only long enough to make two albums. Yet 1992's *Hybris* and 1994's *Epilog* stood out for their unapologetic prog. "We decided very early on that we wanted to be a prog rock band," Olsson said years later. "Not a prog band with leanings toward pop or fusion or anything, just straightup Scandinavian progrock band. I think it helped having a very naïve and open-minded approach to it but a[t] the same time being very focused. Sounds like a contradiction but it worked for us."[24]

Hybris consisted of exactly four songs; the shortest was eight minutes long. *Epilog*, its fatalistically titled follow-up, was completely instrumental. Consisting of three extended tracks and three throwaway, transitional pieces, it offered a uniquely Scandinavian form of musical despair. One live album later, Änglagård was spent. "No, we were all pretty fed up with the whole thing," said Olsson. "I think we felt that it would have been strange [with] someone from the outside. Our own Swedish Trevor Rabin perhaps. A very scary thought indeed."[25]

ROBERT FRIPP, as ever, found a sideways path to the new trend. Shortly after the four-man King Crimson ended, he collaborated with Andy Summers of the similarly defunct Police for two albums of abstract, interlocking guitar music, with no vocals. In 1984, Summers and Fripp were talking with *Musician* magazine, which had so loyally followed experimental music, when Fripp dropped an announcement: "I'm off to clean latrines in West Virginia!" Fripp said cheerfully.[26]

He was announcing what would become "Guitar Craft," a seminar in Charles Town for a few dozen players each year. Fripp modified the lifestyle that had been pounded into him during his 1970s sabbatical, bringing musicians together to eat, play, and find a new way of living. "Within Guitar Craft is the first time I've been able to live in a sane world," he told an interviewer after the project's first few years.[27]

One of the first Guitar Craft attendees was a music student from Texas who could not quite believe his luck. Trey Gunn had

& Charleston

written a sort of "dream list" of the musicians who'd inspired him—people like David Bowie, people like Robert Fripp. "When I was in college studying music, I eventually became kind of a punk rocker," recalled Gunn. "Everyone was anti-know-what-you're-doing. When I was finishing up, I thought, 'This is stupid. I'm working with good people, but none of the people here do what is awesome. What the hell? Why shouldn't it be like the good old days?' "[28]

Gunn arrived in Charles Town to a simple guitar, and to exercises like forming around a table and being instructed to eat soup without using hands or even sitting next to the bowl. "We bowed down and hoped to taste it," said Gunn. "You have to be really smart to think up tests like that. We were really doing practical practices for how to hold the body, practical practices for disciplines of the mind—and disciplines of the heart. It wasn't just that first week; it took years. You came to realize that regular music was just dabbling."[29]

It was difficult to tell who was in Robert Fripp's good graces, and who was not. Gunn figured out that he was. He played bass and stick on the albums Fripp produced with his wife, Toyah Willcox. Gunn was tapped again in 1992 when Fripp collaborated with David Sylvian, the romantic art rocker from the defunct group Japan. Pat Mastelotto, a founding member of the metal-pop one-hitter Mr. Mister, was, to his own surprise, brought on as drummer. "He writes wonderful lyrics, he has a gorgeous voice, and the sounds he makes from his keyboard are stunning," Fripp said of Sylvian. "And then you move on to the third point: I like being with him."[30]

The pieces of King Crimson had spent a decade scattering. Adrian Belew had found a distinct voice with the Bears and with his own music; he'd even had a hit single, 1989's "Oh Daddy," in which his real-life daughter, Audie, asked him for attention and Belew obliged. Bill Bruford had teamed up with the floating Patrick Moraz and then delved deeply, seemingly for good, into jazz. Belew had joined Peter Gabriel for his mid-1980s career reinvention as a socially conscious megastar.

But Fripp wanted to talk to them. "In the beginning I assumed we'd be continuing musically where we left off in 1984 as well," said Bruford. "We were going to return to a sound more from the '70s, more to do with *Red*—a thick, intelligent Metal kind of sound."[31] Instead, Fripp wanted to expand the band's ambition and sound by adding a bassist and a drummer—creating what he called a "double trio." Trey Gunn became the second bassist. "He'll say something like 'I've had this vision of a double trio, I don't particularly want this and I don't know whether it's a good idea or not but that's what we're going to do.' And musicians quite like a plan," said Bruford of Fripp. "Men like to have a kind of hierarchy."

In less than ten years, Gunn had gone from a fan of Fripp's music to a collaborator in King Crimson. "You couldn't be, at my age, thirty-five-ish—you couldn't be in a more uncool genre," he said. "It was awful. I was always trying to say, we're doing this cool thing. All the other guys were all older, and they'd been in it when it was a cool thing. They didn't know or care. It was challenging. Then we kind of pushed through this barrier, kind of like the world caught up to us."[32]

But the group was aware of that. The spiny music they wrote and played did not sound much like the past King Crimsons. "We didn't want to be a bunch of old guys who got together to try and re-create the past or cash in on it—not that the band was ever that popular anyway," said Belew. "I've always seen King Crimson as more influential than affluent. In fact, it was several months before we even played a note of old Crimson songs."[33]

"We've been seeing 18-year-old guys backstage who've bor-rowed *In the Court of the Crimson King* from their fathers and think we're just as hip as anything else around," said Bruford. "They don't seem to mind that we're forty-five years old."[34]

The new music was released in an EP, then an album called *Thrak*, named for the placeholder title of the band's improvisa-tions. After the tour, Fripp was tasked with approving and pro-moting a compilation of the old King Crimson's work. For the first time in decades, the band that had made *In the Court of the Crimson King* was in one room, at a New York hotel, talking to reporters. The Giles brothers, Peter Sinfield, Ian McDonald, and Greg Lake were together; they could not figure out why, since Fripp largely did interviews without them.

"Mike, Ian, and myself wait outside for one hour, and when Robert's finished he leaves the building," said Lake. "Bearing in mind we'd gone all that way to support his record on his fucking record company, I felt that was really out of order."

Fripp had no interest in collaborating with Lake. He did float an idea of a modified reunion tour, playing "the 1969–1974 rep-ertoire," with Wetton on vocals. It was smothered by mutual disinterest. "I really don't like the idea of re-forming because it would seem like it's for the money," said Michael Giles, accord-ing to Ian McDonald. "I hate it when you see things like Fleet-wood Mac and The Eagles."[35]

There never would be a cash-grab reunion of the first King Crimson. What came instead was a purposeful band schism, as Fripp divided the double trio into two of his beloved mobile units—"fraKctals"—who would work on experimental "Pro-jeKcts." The "double trio" would never come back together. Having gone one final round with Fripp, Bruford left to focus fully on Earthworks, his jazz project. Tony Levin left to tour the world with Seal. King Crimson re-formed in 2000 as a four-

piece, with a brittle metal sound and a long-delayed fourth chapter of "Larks' Tongues in Aspic."

In 2001, the new unit got a challenging offer. Tool, a metal
group that had never been shy about its progressive influences,
asked King Crimson to open on its world tour. "It was like a
revolution, practically, when I heard this record," said Tool's
towering drummer Danny Carey of King Crimson's *Discipline*,
in an interview. "There were just so many new textures that I
hadn't heard. . . . The guitars are like playing in 5 over it, and
the drums are like in 15, so it like creates this cycle that only
meets up every, you know, third bar for the guitars."[36]

It was a tribute, and also a demotion. King Crimson, in this
iteration, was comfortable with smaller venues; Tool was playing
arenas. But the band went along. "They had a better dressing
room," said Gunn. "Maynard [James Keenan] had an amazing
espresso machine with porn stars on it. They were total sweet-
hearts about it all."[37] One night, the million-selling metal band
decided to pay tribute to Fripp's band by pulling a switch. King
Crimson played "Red," and at one moment Gunn heard applause
and a slight change in the drum sound. He looked back to see
Danny Carey sitting in on drums—a metal player, with no natural connection to the progressive rock movement, putting his
hands on the torch.

DREAM THEATER HAPPILY shrugged off the skeptics of its progressive approach. *Images and Words* had a painted cover, because they
wanted to be like Yes or Pink Floyd. A reviewer for *Raw* said
the band would "do for prog rock what Nirvana have done for
smelly cardigans."[38]

Elektra's strategy had worked for Aerosmith, which spent the
late '80s rising from a haze of cocaine dust to become a singles

band. But the label could not turn Dream Theater into a singles band. Instead, an unencumbered band delved even further
into experimentation, adding keyboard player Jordan Rudess to
thicken the sound. "I was a very serious young protégé from
the age of nine, going to Juilliard. I knew nothing about rock
music," said Rudess. "That all changed because a friend of mine
in high school brought over Emerson, Lake and Palmer's *Tarkus*
record and played it for me, and I couldn't stop listening to it. I
thought it was incredible."[39]

"Metropolis—Part I: The Miracle and the Sleeper," the fifth
song on *Images and Words*, stretched to nearly ten minutes. Yet it
was never intended as part one of anything. "When we released
Part 1, we only sort of tagged the 'Part 1' just like a joke, just
trying to be pompous," Portnoy said in 2000.[40]

The song enjoyed a lengthy half-life. (*Metropolis Pt. 2: Scenes
from a Memory* was released in 1999, and musically it set the
stage for what would become the band's signature sound.)
"Metropolis—Part I" began with a repeating, three-note figure
played on a synthesizer, then a crash of guitars playing eighth
notes. For a short while, the song was based around a standard
tempo, a standard time signature, and a standard guitar rhythm.
When the verse transitioned into the bridge, the group threw in
an extra beat every other measure. For the verses, it was back to
4/4. Four minutes into the song, the time signature switched to
13/8. Ninety seconds later, the band was in double time, moving
like Motörhead, and soloing over the bars. The time changed to
7/4, for more solos, then ended in 4/4, with repetitions of the
opening theme.

Images and Words was unashamedly progressive—and it found
an audience. The first track on the album, the slightly more
accessible "Pull Me Under," was released as a single, complete
with low-budget video padded with live footage. It made the

metal charts. "I always used to tell them that the songs could be three songs instead of one," said Steve Stone, one of the band's promoters. "I sat back and went, 'you bastards!' They broke it down to a three- or four-minute mentality and look what happened."[41] The breakout—finally.

For the next album, the label, Elektra, was clear: it wanted singles. When they began work on their fourth album, *Falling into Infinity*, Elektra urged the band to craft another single from its tracks. They were led to Desmond Child, a pop rock songwriter with little time for progressive music, but a record of turning hair-metal bands into chart darlings. "It really bothered me that Desmond was going to rewrite one of our songs with only one member," said Mike Portnoy. "But it's not like we had any options, because if we fought it or said no, the whole machine would have been turned off."[42]

The band toyed around with epic songs, splitting them into pieces, and the result was *Awake*. There was no "Pull Me Under"—nothing to threaten the charts. Dream Theater had jumped out of the niche once; it wouldn't happen again. Derek Shulman, citing his own experience with Gentle Giant, advised the group not to change its sound even if urged to, even if groups like Rush and Kansas had gotten pop hits by doing so.

"On our last couple of records, we decided to try and do what they did, and that was the biggest mistake on a creative, business, and fan-appreciation level that we made," said Shulman. "I could recount from those days and say to this band—who played an interesting but not radio-friendly music—not to sell out."[43]

Dream Theater kept plugging. "It was several years before we finally shook that kind of freak hit and were able to finally convince the label to let us be who we are and stop trying to chase the success of 'Pull Me Under,'" Portnoy told the *New York Times*. "We were just interested in a long-term career. A lot of bands that chase their big hits with more and more follow-ups end up dying as soon as the trend does, and we never wanted to be that. We wanted to be a band that had a slow-building foundation and built our success on constant touring and on albums as opposed to singles."[44]

In 2004, Dream Theater got its own version of the call-up: Yes, which had just released an original album of its music accompanied by an orchestra, wanted Dream Theater to open for them. "They're still young and seem to have the same dedication that Yes did all the way through the 70s," Steve Howe told *Raw*. "There just isn't enough of that kind of progressive music around."[45]

By the late 1990s, most of the innovation in progressive rock was in the metal genre. New York's Coheed and Cambria emerged in 1995, with a cohesive, multialbum concept running through its music, courtesy of songwriter Claudio Sanchez. The concept was exemplified in 2003's *In Keeping Secrets of Silent Earth: 3*. "We were still kind of fresh," said Sanchez. "We didn't have that professional sort of rock band attitude, and this was the first time we actually got to be conceptual and go into a studio that's got great equipment and really try to hone [*sic*] in on a sound. *Second Stage* [the band's first album: *The Second Stage Turbine Blade*] was very much done in a bedroom, whereas [*Silent Earth*] had the production and the concept in mind."[46] The title track was eight minutes long, but the centerpiece was a three-song suite called "The Camper Velourium."

"I always thought of the band . . . as a progressive rock band," Sanchez recalled. "The songs are kind of long; there are a lot of things that go in the songs, like a lot of parts. I mean, I don't necessarily dislike the term emo or any name given to a particular style of rock. I just feel that rock music is rock music and the emotion has always been there since the days of traditional blues. But it doesn't really bother me that it's the name given. I've noticed that some bands take it to heart and dislike names or labels, but I don't really care, I've always thought of the band as a progressive rock band."[47]

The Mars Volta discovered the same audience, all on its own. Founded by guitarist-producer Omar Rodríguez-López and Cedric Bixler-Zavala, the group, like Dream Theater, harked back to progressive heroes. It booked Storm Thorgerson to design its covers, and gabbed happily about its ambition of writing progressive epics. "We choose to take the 'prog' label literally," Rodríguez-López told the revivalist magazine *Mojo* in 2004. "For us, 'progressive' means moving forwards, not sounding like our previous bands or our old records. When you think of it in those terms, it's a *positive* association."[48]

Bixler-Zavala was even more adamant. "If, musically, you get in a spot where the sheets are warm and the pillows are comfy, I think it's important to sleep on the floor every once in a while," he said. "When I was fourteen, I didn't want to hear anything but fast punk music. Older friends would make fun of me; 'Oh, you're a *punk*, huh?' I wish I could've had the knowledge back then to say, I'm just fourteen, let me have my fun with this!"[49]

Sweden's Opeth, like Voivod, began as a death metal band. They were already showing signs of impatience with the genre by the time they released their sophomore album, 1996's *Morningrise*, and guitarist-vocalist-songwriter Mikael Åkerfeldt had consistently sung the praises of the prog genre. Critics took notice as early as 1999, with the album *Still Life*. It opened with "The Moor," a midtempo shuffle with minor-key riffing and vocals alternating between death metal growls and melodic singing, and a running concept about a demon-possessed woman named Melinda. That song attracted the attention of Steven Wilson, who agreed to produce the band's follow-up album, *Blackwater Park*. Opeth was "taking a style which

is really contemporary, like death metal which is totally now . . .
and combining it with more progressive elements to create
something new—that, for me, is what progressive music should
be about," Wilson said. "And I think that the album is a true,
true progressive album."[50]

"I don't see the point of playing in a band and going just one
way when you can do everything," Åkerfeldt said. "It would
be impossible for us to play just death metal; that is our roots,
but we are now a mishmash of everything, and not purists to any
form of music. It's impossible for us to do that, and quite frankly
I would think of it as boring to be in a band that plays just metal
music. We're not afraid to experiment, or to be caught with our
pants down, so to speak. That's what keeps us going."[51]

THE 1990S WERE ROUGHER for most of the first-wave progressive bands. Genesis had become one of the biggest bands on the
planet just as its singer surpassed it, and just as Mike Rutherford found solo success of his own. In 1991, the band produced
one last album, a shimmering and ironic collection of pop songs
called *We Can't Dance*.

The next year, Peter Gabriel returned with *Us*, which found a
place between the pop breakthroughs of the 1980s and the world
music he had drunk in to write the soundtrack to Martin Scorsese's
Last Temptation of Christ. A generation of fans had discovered Gabriel
with no living memory of Rael or the Giant Hogweed.

Yes, which had become more fractious with every shuffling
of the lineup, did not adjust so easily. The *Union* lineup fractured again with the end of the torturous tour. For the rest of
the decade, a new version of Yes was built around Chris Squire
every few years. But there was never any question that Yes would
keep playing, or that a fan could count on some version of the
band coming to town.

It was different for Emerson, Lake & Palmer. In 1991, when they announced that they would play again for the first time in thirteen years, it was an event, even though—once again— the players had been pushed together by a hungry label. The reunited ELP avoided the blunders of Emerson, Lake & Powell. Its US tour began in Philadelphia, the mecca where every progressive act could find a crowd, and went on to venues small enough to sell out. Emerson's classic Moog was restored, to complete the picture of a resurrected band.

But the new-old ELP had nothing to say. There was little merit in the comeback album *Black Moon*, or in the new tracks recorded for the box set that every resurrected band seemed destined to make. Lake had thickened since the days of photo shoots in karategis; at the same time, his voice had thinned. And there was a greater problem with Emerson. From the start of the tour, he was rubbing his right hand, struggling to get through shows without pain. When there was time for a checkup, Emerson got the diagnosis: progressive nerve damage, which could be operated on but not reversed.

There would be no tour for the second reunion album. The band picked up again in 1996, touring with Jethro Tull as part of an all-nostalgia progressive package deal. Emerson's hand was steady enough for the gigs, but he did not pretend to be healed. "Keith was having a hard time," Ian Anderson would recall. "He said to me, 'I can only do forty-five minutes at a stretch; otherwise my hand is so sore, and the next day I can't play at all.' He was suffering. Some of the nights on that tour, you could see he was in pain."[52]

As the genre changed around them, Marillion cut its own path. The band kept writing emotional pop music that Steve Hogarth had brought on board, and plugging ahead without an obvious hit. On January 27, 1997, Mark Kelly posted a message on the "Marillion Freaks" message board, apologizing that the losses incurred on the previous tour, along with their label's dwindling financial reserves, meant that an upcoming tour would have to be tacked back. "We are not prepared to put on half a show with second rate equipment and a crap sound system," Kelly wrote, apologetically.[53]

Jeff Pelletier, just a fan on the boards, wrote up his own suggestion. "What if all the US freaks donated to a Marillion Tour the USA fund?" he asked. "I'd gladly throw $50 in the hat if that guaranteed a chance to see them."[54] He logged off and did not immediately see that his idea had been taken up by fans—dozens, then hundreds. The "tour fund" cracked $30,000, which was as much as Kelly claimed to need. It hit $60,000 before the pitch was over. By pure accident, a Marillion fan had invented crowdfunding.

The band took up that cause, with the Internet still mostly accessed by dial-up and streaming video many years away. In 1999, it crowdfunded an album, cheekily named *marillion.com*, and distributed it by itself. In 2002, it hosted the first Marillion Weekend, another effectively crowdfunded endeavor—a festival where the band spent days playing albums in their entirety and hobnobbing with fans.

IN 2002, PORCUPINE TREE went on tour with Yes—as legitimate a torch-passing event as there was. Audiences who showed up early would get to see the future of progressive rock: Steven Wilson and his band. Audiences who showed up to relive their 1970s would see Yes, performing new songs that had been written with an orchestra.

It took no time for Wilson to realize the error. "Lava talked us into it," said Wilson, referring to his management company. "We thought it was a bad idea, and we were proven right, because it was a terrible idea. The truth is, the fans who went to see Yes, even in 2002, were not interested in new music. They were only interested in hearing what they already knew."[55]

By the time he was being asked to let older groups hitch a wagon, Wilson was both a success in his own right and an excavator for lost or hidden progressive music. His work with Opeth was only the start of it. Porcupine Tree's own music seemed to synthesize the entire history of the genre—accessible enough for a new listener, but deep enough to suggest that it had come from somewhere deeper. "Arriving Somewhere but Not Here," the fifth song on the band's 2005 album *Deadwing*, epitomized that over twelve minutes.

The song started with about a minute and a half of ambient sounds, leading into a soft vocal and softer acoustic guitar, strongly flavored by Pink Floyd. The band came in; at six minutes, the band dropped out, leaving just electric guitars until the full band returned, playing a descending riff. This gave way to the heaviest riff in the song, courtesy of Opeth's Mikael Åkerfeldt. At eight minutes, everything dropped out except for a solo electric guitar playing jazzy lines, a piano playing whole notes, and keyboard padding in the background. The full arrangement returned for another verse and chorus, then a fade-out.

Porcupine Tree became known for immaculate music, and ready experimentation. It sounded that way because Wilson was bored with what was familiar. "Progressive metal, what bands like Opeth were doing, was inventive at the start of the twenty-first century," said Wilson. "But then progressive metal, like everything else, became a meme. The world doesn't need any more progressive metal bands. Unfortunately, I get more demos from progressive metal bands than from any other type."[56]

As the decade ended, Wilson was more interested in reviving the progressive rock music he'd grown up with. From his studio at home in Hempstead, not far from where he'd grown up, Wilson began remixing the classic albums—some by Yes, more by King Crimson. With the permission of the artists, he removed noodling that had not worked, chopping off a piece of King Crimson's "Moonchild." He lifted parts that had been buried in the twenty-four-track recordings. "There are some extraordinary ideas going on in those records," said Wilson." I still don't understand how Robert put everything together. He was no help in explaining things to me. He's not about to help you understand how the music was created. In a way, and I mean this positively, he probably doesn't know himself."[57]

EPILOGUE

I'm sitting in the Zoellner Arts Center in Bethlehem, Pennsylvania, right in front of a middle-aged
man wearing a thick beard and a T-shirt that
proves he saw Genesis on their 1977 tour. He's
yelling right into my ear.

"A Plague of Lighthouse Keepers!"

"Refugees!"

"Man-Erg!"

A reunited and rejuvenated Van der Graaf Generator is just
a few feet in front of us, unmoved. "Shouting out requests is
futile, I assure you!" announced Peter Hammill to the crowd of
a thousand-odd obsessives. "We've got a set list."[1]

Van der Graaf Generator is performing at the last-ever North
East Art Rock Festival—NEARfest. They have slimmed down
to Hugh Banton on keyboards, Guy Evans on drums, and Hammill on piano and guitar. Their hair, respectively, is white, nonexistent, and white. They're playing for people who knew them
when that hair was shaggy and black.

In Bethlehem, I want to see who still lives, loves, and listens to
prog. Every day, a crowd files politely into an amphitheater and

watches a short film projected onto a scrim above the stage. An asteroid hurtles toward Earth, picks up momentum, and crashes. The planet cracks and bleeds like a sunburn. It explodes; two new planets are born. One is a lush, green globe painted by Roger Dean, who did the covers for Yes and Asia and Atomic Rooster. The other is a beautifully detailed vision of a burning Earth, courtesy of Marillion cover artist Mark Wilkinson.

Our programs remind us that we will never go to another NEARfest. The organizers are done, moving on. There will never again be micro–tailgating parties in the parking garage, or rooms where rare LPs and Korean reprints of albums are traded like rubies. "We know for certain," write the organizers, "that there will always be musicians with open minds, big ears, and bigger hearts, who are not satisfied to write simple protest, love, or dance songs."

When I look around at the audience throughout NEARfest— imagine the demographics of a Tea Party rally, but put them in Eloy and Magma T-shirts—there is occasional boredom, occasional nodding off and walking out. These are nostalgic, brainy people. (Nobody wants to read rundowns of stereotypes, but every third person I talk to either teaches science or reads about it to distract from a computer-programming day job. Or runs a record shop.) A few of the wristband wearers sport blue T-shirts, obtained at another days-long concert series. The message, spelled out in bold white letters:

> *Progressive Rock isn't dead yet,*
> *but its fans are dying off.*
> *So get off your couches and support the scene,*
> *you apathetic mother f*#kers.*

You do not hear that sentiment at a Depeche Mode show or a Phish show or a De La Soul reunion show. Their fans adapt to trends. Their music comes back into fashion, it goes out, it comes back in.

On the first night of the festival, I follow the masses to the after-party at the Comfort Suites. The bar serves a special NEARFest Apocalypse Ale—9.8 percent alcohol, brewed "in 9/8 time." In the ballroom: an Internet radio station streams the festival, and a local band plays a catchy, King Crimson–y batch of originals. Gary Green, the guitarist from Gentle Giant, has taken up residence near the entrance. I ask him about Kanye West's "Power," and a few other new songs that sample prog. What does prog have to offer them?

"Perhaps it's more interesting music than what's currently about," says Green. "It's pretty thin out there. I'm a bit surprised by the lack of—well, of ability. Maybe they've got technology that can patch them through. But the ability—that I sorely miss, because I grew up on Benny Goodman and Django Reinhardt. Playing your instrument and playing it well—you know, *that's* music."[2]

IT WAS EASY to pinpoint when the culture gave up on progressive rock in Jonathan Coe's nostalgic novel *The Rotters' Club*, named for a Hatfield and the North album, which captured the popular memory of prog rock when its characters formed a band called Gandalf's Pikestaff. Their opus: "Apotheosis of the Necromancer." Their sheet music was "covered with dwarfish runes, Gothic calligraphy, and Roger Dean–style illustrations of dragons and busty elfin maidens in various stages of provocative undress." When the band finally began playing, they were rescued by real music—punk, obviously.

It was the drummer who sounded the first note of rebellion. After tinkling away on his ride cymbal for what must have seemed an eternity,

*as part of an extended instrumental passage that was meant to evoke
the idea of zillions of far-off galaxies springing into life, he suddenly
announced, "Fuck this for a game of soldiers," and started to lay down a
ferocious backbeat in 4/4. Recognizing his cue, the guitarist whacked up
his volume and embarked upon a riotous three-chord thrash over which
the lead vocalist, an aggressive little character called Stubbs, began to
improvise what the charitable might describe as a melody.*

Pop's move away from prog didn't happen that quickly. It was
slow and tortured and involved a ton of moving parts breaking
at about the same time. In the United States, where most of
this music ended up being sold, progressive rock radio slowly,
slowly was assimilated into the Borg of commercial networking.
The popularity of prog metal, of Marillion, and of the other
bands that willingly identified themselves with "prog" never
quite did it.

Progressive music would not have a short-lived comeback,
like swing music or garage rock. Instead, it would receive occasional love letters from the pop world. Years after ELP had dis-
banded for the second time, Keith Emerson got one of them in
the form of a 2002 sketch from the British comedy series *Big
Train*. A jailed Roman warrior, played by the future identified
"nerd'do well" Simon Pegg, was asked to save the empire. He
looked back in his jail cell and asked for the freedom of his mate:
Keith Emerson, portrayed by another comedian, with the power
to repel attacks through synthesizer blasts.

"As you can see, Keith's fascination with the more elaborate
end of prog rock has lumbered him with a vast array of keyboards," said Pegg. "I need two hundred mules for the journey."

"Such a journey's possible without roadies!" said a baffled
prison guard.

"The ELP roadies were sold into slavery in Crete!" said Pegg.[3]

"I thought it was great," Emerson laughed in an interview.

"I was really quite proud actually, and I wondered, who put this together? It was almost like they knew me very, very well. 'He doesn't speak much.' Well, I didn't, back then. I was very reserved."[4]

While no new progressive act made a true mainstream crossover, by the first decade of the twenty-first century, critics and cultural spelunkers were ready to consider the music again. Rush, the second-wave band that had built a fan base when the press thought it impossible, was the one group that had never lost its niche. They seesawed between strange and ironically cool, aided by every rock musician who admitted that he, too, had been to a Rush show.

One by one, then all at once, bands that had faded with the genre found reasons to re-form. Rick Wakeman seemed to be having the most fun, turning his stories of pregig booze and doomed marriages into two "Grumpy Old Rock Star" memoirs. In 2007, he set out on a quasi-cabaret tour—just Rick Wakeman, his piano, and unbelievable stories of excess or inspiration.

That same year, Kevin Ayers made one of the era's least-expected returns. He had gone dark for fifteen years, living the Mallorca life idealized in his music. "This quintessential hippie freak, it seems, has grown into the sweetest possible codger," wrote a patronizing but pleased reviewer.[5] "Like all magnificent terrestrials, no matter how rich in talent, Kevin always played very badly when drunk," said Daevid Allen. "Somehow his extraordinarily rich voice survived in spite of everything and washed convincingly over the wreckage, making it almost sound deliberate."[6]

By 2009, the heroes of the romantic comedy *I Love You, Man* could credibly jam on Rush songs and conspire to gain entry into a secret Rush gig. That same year, the music magazine collective Planet Rock launched *Prog* magazine, to be published nine times a year. They had no trouble meeting that goal; to some surprise, they soon added an issue to the schedule. When the punk songwriter Ted Leo affirmed his love for Rush in *Spin*, the piece was packaged as a "confessional" because Rush were proggy, and you couldn't endorse prog *qua* prog.

"I think at like the intersection of serious virtuosity and rock-iness, that's where some of the greatest music is," said Leo in a follow-up interview. "Some of the most famous punk bands—Wire, Ramones even—there was a certain amount of theory going into even their primitivism, you know? Even their choice to play as primitively as the Ramones or early Wire, that's not pure amateurism. There's a theory behind what they were doing that I think actually enhances the experience for me, so it's not like I shy away from the intellectual or theoretical side of any of this. I mean even my own songwriting; I have done things and continue to do things that are in the twists and turns of a song that are interesting to me more because it's like a little songwrit-ing game."[7]

Prog bands had demoed the electronics, pioneered the found sounds and use of empty space. They'd tweaked the synthesizers and parodied the three-minute pop song. All this was the result of a "remarkable explosion of the creative impulse in popular music," said Robert Fripp in a 2012 interview. Early, experimen-tal progressive rock "came from these young men who didn't know what they were doing, yet were able to do it."[8] You could say the same of the punks.

And when the progressives were *on*, they wrote gooseflesh-raising music. Their follies were grander than anyone else's fol-lies; their strange epics, stranger and more epic. We place an awful lot of emphasis on sincerity in music, and we assume that rawer, more automatic songs are de facto more sincere than music that's overly studied and composed. I don't think that's true. Art, if you trust Carl Jung's opinion, is "constantly at work educating the spirit of the age, conjuring up the forms in which the age is most lacking."[9] That's a perfect description of what the progressives were trying to do.

When I talked to first-wave progressive artists, only a few expressed outright contempt for less complicated music. For most, their feelings about punk are rooted in their resentment of the way the record companies of the late 1970s left them behind. For years, said Van der Graaf's Peter Hammill, prog artists "were given the right to experiment" by record companies. And then, not so much.[10]

The rest of us were lucky that experiment happened at all. Teams of highly trained visionaries paced themselves against their influences and their peers to write songs they were confident no one else would think of writing. They took the music far, far away from the basics, so that some later groups of jerks could take it "back to basics" and be praised for *their* genius. Every new artistic movement rebels against whatever came right before it. But the progressives' rebellion was the weirdest, and the best.

IT WAS NOT BILLED as the final appearance of Emerson, Lake, & Palmer. Twelve years had passed since the disappointment of *In the Hot Seat*. There had been no talk of a new album—lesson very much learned. Emerson had briefly reunited with the Nice. Palmer had reunited with Asia. Lake had toured with a new "Greg Lake Band." When he was asked about the band—and he was asked frequently—Emerson was more likely to criticize Lake for letting his voice go than to reminisce.

But in 2010, finally, ELP returned. An acoustic tour of the United States had knocked off some of the dust, and on July 25 their reunion was the headline event of London's new "High Voltage Festival." A posse of prog rock successors, from Marillion to Pendragon to Focus, warmed up Victoria Park for ninety minutes of ELP.

No one was satisfied. Emerson labored through his hand injuries. Lake's voice, deepened with age, had not improved in the intervening decade. Palmer was the first member of the band to declare the show a bust. "It wasn't to the standard that I liked and I didn't think it sounded that good," he said. "Unless it's as good as what it can be, then I can't do it. I would have carried on if it had been as good as it was. I don't believe it was and I don't believe it would have ever gotten back to that standard."[11]

Lake would admit that Palmer and Emerson were uncomfortable with ELP's sound. They had performed at such a high level—they had won fans, playing at that level—that it was difficult to ask anyone to settle. "I think we owed it to the fans," said Lake of the 2010 show. "I said, 'Look, we might not have been as great as we were, but here it is, you get a chance to hear the band one last time.'"[12]

Instead, ELP scattered, and the three musicians rejoined the ranks of progressive rock legends with fewer opportunities to create and more to cash in. There were always cruises and festivals and opportunities for quick tours in familiar markets. Carl Palmer formed "ELP Legacy," a tribute to his own music, with a guitarist replacing the keyboards. In 2012, Lake began a "Songs of a Lifetime" tour, with electronic backing tracks filling in for Emerson, Palmer, and the bygone orchestra. Every night, he walked out on stage to Kanye West's "Power."

Emerson was more judicious in how and when he played. In 2013, he traveled to Bowling Green, Kentucky, to conduct a piece he'd written for a never-made film, about the Civil War

Battle of Glorieta Pass. In April 2014, Emerson was a guest of honor at the annual Moogfest in Asheville, North Carolina. Named for the late Robert Moog, it was a celebration of all electronic music, but the monolithic box of wires that Emerson had been so identified with was at its center. The company, given new life by the electronic music boom, was unveiling a new product based on the oldest designs: the Emerson Moog Modular System. "This synthesizer represents so much to all of us," said Moog's chief engineer Cyril Lace.[13] Emerson was being canonized by a circuit board, and he could not have sounded prouder. Flanked by his own machine, and by the nearly identical new system, he reflected on how music was changed by it. "There are loads of prog bands, all over the world—internationally, like in Japan, Germany—you name it, all over, and all of them aspire to have this instrument," he said.[14]

On July 10, 2015, Emerson played in England for the first time since the ELP reunion. As part of that country's MoogFest, Emerson and the BBC Concert Orchestra took over the Barbican. The set list mingled ELP with Emerson's solo work, but it ended with him playing conductor again. His long hair falling over his suit, Emerson conducted "Glorieta Pass."

Eight months later, on March 11, 2016, Keith Emerson was dead. The news tumbled out as cruelly as it could. Emerson's social media sites posted a matter-of-fact statement, then a tribute from Carl Palmer. Within a day, reporters confirmed that the Los Angeles coroner was investigating a suicide. Emerson had died of a shotgun wound to the head. The report, when the coroner was finished, listed three maladies:

Arteriosclerotic cardiovascular disease
Valvular heart disease
Depression—chronic alcohol

Both versions of the news—the death itself, and the suicide—rattled the rock world's diaspora. Greg Lake, who had always hoped for one more reunion, told Britain's *Express* newspaper that his friend had been battling the black dog since at least the making of *Works*. "It's a very difficult thing to actually describe what depression is," mused Lake. "We all know what it looks like, people's moods become very black. But it's more complicated than that. It changes someone's personality. Also, Keith got into substance abuse, which made it worse and the whole thing just spiralled. He lived, in the end, this very lonely existence of someone who was deeply troubled. He loved music—that was his main purpose in life. But the music he made after ELP never bore fruit in the same way as it did in the early days."[15]

But Emerson had not been alone. With his girlfriend, Mari Kawaguchi, he had been preparing for, and dreading, a trip to Japan. The hand pain had never receded. Emerson dreaded what might come if he fulfilled the dates, then failed his own standards. "He read all the criticism online and was a sensitive soul," Kawaguchi told a British tabloid. "Last year he played concerts and people posted mean comments such as, 'I wish he would stop playing.' He was tormented with worry that he wouldn't be good enough. He was planning to retire after Japan."[16]

There were tributes immediately—little ones, leading up to a concert in Los Angeles at the end of May. The El Rey, a theater that packed in a little less than eight hundred people, was taken over. One by one, Emerson's friends and admirers filled the bill, and Michelle Moog-Koussa, the daughter of the synthesizer's creator, read a tribute of her own: "Keith took this daunting, sometimes delicate, and highly expressive new technology that was originally designed to sit on a table at some studio, and he boldly brought it to the masses." He traveled the world with it.[17]

Neither Palmer nor Lake appeared at the concert. The musicians who did stretched the show to three full hours, including a complete performance of "Tarkus." As midnight approached, Eddie Jobson got behind the big box of drums and wires for one final tribute to what Emerson had built. The song was "Lucky Man."

ACKNOWLEDGMENTS

O ne summer day in 2012, with the last normal presidential campaign heading into a slow period, I sat across from *Slate*'s David Plotz and Josh Levin and pitched them on my "fresca." Named for (but legally unrelated to) the fruity low-calorie beverage, the fresca was a yearly *Slate* staffer challenge. Whatever we normally covered—politics, in my case—the mission was to report and write for a month about something else.

I started talking about progressive rock, the music I'd wanted to write about since I was a teenager. To my surprise, and to my great reward, they listened. "Prog Spring," a title I wish I could grab the credit for, was a hit, and Howard Yoon saw a book in it. So did Matt Weiland, whose excitement for the project made me fret about delivering something that could earn it.

If I did, Matt's wonderful patience and sharp eye deserve the thanks. He chased me through three jobs, more delays than I want to admit, typically begged for by me from some hotel room in Iowa or New Hampshire or Florida. (America couldn't have had a normal election in 2016, could it? With a normal, boring candidate? I digress.) YAWN

There was plenty of hand-holding on the way to finishing this book, and I am grateful to Stephanie Hiebert for painstaking copyedits, Noah Shannon for research that made me question reality (in a good way), and Fay Torresyap for navigating the wild and expensive world of music photo licensing.

Thank you to Dan Kois for making something great out of the original *Slate* series. Thanks, too, to Alexandra Gutierrez, who read through the chapter I worried most about, and Jeb Lund, who pored over the first proof.

Plenty of musicians, managers, and producers gave me their time to talk through their stories. I'm especially grateful to Ian Anderson, Jon Anderson, Steve Hackett, Adrian Belew, Alan White, Carl Palmer, Steven Wilson, Todd Rundgren, David Hitchcock, Steve Howe, Trey Gunn, Eddie Jobson, Davy O'List, Ian McDonald, Roger Dean, Peter Hammill, the Roches, the organizers of NearFest, and the Cruise to the Edge team. And I am glad beyond the telling to have spoken to Chris Squire, Daevid Allen, John Wetton, Greg Lake, and Keith Emerson before they passed away.

Some wonderful, diligent, and thoughtful music historians tread this territory before I did. Everyone who worked for *Sounds*, *NME*, *ZigZag*, *Creem*, and the rest of the magazines that covered prog in real time helped me live through their typewriters. Sid Smith, Edward Macan, Dan Bukszpan, Paul Stump, and Nick Awde did the same.

Jack Shafer talked me through the project and loaned me libraries worth of material. Richard Morton Jack let me spend several messy days in his paper-stuffed study, where I found some of my favorite stuff. Barney Hoskyns and everyone else at Rock's Back Pages provides a heroic service for a low, low price—$30 per month for access to a curated mega-archive of sources—and were kind enough to let me rifle through the stacks. Thank you to the taxpayers of the UK and USA, too, for indirectly helping the British Library and Library of Congress stock such great archives.

The progressive rock fan community is as smart as any sub-culture you'll find. I am forever indebted to Mark Prindle and the whole Music Babble community, first for giving me my first crack at writing for an audience, and second for years of tape-trading and positive reinforcement. Singing along to "Tarkus" feels more natural when your friends are singing along.

NOTES

INTRODUCTION

1 Unless otherwise noted, all quotes in this Introduction come from conversations with the author during the Cruise to the Edge, April 2014.

2 Lloyd Grossman, "Emerson, Lake & Palmer: *Emerson, Lake & Palmer*," *Rolling Stone*, April 15, 1971.

3 Eric Tamm, *Robert Fripp: From King Crimson to Guitar Craft* (Faber and Faber, 1990), 31.

4 Dave Laing, "Yes: Essay," *Let It Rock*, February 1974.

5 Tim Morse, *Yesstories: Yes in Their Own Words* (St. Martin's Press, 1996), 9.

6 Jon Anderson, interview by the author, 2013.

7 Peter Sinfield, interview by the author, May 2012.

8 John Atkins, *The Who on Record: A Critical History, 1963–1998* (McFarland, 2000), 73.

9 Greg Lake, interview by the author, summer 2013.

10 Ibid.

11 Edward Macan, *Rocking the Classics: English Progressive Rock and the Counterculture* (Oxford University Press, 1997), 34.

12 Paul Stump, *The Music's All That Matters: A History of Progressive Rock* (Quartet Books, 1997), 129.

13 Jon Davison, interview by Jon Kirkman, "Storytellers" series, Cruise to the Edge, April 2014.

CHAPTER ONE: CHILDREN OF THE BLITZ

1 Hans Christian Andersen, *A Poet's Bazaar*, 11.

2 As quoted in "Master Liszt," *Musical Times*, April 1, 1902.

3 Alan Walker, *Franz Liszt*, vol. 3, *The Final Years, 1861–1886* (Knopf, 1996), 174.

4 Alan Walker, *Franz Liszt*, vol. 1, *The Virtuoso Years, 1811–1847* (Knopf, 1983), 371–72.

5   Ibid., 372.

6   O. G. Sonneck, "Heinrich Heine's Musical Feuilletons," *Musical Quarterly* 8, no. 4 (1922), https://books.google.com/books?id=alk5AAAAIAAJ.

7   Edward Macan, *Endless Enigma: A Musical Biography of Emerson, Lake and Palmer* (Open Court, 2006), 36.

8   Kevin Holm-Hudson, "A Promise Deferred: Multiply Directed Time and Thematic Transformation in Emerson Lake and Palmer's 'Trilogy,'" in *Progressive Rock Reconsidered*, ed. Kevin Holm-Hudson (Routledge, 2002), 112.

9   Stephen Walsh, *Musorgsky and His Circle: A Russian Musical Adventure* (Knopf, 2013), 296.

10 C. Hubert H. Parry, *Summary of the History and Development of Mediaeval and Modern European Music* (London: Novello, 1905), 119, https://archive.org/details/summaryof history00parrrich.

11 Ibid.

12 Robert Fripp, *Robert Fripp's Diary: Sunday, 11th March 2001*, Discipline Global Mobile, http://www.dgmlive.com/diaries.htm?entry=899.

13 Roger Nichols, *Ravel* (Dent, 1977), 137.

14 Robin Maconie, *Other Planets: The Music of Karlheinz Stockhausen* (Scarecrow Press, 2005), 178.

15 Karlheinz Stockhausen, "How Times Passes By," *Reihe* (English ed.) 3 (1959): 10–40, http://www.artesonoro.net/artesonoroglobal/HOW%20TIME%20PASSES%20 BY.PDF.

16 Daevid Allen, interview by the author, November 2013.

17 Aidan Smith, "Interview: Daevid Allen, Musician," *Scotsman*, November 19, 2009, http:// www.scotsman.com/what-s-on/music/interview-daevid-allen-musician-1-768818.

18 Marcus O'Dair, *Different Every Time: The Authorised Biography of Robert Wyatt* (Serpent's Tail, 2014), 32.

19 Ibid.

20 Ryan Dombal, "Robert Wyatt," *Pitchfork*, February 21, 2012, http://pitchfork.com/ features/5-10-15-20/8776-robert-wyatt.

21 O'Dair, *Different Every Time*, 28.

22 Rob Chapman, "Soft Machine," *Mojo*, June 1997, http://www.rob-chapman.com/pages/ soft.html.

23 Ibid.

24 O'Dair, *Different Every Time*, 38–39.

25 Ibid., 43.

26 Ibid., 44.

27 Ibid., 45.

28 Anil Prasad, "Terry Riley: Lighting Up Nodes," *Innerviews*, 2014, http://www.inner views.org/inner/riley.html.

29 Ibid.

30 O'Dair, *Different Every Time*, 47.

31 Sid Smith, *In the Court of King Crimson* (Helter Skelter, 2001), 10.

32 Keith Emerson, *Pictures of an Exhibitionist* (John Blake, 2004), 13.

33 Smith, *In the Court*, 14.

34 Ibid., 15.

35 Paul Stump, *Gentle Giant: Acquiring the Taste* (SAF, 2005), 12.

36 Tony Banks et al., *Genesis: Chapter & Verse* (Thomas Dunne Books/St. Martin's Griffin, 2007), 13.

37 "Robert Wyatt Story (BBC Four, 2001)," YouTube, September 22, 2012, https://www.youtube.com/watch?v=CdNKPqG-0ss.

38 Ray Coleman, *Phil Collins: The Definitive Biography* (Simon & Schuster, 1997), 27.

39 Peter Banks and Billy James, *Beyond and Before: The Formative Years of Yes* (Golden Treasures, 2001), 11–12.

40 Nick Awde et al., *Mellotron: The Machine and the Musicians That Revolutionised Rock* (Desert Hearts, 2008), 283.

41 Greg Lake, interview by the author, summer 2013.

42 Awde et al., *Mellotron*, 284.

43 Ibid., 196.

44 Ibid., 500.

45 Smith, *In the Court*, 15.

46 Jean-Gilles Blum, "Interview with Robert Fripp in Best," trans. Louis Courteau, January 1979, ETWiki, http://www.elephant-talk.com/wiki/Interview_with_Robert_Fripp_in_Best.

47 Smith, *In the Court*, 24.

48 Nick Logan, "Easier to Dislike Than to Like," *New Musical Express*, November 7, 1970.

49 David Rees, *Minstrels in the Gallery: A History of Jethro Tull* (Fire Fly, 1998), 45.

50 Awde et al., *Mellotron*, 110.

51 Smith, *In the Court*, 26.

52 Emerson, *Pictures*, 27.

53 Michael Gray, "Emerson, Lake & Palmer Ascending," *Crawdaddy!*, August 1971, Rock's Backpages, http://www.rocksbackpages.com/Library/Article/emerson-lake--palmer-ascending.

54 Emerson, *Pictures*, 35.

55 Ibid.

56 Graham Bennett, *Soft Machine: Out-Bloody-Rageous* (SAF, 2005), 56.

57 Ibid., 62.

58 Ibid., 63.

59 Ibid., 64.

60 Ibid., 65.

61 O'Dair, *Different Every Time*, 58.

62 Jimmy James, "Kevin Ayers Interview," *Perfect Sound Forever*, May 1998, http://www.furious.com/perfect/kevinayers.html.

63 Bennett, *Soft Machine*, 74.

CHAPTER TWO: THE PSYCHADELIC BOOM

1 Henry Scott-Irvine, *Procol Harum: The Ghosts of a Whiter Shade of Pale* (Omnibus, 2012), 18.

2   Keith Emerson, *Pictures of an Exhibitionist* (John Blake, 2004), 43.

3   Mark Blake, *Comfortably Numb: The Inside Story of Pink Floyd* (Da Capo Press, 2008), 58, 61.

4   Ibid., 70.

5   Graham Bennett, *Soft Machine: Out-Bloody-Rageous* (SAF, 2005), 79.

6   Stephen Nardelli, interview by Henry Potts, October–November 2003, http://www .bondegezou.co.uk/iv/sninterview.htm.

7   Peter Banks and Billy James, *Beyond and Before: The Formative Years of Yes* (Golden Treasures, 2001), 19–20.

8   Ibid., 20.

9   Emerson, *Pictures*, 52, 65.

10   Scott-Irvine, *Procol Harum*, 34.

11   Ibid., 35.

12   Ibid., 38.

13   Matthew Fisher, interview by the author, summer 2013.

14   Scott-Irvine, *Procol Harum*, 39.

15   Ibid., 37–38.

16   Ibid., 41.

17   Ibid., 41–42.

18   Ibid., 42.

19   Bennett, *Soft Machine*, 88.

20   Keith Shadwich, *Jimi Hendrix: Musician* (Hal Leonard Corporation, 2012), 91.

21   Bennett, *Soft Machine*, 91.

22   Banks and James, *Beyond and Before*, 26.

23   Chris Welch, *Close to the Edge: The Story of Yes* (Omnibus, 1999), 87.

24   Jim DeRogatis, *Kaleidoscope Eyes: Psychedelic Rock from the '60s to the '90s* (Carol Publishing Group, 1996), 86.

25   "The Story of Caravan," *ZigZag*, May 1975.

26   Bennett, *Soft Machine*, 109.

27   Ibid., 112.

28   Emerson, *Pictures*, 71.

29   Nick Awde et al., *Mellotron: The Machine and the Musicians That Revolutionised Rock* (Desert Hearts, 2008), 92.

30   Ibid., 169.

31   Ibid., 92.

32   David Beard, "Revisit the Moody Blues' Landmark Album, 'Days of Future Passed,'" *Goldmine*, June 12, 2012, http://www.goldminemag.com/article/revisit-the-moody -blues-landmark-album-days-of-future-passed.

33   Awde et al., *Mellotron*, 93.

34   Beard, "Revisit the Moody Blues' Landmark Album."

35   Awde et al., *Mellotron*, 167.

36   Beard, "Revisit the Moody Blues' Landmark Album."

37   Awde et al., *Mellotron*, 170.

38 Ibid., 171.

39 Beard, "Revisit the Moody Blues' Landmark Album."

40 Banks and James, *Beyond and Before*, 29.

41 Ibid., 33, 34.

42 Ibid., 35.

43 Ibid., 38.

44 Welch, *Close to the Edge*, 48.

45 Banks and James, *Beyond and Before*, 39.

46 Welch, *Close to the Edge*, 48.

47 Banks and James, *Beyond and Before*, 40.

48 "Pink Floyd & the Story of Prog Rock," *Mojo* Classic, Collectors Edition, July 2005.

49 Scott-Irvine, *Procol Harum*, 66.

50 [Barry] Miles, "The Who: Pete on *Tommy* #2," *International Times*, June 13, 1969, Rock's Backpages, http://www.rocksbackpages.com/Library/Article/the-who-pete-on -itommyi-2.

51 Armando Gallo, *Genesis: I Know What I Like* (Gallo, 2014), Kindle ed., loc. 367.

52 "Peter Gabriel Talks about the Downs and Ups of Genesis . . . ," *ZigZag*, May 1971, Rock's Backpages, http://www.rocksbackpages.com/Library/Article/genesis.

53 Daryl Easlea, *Without Frontiers: The Life and Music of Peter Gabriel* (Omnibus, 2014), 41.

54 Gallo, *Genesis*, loc. 404–5.

55 Barry Miles, "The Nice: Two Thirds Nice," *International Times*, April 25, 1969.

56 Emerson, *Pictures*, 80.

57 Nick Jones, "London Notes," *Rolling Stone*, November 1967.

58 Ibid.

59 Chris Welch, "1968 the Year of the Nice," *Melody Maker*, July 13, 1968.

60 Emerson, *Pictures*, 100.

61 Ibid., 98.

62 Ibid., 116.

63 The Nice, *Ars Longa Vita Brevis* (Immediate Records, 1968), liner notes.

64 Welch, "1968 the Year of the Nice."

65 David O'List, interview by the author, May 2013.

66 Keith Jordan and Davy O'List, "An Interview with the Nice's Davy O'List," *Pink Floyd Blog*, October 5, 2006, http://www.neptunepinkfloyd.co.uk/tag/keith-emerson.

67 Emerson, *Pictures*, 119.

CHAPTER THREE: A BILLION TIMES THE IMPACT

1 Sid Smith, *In the Court of King Crimson* (Helter Skelter, 2001), 41.

2 Ibid., 44.

3 Nick Awde et al., *Mellotron: The Machine and the Musicians That Revolutionised Rock* (Desert Hearts, 2008), 502–3.

4 Smith, *In the Court*, chap. 2.

5 Ibid., 44.

6 "King Crimson Journal," January 13, 1969, ETWiki, http://www.elephant-talk.com/ articles/fripp-yp.htm.

7 Smith, *In the Court*, 46.

8 Peter Sinfield, interview by the author, May 2012.

9 Paul Stump, *The Music's All That Matters: A History of Progressive Rock* (Quartet Books, 1997), 43.

10 "King Crimson Journal," January 27, 1969.

11 Ibid., February 23–March 1, 1969.

12 "It's Underground? It's Chrysalis! The Whole Scene under One Roof," *Top Pops and Music Now*, September 1969.

13 Daviona Burman, "The Van Der Graff [*sic*] Generator," [*Manchester Independent*], http://www.vandergraafgenerator.co.uk/pawnhearts/68_2a.jpg, accessed November 14, 2016.

14 Jim Christopulos and Phil Smart, *Van der Graaf Generator, the Book: A History of the Band Van der Graaf Generator, 1967 to 1978* ("Phil and Jim," 2005), Kindle ed., loc. 1091.

15 Ibid., loc. 487.

16 Peter Hammill, "The Aerosol Grey Machine CD Sleeve Notes," 1997, http://www .vandergraafgenerator.co.uk/aeronote.htm.

17 Smith, *In the Court*, 37.

18 Ibid.

19 Ibid., 49.

20 Ibid.

21 *Robert Fripp Unplugged! Ultimate Conversations with Robert Fripp* [audio recording] (Musical Concepts, 2007).

22 Smith, *In the Court*, 48.

23 *Robert Fripp Unplugged!*

24 Robert Fripp, "Robert Fripp's Diary: Saturday, 5th July 1969," Discipline Global Mobile, http://www.dgmlive.com/diaries.htm?diarist=3&entry=242.

25 Robert Fripp, "Robert Fripp's Diary: Sunday, 6th July 1969," Discipline Global Mobile, http://www.dgmlive.com/diaries.htm?artist=&show=&member=3&entry=237.

26 Ibid.

27 Smith, *In the Court*, 54.

28 Ibid., 68.

29 "What Pete Townshend Thinks about King Crimson," *Rolling Stone*, December 27, 1969, http://www.songsouponsea.com/Promenade/lyrics/gallery/RS122769.html.

30 Steve Turner, "King Crimson," *Beat Instrumental*, January 1972.

31 Smith, *In the Court*, 74.

32 John Mendelsohn, "King Crimson Opens Its Rock 'n' Roll Stand," *Los Angeles Times*, December 5, 1969.

33 Smith, *In the Court*, 76.

34 John Mendelsohn, "King Crimson: *In the Court of King Crimson*," *Rolling Stone*, December 27, 1969.

35 Michael Wale, "A Long and Rambling Interview with Robert Fripp," *ZigZag*, October 1973.

36 Peter Banks and Billy James, *Beyond and Before: The Formative Years of Yes* (Golden Treasures, 2001), 62.

37 Ibid., 63.

38 Keith Emerson, *Pictures of an Exhibitionist* (John Blake, 2004), 161.

39 Ibid.

40 Ibid., 163.

41 Ibid., 171.

42 Smith, *In the Court*, 83.

43 Ibid., 82.

44 Cameron Crowe, "King Crimson's Fripp: 'Music's Just a Means for Magic' " [*Rolling Stone*, no. 149 (December 6, 1973)], *The Uncool* (blog), http://www.theuncool.com/journalism/rs149-robert-fripp.

45 Smith, *In the Court*, 85.

46 Ibid., 87.

47 Ibid., 88.

48 Richard Williams, "McDonald & Giles: Outside the Court of the Crimson King," *Melody Maker*, November 21, 1970.

49 Smith, *In the Court*, 99.

50 Ibid., 93.

51 Ibid., 78.

52 Gordon Haskell, interview by the author, December 2013.

53 Ibid.

54 Smith, *In the Court*, 111.

55 Ibid., 113.

56 Ibid., 110.

57 Ibid.

58 Ibid., 111.

59 Haskell, interview, December 2013.

60 Tony Norman, "The Crimson 'Lizard,'" *Music Now*, October 26, 1970.

61 Haskell, interview, December 2013.

62 Smith, *In the Court*, 115.

63 Ibid., 114.

64 Haskell, interview, December 2013.

65 Ibid.

66 Norman, "Crimson 'Lizard.' "

67 Ibid.

CHAPTER FOUR: MOOG MEN

1 Keith Emerson, *Pictures of an Exhibitionist* (John Blake, 2004), 174.

2 Dick Meadows, "Carl Palmer," *Sounds*, November 27, 1971.

3   Emerson, *Pictures*, 175–76.

4   Ibid., 178–79.

5   Trevor J. Pinch and Frank Trocco, *Analog Days: The Invention and Impact of the Moog Synthesizer* (Harvard University Press, 2004), 203.

6   Emerson, *Pictures*, 166.

7   Ibid., 180.

8   Ibid.

9   Ibid., 181.

10 Ibid.

11 Ibid.

12 "Gary James' Interview with Greg Lake of Emerson, Lake and Palmer," ClassicBands, [1997], http://www.classicbands.com/GregLakeInterview.html.

13 Emerson, *Pictures*, 186, 187.

14 Chris Welch et al., "The Isle of Wight Festival: Five Days That Rocked Britain," *Melody Maker*, September 5, 1970.

15 Penny Valentine, "Here Comes Another Orgasmic Peak," *Sounds*, October 31, 1970.

16 Peter Banks and Billy James, *Beyond and Before: The Formative Years of Yes* (Golden Treasures, 2001), 100.

17 Chris Squire, "Open Your Eyes (Eagle)" (interview with Anil Prasad, Innerview), January 1998, http://www.progrock.fateback.com/sider/anmeldel/yes/openyour.htm.

18 Banks and James, *Beyond and Before*, 100.

19 Tim Morse, *Yesstories: Yes in Their Own Words* (St. Martin's Press, 1996), 20.

20 Chris Welch, *Close to the Edge: The Story of Yes* (Omnibus, 1999), 89.

21 Joe Bosso, "Steve Howe Talks The Yes Album Track-by-Track," *MusicRadar*, December 17, 2012, http://www.musicradar.com/us/news/guitars/steve-howe-talks-the-yes-album -track-by-track-568616.

22 Morse, *Yesstories*, 978.

23 Tony Norman, "Yes: The Time Is Now, the Word Is Love," *Music Now*, August 8, 1970.

24 Bosso, "Steve Howe Talks."

25 Penny Valentine, "The Anderson Tapes," *Sounds*, March 10, 1973.

26 Morse, *Yesstories*, 25.

27 Ibid., 24.

28 Valentine, "Anderson Tapes."

29 Karen de Groot, "Yes: 'We Owe Our Audiences to Really Sweat for Good Sound Quality,'" *Music Now*, January 30, 1971.

30 Ibid.

31 Emerson, *Pictures*, 190.

32 Ibid., 201.

33 Blair Pethel, *Keith Emerson: The Emergence and Growth of Style: A Study of Selected Works* (UMI, 1988), 19.

34 Emerson, *Pictures*, 203.

35 Ibid., 204.

36 Meadows, "Carl Palmer."

37 "Emerson, Lake & Palmer: The Dagger Does More Than You Think," *Circus*, March 1972, http://ladiesofthelake.com/cabinet/circus72.html.

38 William Neal, "Tarkus," 2009, http://web.archive.org/web/20091109015042/http://www.williamneal.co.uk/index.php?option=com_igallery&view=gallery&id=2&Itemid=18.

39 David Lubin, "Emerson Lake & Palmer: *Tarkus, Rolling Stone*, August 19, 1971.

40 Penny Valentine, "Greg Lake—ELP's Dark Horse," *Sounds*, December 5, 1970.

41 Pete Stone, "Demolishing the Record Cover," *Creem*, June 1971.

42 "Francis Monkman (Curved Air, Sky, Solo)," Progressor: Interviews of Prog, August 25, 2006, http://www.progressor.net/interview/francis_monkman.html.

43 Mont Campbell, interview by the author, May 2013.

44 Nick Awde et al., *Mellotron: The Machine and the Musicians That Revolutionised Rock* (Desert Hearts, 2008), 200–201.

45 "Peter Gabriel Talks about the Downs and Ups of Genesis . . . ," *ZigZag*, May 1971, Rock's Backpages, http://www.rocksbackpages.com/Library/Article/genesis.

46 Awde et al., *Mellotron*, 199–200.

47 Ibid.

48 Tony Banks et al., *Genesis: Chapter & Verse* (Thomas Dunne Books/St. Martin's Griffin, 2007), 107.

49 Caroline Boucher, "Genesis: Too Posh for Fame," *Disc and Music Echo*, March 25, 1972.

50 Notes about the song "Watcher of the Skies," Genesis Museum, http://www.genesismuseum.com/features/songbook77.htm, accessed November 30, 2016.

51 Genesis, *Watcher of the Skies: Genesis Revisited* (Guardian Records, 1996), liner notes.

52 Banks et al., *Genesis: Chapter & Verse*, 122.

53 Jerry Gilbert, "Genesis Doing the Foxtrot," *Sounds*, September 9, 1972.

54 Banks et al., *Genesis: Chapter & Verse*, 122.

55 Ibid., 113.

56 Gilbert, "Genesis Doing the Foxtrot."

57 Banks et al., *Genesis: Chapter & Verse*, 124.

58 Ibid., 123.

59 Richard Williams, "How to Succeed in Pop without Really Trying," *Radio Times*, August 6, 1970.

60 As quoted in Graham Bennett, *Soft Machine: Out-Bloody-Rageous* (SAF, 2005), 214.

61 Ibid.

62 Ibid., 216.

63 Edward Macan, *Endless Enigma: A Musical Biography of Emerson, Lake and Palmer* (Open Court, 2006), 175.

64 Dick Meadows, "Carl Palmer."

65 Penny Valentine, "Keith Emerson in the Talk-In," *Sounds*, July 7, 1971.

66 Don Snowden, "Moog on the State of the Synthesizer," *Los Angeles Times*, June 7, 1981.

67 Jody Breslaw, review in *Sounds*, October 9, 1971.

68 Howard Fielding, untitled concert review, *Sounds*, December 18, 1971.

69 Greg Lake, interview by the author, summer 2013.

CHAPTER FIVE: A HIGHER ART FORM

1   Chris Welch, *Close to the Edge: The Story of Yes* (Omnibus, 1999), 109.

2   Rick Wakeman, *Grumpy Old Rock Star: And Other Wondrous Stories* (Preface Digital, 2009), Kindle ed.

3   https://www.youtube.com/watch?v=6EfPCPqjoAg.

4   Will Romano, *Mountains Come Out of the Sky: The Illustrated History of Prog Rock* (Backbeat Books, 2010), 62.

5   Welch, *Close to the Edge*, 109.

6   Darryl Morden, "Yes's Original Keyboardist Tony Kaye Sues to Stop New Boxed Set," Yes in the Press, July 18, 2002, http://zenponies.com/yitp/2002/jul/jul18_02.html.

7   Nick Awde et al., *Mellotron: The Machine and the Musicians That Revolutionised Rock* (Desert Hearts, 2008), 288.

8   Welch, *Close to the Edge*, 110.

9   Penny Valentine, "Yes: Making It Last," *Sounds*, 1971, Rock's Backpages, http://www.rocksbackpages.com/Library/Article/yes-making-it-last.

10   "Rick Goes Back to Go Forward," *Sounds*, May 19, 1973.

11   Romano, *Mountains Come Out of the Sky*, 62.

12   Tim Morse, *Yesstories: Yes in Their Own Words* (St. Martin's Press, 1996), 31.

13   Ibid., 32.

14   Richard Cromelin, "Yes: *Fragile*," *Rolling Stone*, March 16, 1972, Rock's Backpages, http://www.rocksbackpages.com/Library/Article/yes-fragile.

15   Ibid.

16   Welch, *Close to the Edge*, 118.

17   Steve Peacock, "Dean of the Future," *Sounds*, October 14, 1972.

18   Ibid.

19   *Prog Rock Britannia: An Observation in Three Movements*, directed by Nigel Planer (BBC, January 2, 2009).

20   Ibid.

21   Valentine, "Yes: Making It Last."

22   "After the Pig: Mick's Plans," *Music Now*, October 3, 1970.

23   Ray Telford, "Fresh Soft Mick," *Sounds*, December 11, 1971.

24   Jerry Gilbert, "When It Comes to Mind-Blowing, Hawkwind Are Really into It," *Sounds*, October 17, 1970.

25   Lemmy and Janiss Garza, *White Line Fever: The Autobiography* (Citadel Press, 2004), 71.

26   James Johnson, "The Truth about Hawkwind," *NME*, February 5, 1972.

27   Andrew Means, "Hawkwind: A Space Odyssey," *Melody Maker*, April 29, 1972.

28   John Ingham, "Rock as Electric Wallpaper," *Creem*, October 1971.

29   "Ian Anderson (7 of 11)—Recording Aqualung" (Living Legends Music interview), YouTube, January 9, 2008, https://www.youtube.com/watch?v=OhxbbiJ27vU.

30   *Jethro Tull: Their Fully Authorised Story* (Pinnacle Vision, 2008), DVD.

31   David Rees, *Minstrels in the Gallery: A History of Jethro Tull* (Fire Fly, 1998), Kindle ed., loc. 614.

32 Ibid., loc. 597.

33 Romano, *Mountains Come Out of the Sky*, 86.

34 Keith Altham, "Jethro Tull: God Is Alive and Starring On . . . ," *Record Mirror*, March 27, 1971.

35 Jethro Tull, *Thick as a Brick*, 40th anniversary special ed. (Chrysalis Records, 2012), liner notes.

36 Chris Welch, "Tull's Tommy?" *Melody Maker*, March 11, 1972.

37 Ibid.

38 Jordan Blum, "Looking Back (and Forward) on Jethro Tull's 'Thick as a Brick,'" *Pop-Matters*, March 12, 2013.

39 Dave Marsh, "Jethro Tull: Thick as a Brick," *Creem*, August 1972.

40 John Swenson, "Jethro Tull: Thick as a Brick," *Crawdaddy!*, August 1972.

41 Bill Bruford, "America," *Melody Maker*, March 11, 1972.

42 "03/27/1972 Boston, Massachusetts," Forgotten Yesterdays: A Comprehensive Guide to Yes Shows, http://forgotten-yesterdays.com/dates.asp?ftype=1&qdec=1970&qdateid=496, accessed June 2014.

43 J. P. Dolan, "Crimso [*sic*] in Boston," *Melody Maker*, April 15, 1972.

44 Ibid.

45 Welch, *Close to the Edge*, 127.

46 Morse, *Yesstories*, 36.

47 Welch, *Close to the Edge*, 122.

48 Chris Welch, "The What, Where and Why of Howe," *Melody Maker*, January 8, 1972.

49 Tim Morse, "Conversation with Eddy Offord, from NFTE #234," *Notes from the Edge* (blog), 2002, http://www.nfte.org/interviews/EO234.html.

50 Welch, *Close to the Edge*, 124.

51 Penny Valentine, "The Anderson Tapes," *Sounds*, March 10, 1973.

52 Morse, *Yesstories*, 36.

53 Steve Turner, "The Great Yes Technique Debate," *Rolling Stone*, March 30, 1972, Rock's Backpages, http://www.rocksbackpages.com/article.html?ArticleID=1837.

54 Bill Bruford, *Bill Bruford: The Autobiography: Yes, King Crimson, Earthworks, and More* (Jawbone Press, 2009), 56, 57.

55 Ibid., 58.

56 Jim Christopulos and Phil Smart, *Van der Graaf Generator, the Book: A History of the Band Van der Graaf Generator, 1967 to 1978* ("Phil and Jim," 2005), Kindle ed., loc. 2012.

57 Steve Peacock, "Van der Graaf—Opening a Chink in the Curtain," *Sounds*, January 29, 1972.

58 Ibid.

59 David Hitchcock, interview by the author, September 2013.

60 Romano, *Mountains Come Out of the Sky*, 99.

61 Richard Sinclair, interview by the author, September 2013.

62 Andrew Tyler, "Caravan: Missing Out on Hysteria," *Disc*, June 24, 1972, Rock's Back-pages, http://www.rocksbackpages.com/Library/Article/caravan-missing-out-on-hysteria.

63 Romano, *Mountains Come Out of the Sky*, 101.

64 Derek Shulman, interview by the author, 2014.

65 Thodoris, "Interview: Derek Shulman (Gentle Giant)," *Hit Channel*, April 22, 2014, http://www.hit-channel.com/interviewderek-shulman-gentle-giant/62545.

66 Richard Williams, "Have Egg Finally Cracked It?" *Melody Maker*, January 1, 1972.

67 Ibid.

68 Ibid.

69 "Learning How to Be Independent," *Sounds*, January 27, 1973.

70 Welch, *Close to the Edge*, 135.

71 Jon Anderson, interview by the author, summer 2012.

72 Penny Valentine, "The Six Wives of a Yes Man," *Sounds*, January 27, 1973.

73 Jethro Tull, *A Passion Play* (Chrysalis Records, 1973), liner notes.

74 Chris Welch, "Jethro Tull: A Passion Play," *Melody Maker*, July 21, 1973.

75 Ian Anderson, interview by the author, summer 2012.

76 *New Musical Express.*

77 Welch, *Close to the Edge.*

78 *New Musical Express.*

79 *Prog Rock Britannia.*

80 Roger Dean, interview by the author, August 2012.

81 Tony Palmer, *Observer.*

82 Wakeman, *Grumpy Old Rock Star*, loc. 1634.

83 Ibid., loc. 1616.

84 Ibid., loc. 1636.

85 Ibid., loc. 1631.

86 Morse, *Yesstories*, 45.

87 Steve Howe, interview by the author, April 2014.

88 Jon Anderson, interview by the author, 2013.

89 Howe, interview, April 2014.

90 Chris Welch, "Why I Said No to Yes," *Melody Maker*, July 20, 1974.

CHAPTER SIX: HAMMERS AND BELLS

1 John Harris, *The Dark Side of the Moon: The Making of the Pink Floyd Masterpiece* (Harper Perennial, 1992), 74.

2 Ibid., 84–85.

3 Ibid., 85.

4 Mike Oldfield, *Changeling: The Autobiography of Mike Oldfield* (Virgin, 2007), 110–11.

5 Ibid., 110.

6 Richard Williams, "Fresh Ayers," *Melody Maker*, March 4, 1972.

7 Ibid.

8 Johnny Black, "Mike Oldfield: The Making of *Tubular Bells*," *Q Magazine*, August 2001, Rock's Backpages, www.rocksbackpages.com/Library/Article/mike-oldfield-the-making-of-itubular-bellsi.

9 Mick Brown, "Investigation of a Citizen above Suspicion," *Sounds*, January 31, 1976.

10 Simon Heyworth, Tom Newman, and Mike Oldfield, "The Making of Tubular Bells," *Q Magazine*, August 2001, http://tubular.net/articles/2001_08/The-Making-of -Tubular-Bells.

11 Richard Branson, *Losing My Virginity: The Autobiography* (Virgin, 1998), 115.

12 Fred Deller, "The Man Who Taped the Tubular Bells," *NME*, February 8, 1975.

13 Heyworth et al., "Making of Tubular Bells."

14 Ibid.

15 Oldfield, *Changeling*, 127.

16 Ibid.

17 Deller, "Man Who Taped."

18 Oldfield, *Changeling*, 129.

19 Heyworth et al., "Making of Tubular Bells."

20 Oldfield, *Changeling*, 137.

21 Ibid., 138.

22 Ibid.

23 Cameron Crowe, "King Crimson's Fripp: 'Music's Just a Means for Magic'" [*Rolling Stone*, no. 149 (December 6, 1973)], *The Uncool* (blog), http://www.theuncool.com/ journalism/rs149-robert-fripp.

24 Sid Smith, *In the Court of King Crimson* (Helter Skelter, 2001), 155.

25 Ibid., 157.

26 Steve Peacock, "Crimson: Head Heart and Hips," *Sounds*, October 14, 1972.

27 Steve Peacock, "Crimson, Inside and Outside," *Sounds*, March 17, 1973.

28 Mike Dickson, "Interview with Jamie Muir in Ptloemaic [*sic*] Terrascope," November 20, 1996, ETWiki, http://www.elephant-talk.com/wiki/Interview_with_Jamie_ Muir_in_Ptloemaic_Terrascope.

29 David Sheppard, *On Some Faraway Beach: The Life and Times of Brian Eno* (Chicago Review Press, 2009), 104.

30 Steven Rosen, "King Crimson's Robert Fripp," *Guitar Player*, May 1974, Rock's Backpages, http://www.rocksbackpages.com/Library/Article/king-crimsons-robert-fripp.

31 Ian MacDonald, "Robert Fripp: The Sexual Athlete," *New Musical Express*, September 1, 1973, Rock's Backpages, http://www.rocksbackpages.com/Library/Article/robert-fripp -the-sexual-athlete.

32 Caroline Frost, "Sir Richard Branson Reveals John Peel Fell for Mike Oldfield's Tubu- lar Bells over Dinner, Helped Start Virgin Empire," *Huffington Post UK*, August 7, 2012, http://www.huffingtonpost.co.uk/2012/08/07/richard-branson-john-peel-mike -oldfield-tubular-bells_n_1751752.html.

33 "John Peel—*Top Gear*—Introducing Tubular Bells," YouTube, May 3, 2012, https:// www.youtube.com/watch?v=yDi7qhBO5q4.

34 John Peel, "Tubular Bells" (originally published in *Listener*, June 7, 1973), in *The Olivetti Chronicles* (Bantam Press, 2008), 311–13.

35 Oldfield, *Changeling*, 140–41.

36 Ibid., 142.

37 Branson, *Losing My Virginity*, 125.

38   Steve Peacock, "A Young Virgin Will Never Let You Down," *Sounds*, June 9, 1973.

39   Oldfield, *Changeling*, 144.

40   Branson, *Losing My Virginity*, 125.

41   Tony Palmer et al., *All You Need Is Love: The Story of Popular Music*, episode 16: "Imagine: New Directions" (Isolde Films, 2008), DVD.

42   Oldfield, *Changeling*, 146.

43   Ibid., 152.

44   "Robert Wyatt Story (BBC Four, 2001)", YouTube, September 22, 2012, https://www.youtube.com/watch?v=CdNKPqG-0ss.

45   *Prog Rock Britannia: An Observation in Three Movements*, directed by Nigel Planer (BBC, January 2, 2009).

46   Marcus O'Dair, "Robert Wyatt at 70: Happy Birthday, Old Rottenhat!" *Guardian*, January 27, 2015, https://www.theguardian.com/music/musicblog/2015/jan/27/robert-wyatt-at-70-happy-birthday-old-rottenhat.

47   Allan Jones, "Ruth, Richard, and Robert . . . ," *Melody Maker*, June 14, 1975.

48   From a Virgin Records ad in *Sounds*, date unknown.

49   Richie Unterberger, "Robert Wyatt: Interview" [November, 18, 1996], *Perfect Sound Forever*, http://www.furious.com/perfect/wyatt.html.

50   Nick Mason and Philip Dodd, *Inside Out: A Personal History of Pink Floyd* (Chronicle Books, 2005), 167.

51   Graham Bennett, *Soft Machine: Out-Bloody-Rageous* (SAF, 2005), 263.

52   "British Rock: Are We Facing Disaster?" *Melody Maker*, September 21, 1974.

53   Ibid.

54   Ibid.

55   "Emerson, Lake and Palmer's 'Brain Salad Surgery'—The Dirty Dinner Game Becomes a Masterpiece," *Circus*, January 1974.

56   Greg Lake, interview by the author, summer 2012.

57   Ibid.

58   Chris Welch, "Greg Lake: Rock Will Go Back to Its Roots," *Melody Maker*, August 3, 1974, Rock's Backpages, http://www.rocksbackpages.com/Library/Article/greg-lake-rock-will-go-back-to-its-roots.

59   "Karn Evil 9: Songs," *Brain Salad Surgery: Emerson, Lake & Palmer*, last update July, 24, 2016, http://www.brain-salad-surgery.de/karn_evil_9.html, accessed November 14, 2016.

60   Ian Dove, "They Won't Bach around the Clock," *New York Times*, December 16, 1973.

61   Trevor J. Pinch and Frank Trocco, *Analog Days: The Invention and Impact of the Moog Synthesizer* (Harvard University Press, 2004), 194.

62   "Gear Common to the Group," *Brain Salad Surgery: Emerson, Lake & Palmer*, http://www.brain-salad-surgery.de/gear_common_to_the_group.html, accessed summer 2014.

63   Chris Welch, "You Can't Bluff Your Way through Yes," *Melody Maker*, March 29, 1975.

64   Chris Salewicz, "The Rick Wakeman Consumer's Guide to Beers of the World," *NME*, December 21, 1974.

65   Ibid.

66   Steve Clarke, "New Music and Old Arguments," *NME*, November 15, 1975.

67   *Creem*, September 1974.

68   David Rees, *Minstrels in the Gallery: A History of Jethro Tull* (Fire Fly, 1998), Kindle ed., loc. 934.

69   Ibid., loc. 971.

70   Chris Charlesworth, "Tull Put Back the Fun," *Melody Maker*, November 16, 1974, http://www.tullpress.com/mm16nov74.htm.

71   "Lemmy Quits Hawkwind," *Sounds*, May 31, 1975.

72   "Interview: Richard Sinclair (Caravan, Hatfield and the North, Camel)," *Hit Channel*, April 2, 2016, http://www.hit-channel.com/interview-richard-sinclair-caravan-hatfield-and-the-north-camel/97681.

73   Karl Dallas, "Mike Oldfield: High on the Ridge," *Melody Maker*, August 24, 1974, Rock's Backpages, http://www.rocksbackpages.com/Library/Article/mike-oldfield-high-on-the-ridge.

74   John Robinson, "Kevin Ayers—Album by Album," December 2008, *Uncut*, http://www.uncut.co.uk/features/kevin-ayers-album-by-album-25705#S5zhqZwXahgYtODV.99.

75   Ibid.

76   Karl Dallas, "I Can't Stand People Who Play Things Blandly," *Melody Maker*, September 28, 1974.

77   Brown, "Investigation of a Citizen."

78   Karl Dallas, "Beyond the Ridge," *Melody Maker*, October 25, 1975.

79   Ibid.

80   Ibid.

81   Palmer, *All You Need Is Love*.

82   Ibid.

83   Oldfield, *Changeling*, 163.

CHAPTER SEVEN: COMPLEXITY FREAKS

1   Scott McFadyen et al., *Rush: Beyond the Lighted Stage* (Rush Doc Films, 2010), DVD.

2   Skip Daly, "Ian Grandy Interview: Rush's First Roadie," *Guitar International*, http://web.archive.org/web/20120222034607/http://guitarinternational.com/2009/09/16/a-talk-with-ian-grandy-rushs-first-roadie, accessed June 2015.

3   Deborah Frost, "Rush: A Canadian Rush," *Circus*, February 14, 1977.

4   Martin Popoff, *Contents under Pressure: 30 Years of Rush at Home and Away* (ECW Press, 2004), 17–18.

5   Ibid., 25–26.

6   Geoff Barton, "Rush Judgment," *Sounds*, July 16, 1977.

7   Frost, "Rush: A Canadian Rush."

8   Popoff, *Contents under Pressure*, 42.

9   Kory Grow, "Rush's Alex Lifeson on 40 Years of '2112': 'It Was Our Protest Album,'" *Rolling Stone*, March 29, 2016, http://www.rollingstone.com/music/news/rushs-alex-lifeson-on-40-years-of-2112-it-was-our-protest-album-20160329#ixzz496s5UnpL.

10   Frost, "Rush: A Canadian Rush."

11 Mark Powell, *Prophets and Sages: 101 Great Progressive and Underground Rock Albums* (Cherry Red, 2010), 200.

12 Rex Anderson, "Greek Keyboard Revolutionary," *New Musical Express*, October 12, 1974.

13 Steven Rosen, "Jan Akkerman: Dutch Treat," *Guitar Player*, May 1975.

14 Ibid.

15 Hans Beckes, "Interview with Jan Akkerman," *Radio 538*, November 24, 1973, 197.

16 "Interview: Franz Di Cioccio (Premiata Forneria Marconi)," *Hit Channel*, March 19, 2015, http://www.hit-channel.com/interviewfranz-di-cioccio-premiata-forneria-marconi/79130.

17 Ibid.

18 Roy Carr, "You Laugh at da Italian Rock, You Sleep-a wit' da Fishes," *NME*, April 5, 1975.

19 David McKenna and Ludovic Merle, "'Magma, c'est moi': Christian Vander Interview Pt 2," translated by David McKenna, *Rockfort*, http://rockfort.info/content.aspx?cid=160, accessed January 2016.

20 Daevid Allen, interview by Richie Unterberger, RichieUnterberger.com, http://www.richieunterberger.com/allen.html, accessed October 2015.

21 Todd Rundgren, interview by the author, summer 2015.

22 Ibid.

23 Ibid.

24 Geoff Brown, "Rundgren: Rock Is Dead!" *Melody Maker*, July 12, 1975.

25 Rundgren, interview, summer 2015.

26 Max Bell, "Kansas: *Kansas*," *New Musical Express*, April 26, 1975.

27 "Kerry Livgren (Kansas, AD & solo fame)," Progressor: Interviews of Prog, July 1, 2002, http://www.progressor.net/interview/kerry_livgren.html.

28 Bruce Pollock, "Kerry Livgren of Kansas," May 1984, Songfacts, http://www.songfacts.com/blog/interviews/kerry_livgren_of_kansas.

29 Frost, "Rush: A Canadian Rush."

30 Paul Morley and Paul Rambali, "The Rush Phenomenon," *New Musical Express*, June 11, 1977.

31 Paul Elliot, "Q Classic's *Pink Floyd & the Story of Prog Rock*," July 2005, Power Windows, http://www.2112.net/powerwindows/transcripts/20050700qclassicprogspecial.htm.

32 Barry Miles, "Is Everybody Feelin' All Right? (Geddit . . . ?)" *New Musical Express*, March 4, 1978.

33 Ibid.

34 Ibid.

35 Paul Morley, "Power, Pomp, Purity, Pretention, Popularity . . . : The Rush Problem," *New Musical Express*, June 24, 1978.

36 Geoff Barton, "Rush: This Man Has Nightmares," *Sounds*, September 30, 1978.

37 Elliot, "Q Classic's *Pink Floyd*."

38 Popoff, *Contents under Pressure*, 88.

39 Ibid., 102.

40 Ibid.
41 Ibid., 103.

CHAPTER EIGHT: FRIPPERIES

1 Robert Partridge, "Why I Killed the King: An Interview with Robert Fripp," *Melody Maker*, October 5, 1974, ETWiki, http://www.elephant-talk.com/wiki/Interview_with_Robert_Fripp_in_Melody_Maker_(1974).

2 Ibid.

3 Ian Dove, "Fripp: After King Crimson, the Apocalypse," *Rolling Stone*, December 19, 1974, ETWiki, http://www.elephant-talk.com/wiki/Interview_with_Robert_Fripp_in_Rolling_Stone.

4 Partridge, "Why I Killed the King."

5 Chris Salewicz, "Uriah Heep: Ex-Crimson Bass Man Seduced," *New Musical Express*, March 22, 1975, Rock's Backpages, http://www.rocksbackpages.com/Library/Article/uriah-heep-ex-crimson-bass-man-seduced.

6 Glenn O'Brien, "Eno at the Edge of Rock," *Interview*, June 1978, 31.

7 Ian MacDonald, "Before and After Science: Thinking about Music with Brian Eno," *New Musical Express*, November 26, 1977, EnoWeb, http://www.eno-web.co.uk/interviews/nme77a.html.

8 "Lester Bangs Interviews Eno," *Musician*, 1979, EnoWeb, http://www.eno-web.co.uk/interviews/musn79.html.

9 "Gurdjieff's Aphorisms," *Gurdjieff International Review*, April 1, 2000, http://www.gurdjieff.org/aphorisms.htm.

10 "Robert Fripp Prt 2 Interviewed by Bas Andriessen July 13 1999," YouTube, October 5, 2012, https://www.youtube.com/watch?v=dHdRci7Kqzk.

11 Jimmy James, "Kevin Ayers Interview," *Perfect Sound Forever*, May 1998, http://www.furious.com/perfect/kevinayers.html.

12 Stephe Pritchard and Thos. Brooman, "Interview with Robert Fripp for Recorder Three," ETWiki, http://www.elephant-talk.com/wiki/Interview_with_Robert_Fripp_by_Stephe_Pritchard_and_Thos._Brooman_for_Recorder_Three, accessed June 2015.

13 Eric Tamm, *Robert Fripp: From King Crimson to Guitar Craft* (Faber and Faber, 1990), 85.

14 Richard Cromelin, "Genesis: Short on Hair, Long on Gimmicks," *Rolling Stone*, March 28, 1974, Rock's Backpages, http://www.rocksbackpages.com/Library/Article/genesis-short-on-hair-long-on-gimmicks.

15 Chris Welch, "Genesis: The New Face of Gabriel," *Melody Maker*, October 26, 1974, Rock's Backpages, http://www.rocksbackpages.com/Library/Article/genesis-the-new-face-of-gabriel.

16 Ibid.

17 Spencer Bright, *Peter Gabriel: An Authorized Biography* (Sidgwick & Jackson, 1988), 61.

18 Kevin Holm-Hudson, *Genesis and the Lamb Lies Down on Broadway* (Ashgate, 2008), 2.

19 Bright, *Peter Gabriel*, 63.

20 Peter Gabriel, "Gabriel Out of Genesis; Looking Back It Was a Good Decision,"

Musical Brick, July 30, 2015, www.musicalbrick.com/gabriel-out-of-genesis-looking -back-it-was-a-good-decision.

21 Max Bell, "Former Genesis Star Braves Humiliation of Nude Stunt," *NME*, December 27, 1975.

22 Paul Myers, *A Wizard, a True Star: Todd Rundgren in the Studio* (Jawbone, 2010), 180.

23 Karl Dallas, "Here Beginneth the Second Chapter of Genesis," *Melody Maker*, September 27, 1975.

24 Ibid.

25 Barbara Charone, "Genesis: Chapter II," *Sounds*, February 14, 1976.

26 Tony Banks et al., *Genesis: Chapter & Verse* (Thomas Dunne Books/St. Martin's Griffin, 2007), 169.

27 Ibid., 170.

28 Karl Dallas, "Re-generation," *Melody Maker*, August 2, 1975.

29 Jim Christopulos and Phil Smart, *Van der Graaf Generator, the Book: A History of the Band Van der Graaf Generator, 1967 to 1978* ("Phil and Jim," 2005), Kindle ed., loc. 1875.

30 Daevid Allen, interview by the author, November 2013.

31 Ibid.

32 Ibid.

33 Mike Atkinson, "Interview: Kevin Ayers," *Stylus*, October 23, 2007, http://www .stylusmagazine.com/articles/interview/kevin-ayers.htm.

34 Jean-Gilles Blum, "The Anti-dinosaur," *Best*, January 1979, More Dark than Shark, http://www.moredarkthanshark.org/eno_int_best-jan79.html.

35 Jean-Gilles Blum, "Interview with Robert Fripp in Best," trans. Louis Courteau, January 1979, ETWiki, http://www.elephant-talk.com/wiki/Interview_with_Robert_ Fripp_in_Best.

36 Larry Fast, interview by the author, January 2014.

37 Tony Levin, *Beyond the Bass Clef* (Papa Bear Records, 1998), 52.

38 Ibid., 52–54.

39 Jon Pareles, "Music without Frontiers: Peter Gabriel," *Musician*, October 1980.

40 Robert Fripp, "Exposure Re-issues," Discipline Global Mobile, http://www.dgmlive .com/archive.htm?show=1096, accessed summer 2015.

41 Sid Smith, *In the Court of King Crimson* (Helter Skelter, 2001), 208.

42 "Robert Fripp Gets the Call from David Bowie: #LadyChamps15," YouTube, October 8, 2014, https://www.youtube.com/watch?v=XlyJ-v871Og.

43 Allan Jones, "Riding on the Dynamic of Disaster: An Interview with Robert Fripp," *Melody Maker*, April 28, 1979, ETWiki, http://www.elephant-talk.com/wiki/Interview_ with_Robert_Fripp_in_Melody_Maker_(1979).

44 Ibid.

45 Richard Buskin, "Classic Tracks: Heroes," *Sound on Sound*, October 2004, http:// www.soundonsound.com/sos/Oct04/articles/classictracks.htm.

46 David Sheppard, *On Some Faraway Beach: The Life and Times of Brian Eno* (Chicago Review Press, 2009), 256.

47 Chris Dahlen, "Daryl Hall: Interview," *Pitchfork*, August 21, 2007, http://pitchfork.com/ features/interviews/6673-daryl-hall.

48 Tamm, *Robert Fripp*, 91.

49 Blum, "Interview with Robert Fripp."

50 Dahlen, "Daryl Hall: Interview."

51 Ira Robbins, "David Bowie: Heroes (RCA)," *Crawdaddy!*, January 1978.

52 Daryl Easlea, *Without Frontiers: The Life and Music of Peter Gabriel* (Omnibus, 2014), 176.

53 Jim O'Connor, "ELP Split for Solo Exploits," *Circus*, November 1974.

54 Keith Emerson, *Pictures of an Exhibitionist* (John Blake, 2004), 275.

55 Ibid., 280, 281.

56 Charles M. Young, "Emerson, Lake, and Palmer Go Broke," *Rolling Stone*, July 14, 1977.

57 Emerson, *Pictures*, 291.

58 "Greg Lake: Still He Turns Them On," Ladies of the Lake, http://ladiesofthelake.com/cabinet/musicscene.html, accessed June 2015.

59 Peter Sinfield, interview by the author, May 2012.

60 Emerson, *Pictures*, 299.

61 Sinfield, interview, May 2012.

62 Emerson, *Pictures*, 296.

63 *Conversations: Emerson, Lake and Palmer* (Trouser Press, 1978).

64 Sinfield, interview, May 2012.

65 Emerson, *Pictures*, 187.

66 Barbara Charone, "The $2m Show That Never Ends: Emerson, Lake & Palmer," *Sounds*, July 2, 1977, Rock's Backpages, http://www.rocksbackpages.com/Library/Article/the-2m-show-that-never-ends-emerson-lake--palmer.

67 Emerson, *Pictures*, 306.

68 Ibid., 307.

69 Charley Walters, "Album Reviews: Emerson, Lake & Palmer: Works, Vol. 1," *Rolling Stone*, June 2, 1977, http://web.archive.org/web/20071110210624/http://www.rollingstone.com/artists/emersonlakepalmer/albums/album/133206/review/5941527/works_vol_1.

70 Jason Heller, Richard Gehr, and Dan Epstein, "Emerson, Lake and Palmer: 10 Essential Songs," *Rolling Stone*, March 11, 2016, http://www.rollingstone.com/music/lists/emerson-lake-and-palmer-10-essential-songs-20160311/fanfare-for-the-common-man-1977-20160311.

71 Al Rudis, "Guess Who's Back with an Orchestra and 35 Tons of Equipment?" *Sounds*, May 21, 1977.

72 Gordon Reid, "Keith Emerson's Keyboard Clearout: Exploration," *Sound on Sound*, May 1995, http://www.soundonsound.com/sos/1995_articles/may95/keithemerson.html.

73 Young, "Emerson, Lake, and Palmer Go Broke."

74 Charone, "The $2m Show."

75 Ibid.

76 Young, "Emerson, Lake, and Palmer Go Broke."

77 Emerson, *Pictures*, 310.

78 Smith, *In the Court*, 208–9.

79 Ibid.

80 Blum, "Conversation."

81 John Piccarella, "Robert Fripp Thrives on a Loop," *Village Voice*, February 13, 1978.

82 Ibid.

83 Terre Roche, interview by the author, September 2014.

84 Suzzy Roche, interview by the author, September 2014.

85 Ibid.

86 Ibid.

87 "Robert Fripp—The Complete Boffomundo Interview 1979," YouTube, June 24, 2015, https://youtu.be/k96zkPrXQh4.

CHAPTER NINE: DEATH KNELL

1   Tony Banks et al., *Genesis: Chapter & Verse* (Thomas Dunne Books/St. Martin's Griffin, 2007), 332.

2   Hugh Fielder, "Then There Were Three," *Sounds*, October 22, 1977.

3   Banks et al., *Genesis: Chapter & Verse*, 189.

4   Ibid., 201.

5   "Michael Bloom" *Rolling Stone*, August 10, 1978.

6   Banks et al., *Genesis: Chapter & Verse*, 332.

7   Paul Stump, *The Music's All That Matters: A History of Progressive Rock* (Quartet Books, 1997), 242.

8   Andrea Swensson, "40 Years of Album Sales Data in Two Handy Charts," *Local Current Blog*, February 20, 2014, http://blog.thecurrent.org/2014/02/40-years-of-album-sales-data-in-one-handy-chart.

9   "Ian Anderson of Jethro Tull Rare 1980 Interview," YouTube, April 6, 2009, https://youtu.be/Cmjeip14VEE.

10 Derek Shulman, interview by the author, September 2013.

11 Greg Lake, interview by the author, July 2012.

12 Ibid.

13 Chris Welch, *Close to the Edge: The Story of Yes* (Omnibus, 1999), 178–79.

14 Ibid., 180.

15 Ibid., 194.

16 Ibid., 189.

17 Fred Deller, "Horn Buggles," *Smash Hits*, February 21, 1980.

18 Welch, *Close to the Edge*, 195.

19 Ibid., 196.

20 Tim Morse, *Yesstories: Yes in Their Own Words* (St. Martin's Press, 1996), 71.

21 Welch, *Close to the Edge*, 189.

22 Robert Palmer, "Rock: Yes Plays Trio at Garden," *New York Times*, September 7, 1980.

23 John Mendelsohn, "Yes: The Band That Punks Say Is a 'No,'" *Los Angeles Times*, September 28, 1980.

24 David Fricke, "The New Yes: Still Living in the Past," *Rolling Stone*, November 27, 1980.

25 Welch, *Close to the Edge*, 193–94.

26 Ibid.

27 Ibid., 198.

28 Ibid.

29 Ibid.

30 Ibid.

31 Ibid., 200.

32 Kim Dancha, *My Own Time: The Authorized Biography of John Wetton* (Northern Line, 1997), 64.

33 Ibid., 65.

34 Bill Bruford, *When in Doubt, Roll!* (Foruli Classics, 1998), 38.

35 Anil Prasad, "Creating Imaginary Backdrops," *Innerviews*, January 15, 1993, https://web.archive.org/web/20140826114441/http://www.therealallanholdsworth.com/allans interviewinner.htm.

36 Bruford, *When in Doubt, Roll!*, 102.

37 Ibid., 101.

38 Dancha, *My Own Time*, 64.

39 Bruford, *When in Doubt, Roll!*, 39.

40 Eddie Jobson, interview by the author, June 2014.

41 Bruford, *When in Doubt, Roll!*, 38.

42 Prasad, "Creating Imaginary Backdrops."

43 Olga Potekhina, "John Wetton (King Crimson, UK, Asia)," Progressor: Interviews of Prog, November 21, 2009, http://www.progressor.net/interview/john_wetton.html.

44 Dancha, *My Own Time*, 80.

45 Ibid.

46 Ibid., 83–84.

47 Ibid., 84.

48 Shawn Perry, "The Carl Palmer Interview," Vintage Rock, http://www.vintagerock.com/index.php?option=com_content&view=article&id=60, accessed June 2014.

49 John Wetton, interview by the author, October 2013.

50 "Backstage Pass: A Trip to Asia and Beyond with Steve Howe," *Goldmine*, January 16, 2010, http://www.goldminemag.com/article/backstage-pass-a-trip-to-asia-and-beyond-with-steve-howe#sthash.TFIoWLV6.dpuf.

51 Boo Browning, "Heavenly Pap Out of 'Asia,'" *Washington Post*, April 23, 1982.

52 Jon Pareles, "Rock: Asia Plays Forest Hills," *New York Times*, August 22, 1983.

53 Dancha, *My Own Time*, 84.

54 Sylvie Simmons, "What This Bloke Is Doing Now," *Sounds*, April 15, 1978.

55 Steve Hackett, interview by the author, September 2013.

56 Rob Hoerburger, "Phil Collins Beats the Odds," *Rolling Stone*, May 23, 1983, http://www.rollingstone.com/music/news/phil-collins-beats-the-odds-19850523.

57 Lynden Barber, "Phil Collins: Facing Up to New Values," *Melody Maker*, February 7, 1981.

58 Ray Coleman, *Phil Collins: The Definitive Biography* (Simon & Schuster, 1997), 108.

59 Polly Dunbar, "Phil Collins' Ex-wife Breaks Her Silence 35 Years after Split That

Inspired Hit 'In the Air Tonight' to Deny That She Ran Away with the Decorator . . . and Says He's Still Cashing in on That False Version of Their Separation," *Daily Mail*, April 18, 2015, http://www.dailymail.co.uk/femail/article-3045045/No-Phil-didn-t -run-away-decorator-broke-vows-cashing-divorce-Genesis-star-s-wife-breaks-silence -35-years-split.html.

60 Phil Sutcliffe, "Genesis: Help!" *Mojo*, April 2007, Rock's Backpages, http://www .rocksbackpages.com/Library/Article/genesis-help.

61 Rick Wakeman and Steve Hackett, *Gastank* (TV show), 1983, https://www.reddit.com/ r/progrockmusic/comments/3jawf5/rick_wakeman_and_steve_hackett_gastank_ tv_session.

62 Ibid.

63 Hackett, interview, September 2013.

64 Dick Tooley, "Interview with Robert Fripp," August 9, 1979, ETWiki, http://www .elephant-talk.com/wiki/Interview_with_Robert_Fripp_by_Dick_Tooley.

65 Robert Fripp, *God Saves the Queen/Under Heavy Manners* (Polydor Records, 1980), liner notes.

66 Michael Davis, "Records: Bobby Go Loop-de-Loop, Terry Go Loop-de-Li: Robert Fripp, God Save the Queen/Under Heavy Manners; Terry Riley, Shri Camel," *Creem* July 12, 1980.

67 Karl Dallas, "Caught in the Act: Robert Fripp, ICA, London," *Melody Maker*, October 4, 1980.

68 Eric Tamm, *Robert Fripp: From King Crimson to Guitar Craft* (Faber and Faber, 1990), 105, 106.

69 Kurt Loder, "Performance: Robert Fripp Returns to Form—His First Band since King Crimson: The League of Gentlemen, Irving Plaza, New York City," *Rolling Stone*, September 4, 1980.

70 Adrian Belew, interview by the author, September 2015.

71 Richard Grabel, "King Crimson: Robert Fripp's Chocolate Cake Discipline," *Creem*, February 1982.

72 Sid Smith, *In the Court of King Crimson* (Helter Skelter, 2001), 216.

73 Ibid., 217.

74 Ibid., 219.

75 Grabel, "King Crimson."

76 "Jon Anderson Recount's [sic] His First Meeting with Vangelis and Sings 'I'll Find My Way Home,'" YouTube, June 20, 2012, https://www.youtube.com/watch?v=ItV5 h3Arl5M.

77 Mark J. T. Griffin, *Vangelis: The Unknown Man: An Unauthorised Biography* (Griffin, 1994), Kindle ed., loc. 1157.

78 Ibid., loc. 1351.

79 Daevid Allen, interview by the author, November 2013.

80 Ibid.

81 Banks et al., *Genesis: Chapter & Verse*, 222.

82 Larry Fast, interview by the author, January 2014.

83 Banks et al., *Genesis: Chapter & Verse*, 231.

84 Daryl Easlea, *Without Frontiers: The Life and Music of Peter Gabriel* (Omnibus, 2014), 211.

85 Banks et al., *Genesis: Chapter & Verse*, 220.

86 Ibid., 221.

87 Easlea, *Without Frontiers*, 225.

88 Gavin Martin, "Peter Gabriel: *Four* (Charisma)," *New Musical Express*, September 11, 1982.

89 "Peter Gabriel South Bank Show 1983," YouTube, September 30, 2014, https://www .youtube.com/watch?v=o21nJYvyZaM.

90 Easlea, *Without Frontiers*, 216.

CHAPTER TEN: NEO-PROG

1 Phil Bell, "Marillion: The Dial Inn, Glasgow," *Sounds*, May 20, 1982, Rock's Backpages, http://www.rocksbackpages.com/Library/Article/marillion-the-dial-inn-glasgow.

2 Ibid.

3 Ibid.

4 Jon Collins, *Marillion/Separated Out: The Complete History of the Band and Its Fans, 1979–2002* (Helter Skelter, 2003), 15.

5 "Steve Rothery Interview," April 5, 2013, Tone World blog, https://web.archive .org/web/20140111120721/http://www.toneworld.co.uk/blog/2013/04/steve-rothery -interview.

6 Collins, *Marillion/Separated Out*, 11.

7 Ibid., 19.

8 Koldo Barroso, "Interview—Diz Minnitt of Marrillion," Marquee Club, August 2006, https://web.archive.org/web/20080724184948/http://themarqueeclub.net/interview -diz-minnitt-of-marillion.

9 Paul Morley, "Marillion: Just When You Thought It Was Safe to Go Back into the Water," *New Musical Express*, April 28, 1984, Rock's Backpages, http://www.rocks backpages.com/Library/Article/marillion-just-when-you-thought-it-was-safe-to-go -back-into-the-water.

10 Collins, *Marillion/Separated Out*, 23.

11 Tim Morse, *Yesstories: Yes in Their Own Words* (St. Martin's Press, 1996), 77.

12 Collins, *Marillion/Separated Out*, 41.

13 Tony Banks et al., *Genesis: Chapter & Verse* (Thomas Dunne Books/St. Martin's Griffin, 2007), 259.

14 Ibid.

15 Mike Rutherford, *The Living Years: The First Genesis Memoir* (Thomas Dunne Books/St. Martin's Press, 2015), 239.

16 Banks et al., *Genesis: Chapter & Verse*, 276.

17 Ibid., 263.

18 Ibid., 286.

19 Ibid.

20 Nick DeRiso, "John Wetton of Asia, King Crimson and the UK: Something Else! Interview," *Something Else!*, April 18, 2012, http://somethingelsereviews.com/2012/04/18/something-else-interview-john-wetton-of-asia-king-crimson-and-uk/#sthash.SGpaxUSI.dpuf.

21 Dancha, *My Own Time*, 93, 95.

22 Ibid., 94.

23 Ibid., 97.

24 Ibid., 99.

25 Craig Marks and Rob Tannenbaum, *I Want My MTV: The Uncensored Story of the Music Video Revolution* (Dutton, 2011), 101.

26 Anil Prasad, "Greg Lake: New Perspectives," *Innerviews*, 2011, http://www.innerviews.org/inner/lake.html.

27 Kim Dancha, *My Own Time: The Authorized Biography of John Wetton* (Northern Line, 1997), 102.

28 Jeff Giles, "30 Years Ago: Asia Go through Changes to Make 'Astra,'" Ultimate Classic Rock, November 30, 2015, http://ultimateclassicrock.com/asia-astra.

29 Prasad, "Greg Lake: New Perspectives."

30 Morse, *Yesstories*, 75.

31 Ibid.

32 Chris Welch, *Close to the Edge: The Story of Yes* (Omnibus, 1999), 76.

33 Welch, *Close to the Edge*, 204.

34 Ibid., 208.

35 Morse, *Yesstories*, 71.

36 Ibid., 72.

37 "Emerson, Lake and Palmer," Ladies of the Lake, http://ladiesofthelake.com/cabinet/Goldmine.html, accessed November 28, 2016.

38 Edward Macan, *Endless Enigma: A Musical Biography of Emerson, Lake and Palmer* (Open Court, 2006), 486.

39 Ibid., 491.

40 Jim Farber, "Emerson, Lake, and Powell," *Rolling Stone*, June 28, 1986.

41 Macan, *Endless Enigma*, 501.

42 Shawn Perry, "The Keith Emerson Interview," Vintage Rock, http://vintagerock.com/index.php?option=com_content&view=article&id=49, accessed September 2014.

43 Macan, *Endless Enigma*, 506.

44 Simon Reynolds, "Songs for Insane Times: An Anthology 1969–1980 (Harvest/EMI)," *Observer Music Monthly*, August 10, 2008.

45 Anil Prasad, "Mike Oldfield: The Messenger," *Innerviews*, 2013, http://www.innerviews.org/inner/oldfield.html.

46 Daevid Allen, interview by the author, November 2013.

47 Collins, *Marillion/Separated Out*, 19.

48 Ibid., 39.

49 "Pink Floyd & the Story of Prog Rock," *Mojo* Classic, Collectors Edition, July 2005.

50 Collins, *Marillion/Separated Out*, 36.

51 Ibid., 54.

52 Morley, "Marillion."

53 Bell, "Marillion."

54 Phil Bell, "Sob Standard: Marillion: *Script for Jester's Tear* (EMI)," *Sounds*, March 12, 1983, Rock's Backpages, http://www.rocksbackpages.com/Library/Article/sob-standard -marillion-iscript-for-a-jesters-teari-emi-.

55 Lucy O'Brien, "Marillion: Bournemouth Winter Gardens," *New Musical Express*, April 9, 1983, Rock's Backpages, http://www.rocksbackpages.com/Library/Article/marillion -bournemouth-winter-gardens.

56 Bill Holdship, "Marillion Conquer America," *Creem*, July 1986.

57 Collins, *Marillion/Separated Out*, 44.

58 Pete Pardo, "Arena's Mick Pointer in the Spotlight!" Sea of Tranquility, May 21, 2005, http://www.seaoftranquility.org/article.php?sid=395.

59 Collins, *Marillion/Separated Out*, 47.

60 Ibid., 49.

61 Paul Stump, *The Music's All That Matters: A History of Progressive Rock* (Quartet Books, 1997), 260–61.

62 Collins, *Marillion/Separated Out*, 59.

63 Ibid., 62.

64 Ibid., 67.

65 Ibid., 72.

66 Ibid., 84.

67 Ibid., 112, 116.

68 Robert Fripp, "The Diary of the Return of King Crimson," *Musician*, November 1981.

69 David Fricke, "Old Cult Groups Never Die (They Just Become More Popular), March 1982, ETWiki, http://www.elephant-talk.com/wiki/Interview_with_King_ Crimson_in_Trouser_Press.

70 Adrian Belew, interview by the author, September 2015.

71 Robert Fripp, "The Diary of the Return of King Crimson," *Musician*, November 1981.

72 Sid Smith, *In the Court of King Crimson* (Helter Skelter, 2001), 217.

73 Lynden Barber, "King Crimson: *Discipline*," *Melody Maker*, September 1981.

74 Smith, *In the Court*, 243.

75 Steven Rosen, "Adrian Belew: 'I Fit a Dissonant Note in There Every Now and Then Just to Wake People Up,'" Ultimate-Guitar.com, September 22, 2014, https://www .ultimate-guitar.com/news/interviews/adrian_belew_i_fit_a_dissonant_note_in_ there_every_now_and_then_just_to_wake_people_up.html.

76 Belew, interview, September 2015.

77 Ibid.

78 Bill Bruford, *When in Doubt, Roll!* (Foruli Classics, 1998), 125.

79 Ibid.

80 Collins, *Marillion/Separated Out*, 91.

81 Dave Ling, "Marillion: An Interview with Steve Hogarth," previously published in *Classic Rock* magazine, Dave Ling Online, May 2001, http://www.daveling.co.uk/doc -marillion.htm.

82 Collins, *Marillion/Separated Out*, 119.

83 Ibid., 91.

84 Ibid., 92.

85 Ibid., 96.

86 Ibid., 342.

87 Ibid., 239.

88 "Interview with Steve Hogarth—Marillion (Rock Steady 1990)," YouTube, January 21, 2008, https://www.youtube.com/watch?v=viRKMe0R6ag.

89 Ibid.

90 Collins, *Marillion/Separated Out*, 103.

91 Ibid., 97.

92 Ling, "Marillion."

CHAPTER ELEVEN: THE NOSTALGIA FACTORY

1 Steven Wilson, interview by the author, September 2013.

2 Jon Collins, *Marillion/Separated Out: The Complete History of the Band and Its Fans, 1979–2002* (Helter Skelter, 2003), 13–14.

3 Wilson, interview, September 2013.

4 Ibid.

5 Richard Allen, "Porcupine Tree—Strange but True," Terrascope, http://www.terrascope.co.uk/MyBackPages/Porcupine_Tree.htm, accessed November 30, 2016.

6 Ed Sander, "Porcupine Tree: Stupid Dream," Dutch Progressive Rock Page, http://www.dprp.net/proghistory/index.php?i=1999_01, accessed June 2015.

7 Kevin Rathert, "Richard Allen Interview (The Freak Emporium, Delerium Records)," *Psychedelic Baby* (blog), October 10, 2012, http://psychedelicbaby.blogspot.com/2012/10/richard-allen-interview-freak-emporium.html.

8 Steven Rosen, "Steven Wilson: 'Porcupine Tree Was Gonna Be a One-Off Thing,'" Ultimate-Guitar.com, December 14, 2011, http://www.ultimate-guitar.com/interviews/interviews/steven_wilson_porcupine_tree_was_gonna_be_a_one-off_thing.html?no_takeover.

9 Yiannis to Ozric Tentacles: Ozric Message Board, "Richard Allen Tribute," January 11, 2014, http://ozrics.proboards.com/thread/1978/richard-allen-tribute.

10 Wilson, interview, September 2013.

11 "Porcupine Tree—*Up the Downstair*," Delerium Records, 2000, http://web.archive.org/web/20070826202210/http://www.delerium.co.uk/delerium/releases/delec020.html.

12 Anil Prasad, "Porcupine Tree: Dream Logic," *Innerviews*, 2010, http://www.innerviews.org/inner/ptree3.html.

13 "Dream Theater—The Score So Far (Documentary): Part 1," YouTube, April 14, 2011, https://youtu.be/nnyy0Dxmn5M.

14 Ibid.

15 "Dream Theater—The Score So Far."

16 Rich Wilson, *Lifting Shadows: The Authorized Biography of Dream Theater* (Rocket 88, 2013), 49.

17 Ibid., 55.

18 Derek Oliver, "Where Seventeen Universes Intersect: Dream Theater 'When Dream and Day Unite,'" *Kerrang!*, March 11, 1989, reprinted without permission by Graham Boyle on YTSEJAM Digest 3062, October 3, 1997, http://www.interzone.com/Music/Ytsejam/1997/Oct/0012.html.

19 "Awesome Metallica Rips Jethro Tull Wins Best Metal Performance 1992 Grammys," YouTube, March 28, 2011, https://www.youtube.com/watch?v=r5fTtd_hdok.

20 Chris Welch, *Close to the Edge: The Story of Yes* (Omnibus, 1999), 227.

21 Tim Morse, *Yesstories: Yes in Their Own Words* (St. Martin's Press, 1996), 90.

22 Ibid., 235.

23 "Exclusive Interview: Prog Rock Band Spock's Beard," StarTrek.com, October 27, 2015, http://www.startrek.com/article/exclusive-interview-prog-rock-band-spocks-beard.

24 Mattias Olsson, "Interviews," Anglagard.net, September 2002, http://www.anglagard.net/interview01.htm.

25 Ibid.

26 Eric Tamm, *Robert Fripp: From Crimson King to Crafty Master* (1990), Scribd e-book, https://www.scribd.com/doc/19690511/Robert-Fripp-From-Crimson-King-to-Crafty-Master-E-book.

27 Ted Drozdowski, "Robert Fripp: A Plectral Purist Answers the Dumb Questions," *Musician*, February 1989.

28 Trey Gunn, interview by the author, November 2015.

29 Ibid.

30 "David Sylvian & Robert Fripp—Redemption TV Special," YouTube, March 10, 2010, https://youtu.be/3yjJtysafXA.

31 Sid Smith, *In the Court of King Crimson* (Helter Skelter, 2001), 205.

32 Gunn, interview, November 2015.

33 Adrian Belew, interview by the author, September 2015.

34 Smith, *In the Court*, 209.

35 Ibid., 256, 283.

36 "Tool—Danny Carey Talks about King Crimson," YouTube, October 16, 2013, https://www.youtube.com/watch?v=knJPCffGyE4.

37 Gunn, interview, November 2015.

38 Wilson, *Lifting Shadows*, 108.

39 Kory Grow, "Dream Theater's Jordan Rudess Remembers Keith Emerson: 'He Was My Idol,'" *Rolling Stone*, March 11, 2016, http://www.rollingstone.com/music/news/dream-theaters-jordan-rudess-remembers-keith-emerson-he-was-my-idol-20160311.

40 Jerry van Kooten and Hans van der Meer, "A Certain Limitlessness: An Interview with Mike Portnoy," Dutch Progressive Rock Page, April 8, 2000, http://www.dprp.net/specials/mp20000408.html.

41 Wilson, *Lifting Shadows*, 114.

42 Ibid., 169.

43 Ibid., 96.

44 Allan Richter, "Music; A Long Island Sound by Way of Topographic Oceans," *New York Times*, August 22, 2004.

45 Wilson, *Lifting Shadows*, 144.

46 Gary Graff, "Coheed and Cambria Announces 'In Keeping Secrets of Silent Earth: 3' Reissue: Exclusive," *Billboard*, August 18, 2014, http://www.billboard.com/articles/news/6221762/coheed-and-cambria-announces-in-keeping-secrets-of-silent-earth-3-reissue.

47 Moe Castro, "Interview with Coheed and Cambria," Delusions of Adequacy, June 1, 2000, http://web.archive.org/web/20080202075046/http://www.adequacy.net/interview.php?InterviewID=56.

48 "Pink Floyd & the Story of Prog Rock," *Mojo* Classic, Collectors Edition, July 2005.

49 Ibid.

50 Joakim Jahlmar, "An Interview with Steven Wilson of Porcupine Tree," Dutch Progressive Rock Page, 2001, http://www.dprp.net/specials/porcupinetree.

51 "Opeth Mainman: 'We Don't Want to Be Different for the Sake of Being Different,'" BlabberMouth.net, October 27, 2006, http://www.blabbermouth.net/news/opeth-mainman-we-don-t-want-to-be-different-for-the-sake-of-being-different.

52 "Ian Anderson on Keith Emerson," YouTube, June 13, 2016, https://www.youtube.com/watch?v=RmpFbggjQI8.

53 Mark Kelly, online post to Marillion Freaks message board, January 27, 1997.

54 Jeff Pelletier, online post to Marillion Freaks message board.

55 Wilson, interview, September 2013.

56 Ibid.

57 Prasad, "Porcupine Tree."

EPILOGUE

1 North East Art Rock Festival, Zoellner Arts Center, Bethlehem, Pennsylvania, June 22–24, 2012.

2 Gary Green, interview by the author, June 2012.

3 *Big Train*. series 2, episode 1 (BBC Two, January 7, 2002).

4 Keith Emerson, interview by the author, May 2012.

5 Jim Farber, "Kevin Ayers Is an English Eccentric," *New York Daily News*, March 8, 2008, http://www.nydailynews.com/entertainment/music-arts/kevin-ayers-english-eccentric-article-1.287569.

6 Daevid Allen, interview by the author, November 2013.

7 Ted Leo, interview by the author, August 2012.

8 Ludovic Hunter-Tilney, "The Day the Music Died," *Financial Times*, August 3, 2012, https://www.ft.com/content/f588e100-d7ee-11e1-9980-00144feabdc0#axzz25cH32luq.

9 C. G. Jung, *The Spirit of Man, Art, and Literature* (Princeton University Press, 1966), 82.

10 Peter Hammill, interview by the author, August 2013.

11 Nick DeRiso, "Carl Palmer Says Failed 2010 Show Killed Chances for Larger ELP Reunion," Ultimate Classic Rock, April 11, 2013, http://ultimateclassicrock.com/carl-palmer-2010-elp-reunion/?trackback=tsmclip.

12 Sid Smith, "Keith Emerson 1944–2016: The Endless Enigma," *Prog*.

13 "Emerson Moog Modular Unveiling Part 3—Moogfest 2014—BBoyTechReport.com,"
    YouTube, April 28, 2014, https://www.youtube.com/watch?v=VjvytlOd0PI.

14 "Emerson Moog Modular Unveiling Part 1—Moogfest 2014—BBoyTechReport.com,"
    YouTube, April 28, 2014, https://www.youtube.com/watch?v=y3KRxDs8hd4.

15 Martin Townsend, "Bandmate: I Feared for ELP Star Keith," *Express*, March 13, 2016,
    https://www.express.co.uk/news/obituaries/652126/Emerson-Lake-Palmer-bandmate
    -feared-for-ELP-star-Keith-Emerson.

16 Caroline Graham, "ELP Star Keith Emerson 'Shot Himself Because He Could No
    Longer Perform Perfectly for His Fans,'" *Daily Mail*, March 12, 2016, http://www.daily
    mail.co.uk/news/article-3489624/ELP-star-Keith-Emerson-shot-no-longer-perform
    -perfectly-fans.html.

17 Mike Barnes, "All-Star Musicians Pay Respect to Keith Emerson at Tribute Concert
    in Los Angeles," *Billboard*, May 29, 2016, http://www.billboard.com/articles/news/
    7386085/keith-emerson-tribute-concert-los-angeles-el-rey-theatre.

PHOTO CREDITS

Page 1. Top, Pictorial Press Ltd / Alamy Stock Photo. Bottom, Photo by Petra Niemeier – K & K / Redferns/ Getty Images.

Page 2. Top, LFI / Photoshot / Newscom. Middle, Photo by John Williams / BIPs / Getty Images. Bottom, Jak Kilby / ArenaPAL.

Page 3. Top, AFP / Getty Images. Middle, Photo by Michael Ochs Archives / Getty Images. Bottom, Photo by Waring Abbott / Getty Images.

Page 4. Top, Photo by Jack Robinson / Hulton Archive / Getty Images. Bottom, AF archive / Alamy Stock Photo.

Page 5. Top, Photo by John Dickinson / Getty Images. Middle, Photo by Gems / Redferns / Getty Images. Bottom, Photo by Michael Ochs Archives / Getty Images.

Page 6. Top, Photo by Michael Putland / Getty Images. Middle, Photo by Michael Ochs Archives / Getty Images. Bottom, Photo by Fin Costello / Redferns / Getty Images.

Page 7. Top, Photo by Richard E. Aaron / Redferns / Getty Images. Middle, Photo by Fin Costello / Redferns / Getty Images. Bottom, © Mike Black Photography.

Page 8. Both, Photo by Michael Putland / Getty Images.

INDEX